THE IRWIN SERIES IN ECONOMICS

CONSULTING EDITOR

LLOYD G. REYNOLDS

YALE UNIVERSITY

BOOKS IN THE IRWIN SERIES IN ECONOMICS

THE THEORY OF
ECONOMIC INTEGRATION

THE THEORY OF
ECONOMIC INTEGRATION

BY

BELA BALASSA J.D., Ph.D.

Assistant Professor
Yale University

GREENWOOD PRESS, PUBLISHERS
WESTPORT, CONNECTICUT

Library of Congress Cataloging in Publication Data

Balassa, Bela A.
  The theory of economic integration.

  Reprint. Originally published: Homewood, Ill. :
R.D. Irwin, 1961. (Irwin series in economics)
  Bibliography: p.
  Includes indexes.
  1. International economic integration. I. Title.
II. Series: Irwin series in economics.
[HF1418.5.B34 1981]   337.1   82-2971
ISBN 0-313-23543-0 (lib. bdg.)   AACR2

Reprinted with the permission of Richard D. Irwin, Inc.

Reprinted in 1982 by Greenwood Press,
A division of Congressional Information Service, Inc.
88 Post Road West, Westport, Connecticut 06881

Printed in the United States of America

10 9 8 7 6 5 4 3 2 1

TO MY PARENTS

PREFACE

This book finds its origin in my long-standing interest in problems of economic integration in Europe. I soon realized that a discussion of present-day integration projects, in Europe or elsewhere, would bear little fruit without considering the theoretical issues involved. At the same time, a perusal of recent writings on the customs union issue has shown that—following the time-honored tradition of international trade theory—these contributions concentrated on problems of resource allocation in a static framework and paid little attention to the dynamic effects of integration. Yet the economic consequences of a fusion of national markets can be but imperfectly explained under static assumptions, since in the European area, and especially in Latin America, the impact of integration on economic growth assumes great importance.

These considerations induced me to focus my attention on the theoretical problems in the integration of independent national economies, and to endeavor to present a unified theory of economic integration that would include, over and above the received theory, the dynamic aspects of economic integration, and would bring together the theoretical problems involved in co-ordinating economic policies in a union. In the course of the discussion, distinction will also be made between various forms of integration, such as a free trade area, customs union, common market, economic union, and total integration. In addition, at various points of the argument, the theoretical principles will be applied to present-day integration projects, such as the European Common Market and Free Trade Association, and the proposed Latin American unions.

The book is designed for economists, but I assume that the nonprofessional reader with interest in international problems will also find it useful. He will want to skim certain sections that require greater familiarity with economic theory. The selected bibliography is designed to assist the reader in further study and research.

I am heavily indebted to Gottfried Haberler and Harry G. Johnson whose comments and criticism not only helped to remove several errors and obscurities in the argument but also stimulated the reworking of substantial portions of the text. William Fellner, Charles P. Kindleberger, Egon Sohmen, Robert Triffin, and Jacob Viner read several chapters of a previous draft and offered valuable suggestions. Further thanks are due to Lloyd G. Reynolds for his freely given advice during the preparation of this work and to Gerald M. Meier for an attentive final reading of the manuscript.

I also want to state my indebtedness to friends and acquaintances in Europe and Latin America for the interest expressed in this work and for valuable suggestions and information. I cannot forgo mentioning François Perroux of the Institut de Science Economique Appliquée; Claudio Segré of the European Economic Community and L. Duquesne de la Vinelle (formerly with the E.E.C.); Raymond Bertrand of the Organisation for European Economic Co-operation; Richard Thorn of the International Monetary Fund, European Office; and Nuno Fidelino de Figueiredo of the United Nations Economic Commission for Latin America. None of them should be held responsible, however, if the author did not take their good advice.

A grant from the Ford Foundation assisted me in the initial stage of research, while financial assistance given by the Stimson Fund helped at later stages. Some findings of the study have appeared in article form in *Economia Internazionale, Kyklos, Revista de Ciencias Económicas* and *Weltwirtschaftliches Archiv;* the publishers of these journals kindly gave permission for the use of published material. I also want to express my appreciation to Stanley Besen who was very helpful in checking references and statistical information, and to Suzanne Addiss and Rosemarie Arena who did a valiant job of typing and retyping. Mrs. Arena also attempted to remove numerous blemishes of style.

BELA BALASSA

TABLE OF CONTENTS

LIST OF TABLES

Chapter 1 INTRODUCTION

Dans la hiérarchie des mots obscurs et sans beauté dont les discussions économiques encombrent notre langue, le terme d'intégration occupe un bon rang.

—François Perroux, *L'Europe sans rivages* (Paris: Presses Universitaires de France, 1954), p. 419

The term *economic integration*, whatever might have been its earlier history, only recently became a slogan for action, or what the French call more respectfully, *une idée force*.

—M. A. Heilperin, "Economic Integration: Commercial and Financial Postulates," in *European Integration*, ed. C. C. Haines (Baltimore: Johns Hopkins Press, 1957), p. 126

The Concept and Forms of Integration

In everyday usage the word "integration" denotes the bringing together of parts into a whole. In the economic literature the term "economic integration" does not have such a clear-cut meaning. Some authors include social integration in the concept, others subsume different forms of international cooperation under this heading, and the argument has also been advanced that the mere existence of trade relations between independent national economies is a sign of integration.[1] We propose to define economic integration as a process and as a state of affairs. Regarded as a process, it encompasses measures designed to abolish discrimination between economic units belonging to different national states; viewed as a state of affairs, it can be represented by the absence of various forms of discrimination between national economies.[2]

[1] For a critical survey of these definitions and references, see Bela Balassa, "Towards a Theory of Economic Integration," *Kyklos*, No. 1 (1961), pp. 1–5.

[2] It should be noted that this definition is based on the implicit assumption that discrimination actually affected economic intercourse. The suppression of tariff barriers between Iceland and New Zealand, for example, will not integrate the two economies in the absence of a substantial amount of foreign trade, since without trade relations there was no effective discrimination anyway.

1

In interpreting our definition, distinction should be made between integration and cooperation. The difference is qualitative as well as quantitative. Whereas cooperation includes actions aimed at lessening discrimination, the process of economic integration comprises measures that entail the suppression of some forms of discrimination. For example, international agreements on trade policies belong to the area of international cooperation, while the removal of trade barriers is an act of economic integration. Distinguishing between cooperation and integration, we put the main characteristics of the latter—the abolition of discrimination within an area—into clearer focus and give the concept definite meaning without unnecessarily diluting it by the inclusion of diverse actions in the field of international cooperation.

Economic integration, as defined here, can take several forms that represent varying degrees of integration. These are a free-trade area, a customs union, a common market, an economic union, and complete economic integration. In a free-trade area, tariffs (and quantitative restrictions) between the participating countries are abolished, but each country retains its own tariffs against nonmembers. Establishing a customs union involves, besides the suppression of discrimination in the field of commodity movements within the union, the equalization of tariffs in trade with nonmember countries. A higher form of economic integration is attained in a common market, where not only trade restrictions but also restrictions on factor movements are abolished. An economic union, as distinct from a common market, combines the suppression of restrictions on commodity and factor movements with some degree of harmonization of national economic policies, in order to remove discrimination that was due to disparities in these policies. Finally, total economic integration presupposes the unification of monetary, fiscal, social, and countercyclical policies and requires the setting-up of a supra-national authority whose decisions are binding for the member states.[3]

Adopting the definition given above, the theory of economic integration will be concerned with the economic effects of integration

---

[3] Social integration can also be mentioned as a further precondition of total economic integration. Nevertheless, social integration has not been included in our definition, since—although it increases the *effectiveness* of economic integration—it is not necessary for the lower forms of integration. The removal of trade barriers in a free-trade area, for example, is an act of economic integration even in the absence of developments in the social field.

in its various forms and with problems that arise from divergences in national monetary, fiscal, and other policies. The theory of economic integration can be regarded as a part of international economics, but it also enlarges the field of international trade theory by exploring the impact of a fusion of national markets on growth and examining the need for the coordination of economic policies in a union. Finally, the theory of economic integration should incorporate elements of location theory, too. The integration of adjacent countries amounts to the removal of artificial barriers that obstruct continuous economic activity through national frontiers, and the ensuing relocation of production and regional agglomerative and deglomerative tendencies cannot be adequately discussed without making use of the tools of locational analysis.[4]

The Recent Interest in Economic Integration

In the twentieth century no significant customs unions were formed until the end of the Second World War, although several attempts had been made to integrate the economies of various European countries.[5] Without going into a detailed analysis, political obstacles can be singled out as the main causes for the failure of these projects to materialize. A certain degree of integration was achieved during the Second World War via a different route, when—as part of the German *Grossraum* policy—the Hitlerites endeavored to integrate economically the satellite countries and the occupied territories with Germany. In the latter case, economic integration appeared as a form of imperialist expansion.

The post–Second World War period has seen an enormous increase in the interest in problems of economic integration. In Europe the customs union and later the economic union of the Benelux countries, the European Coal and Steel Community,[6] the European Economic Community (Common Market),[7] and the European Free Trade

[4] On the interrelationship of location theory and the theory of economic integration, see my "Towards a Theory of Economic Integration," pp. 6–8.

[5] For a description of these plans, see H. D. Gideonse, "Economic Foundations of Pan-Europeanism," *Annals of the American Academy of Political and Social Science*, May, 1930, pp. 150–56, and *Customs Unions: A League of Nations Contribution to the Study of Customs Union Problems* (Lake Success, N.Y.: United Nations, 1947), pp. 21–28.

[6] Established on February 10, 1953, between the Benelux countries (Belgium, the Netherlands, and Luxembourg), France, the German Federal Republic, and Italy.

[7] Established on January 1, 1958, between the countries of the European Coal and Steel Community. At the same time, these countries created the European Atomic Energy Community (Euratom) for the exploitation of nuclear energy.

Association (the "Outer Seven")[8] are manifestations of this movement. Plans have also been made for the establishment of a free-trade area encompassing the countries of the Common Market and the Outer Seven, but negotiations in the years 1957–60 did not meet with success. However, concessions offered in early 1961 by the United Kingdom with regard to the harmonization of tariffs on non-agricultural commodities give promise for the future enlargement of the Common Market in some modified form.[9]

Besides the European area, Latin America shows the greatest progress in economic integration. The United Nations Economic Commission for Latin America prepared plans for creating a free-trade area to include all Latin-American economies,[10] with a view to eventually transforming this free-trade area into a full-fledged customs union. The proposal was not accepted, but agreements have actually been reached in two groupings of these countries. In 1960, six South American states[11] and Mexico concluded an agreement (the Montevideo Treaty) to establish the Latin American Free Trade Association, while four Central American countries signed a treaty creating the Central American Common Market.[12]

The establishment of a customs union is in progress in the West Indies, too. On the Asian continent the possibilities for integration have been considered in Southern Asia, while in Africa different groupings of the newly independent states prepared proposals for eventual economic integration. Such plans have been discussed in regard to the North African Arab countries, between Ghana, Guinea, and the Mali, and between a number of former French dependencies.

The considerations that have prompted these plans for the integration of independent national economies are by no means uniform; various factors must be given different weights in the movement toward economic integration in Europe and on other continents. Leaving aside political considerations for the moment, we shall presently review some of the economic factors operating in Europe and in underdeveloped countries.

---

8 Established on July 1, 1960, between Austria, Denmark, Great Britain, Norway, Portugal, Sweden, and Switzerland. In March, 1961, Finland joined as associate member. This change came too late, however, to be considered in the present discussion.

9 The economic effects of a prospective accommodation between the Six and the Seven will not be dealt with in the present study. The author hopes to explore this problem at a later date.

10 South America, Central America, and Mexico.

11 Argentina, Brazil, Chile, Paraguay, Peru, and Uruguay.

12 El Salvador, Guatemala, Honduras, and Nicaragua.

The interwar period has witnessed a considerable degree of disintegration of the European and the world economy. On the European scene the mounting trade-and-payments restrictions since 1913 deserve attention. Ingvar Svennilson has shown that, as a result of the increase in trade impediments, the import trade of the advanced industrial countries of Europe shifted from the developed to the less developed economies of this area, which did not specialize in manufactured products.[13] This shift implies a decline in competition between the industrial products of the more advanced economies and a decrease in specialization among these countries. But lessening of specialization was characteristic not only among the more advanced European economies but also of the European economy as a whole. This development can be demonstrated by trade and production figures for the period of 1913–38. While the volume of commodity production in Europe increased by 32 per cent during those years, intra-European trade decreased by 10 per cent.[14] The formation of a European union can be regarded, then, as a possible solution for the reintegration of European economies.

Another factor responsible for the disintegration of the European economy has been the stepping-up of state intervention in economic affairs in order to counteract cyclical fluctuations, sustain full employment, correct income distribution, and influence growth. Plans for economic integration are designed partly to counteract the element of discrimination inherent in the increased scope of state intervention.

A related argument regards the establishment of customs unions as desirable for mitigating cyclical fluctuations transmitted through foreign-trade relations. The foreign-trade dependence of the European Common Market countries decreases, for example, by about 35 per cent if trade among the six countries is regarded as internal trade. The memory of the depression in the 1930's gives added weight to this argument. Note, however, that for this proposition to be valid, there is need for some degree of coordination in countercyclical policies among the participating countries.

Last but not least, it is expected that integration will foster the growth of the European economies. This outcome is assumed to be the result of various dynamic factors, such as large-scale economies on

13 *Growth and Stagnation in the European Economy* (Geneva: United Nations Economic Commission for Europe, 1954), p. 197.

14 United Nations Economic Commission for Europe, *Economic Survey of Europe since the War* (Geneva, 1953), p. 214.

a wider market, lessening of uncertainty in intra-area trade, and a faster rate of technological change. In this regard, the increased interest in economic growth has further contributed to the attention given to possibilities of economic integration.

Turning to underdeveloped countries, economic development appears as the primary consideration. Countries following the advice given by protagonists of the balanced-growth doctrine may strive for economic integration in order to ensure a sufficiently large market for the parallel development of new industries. In carrying out programs for industrialization, the exploitation of economies of scale unattainable in the small national markets will assume importance. It is also alleged that establishing a union furthers economic development by increasing the bargaining power and reducing the external vulnerability of the member countries. Finally, the increased interest in integration in the underdeveloped countries may be attributed in part to a desire to imitate the European example and to deliberate efforts to counteract possible trade-diverting effects of the European Common Market.

To summarize, economic integration in Europe serves to avoid discrimination caused by trade-and-payments restrictions and increased state intervention, and it is designed to mitigate cyclical fluctuations and to increase the growth of national income. In underdeveloped countries, considerations of economic development are of basic importance; further contributing factors are imitative behavior and the endeavor to protect these economies from possible adverse effects of European economic integration.

Integration and Politics

In examining the recent interest in economic integration, we have yet to comment on the role of political factors. There is no doubt that—especially in the case of Europe—political objectives are of great consequence. The avoidance of future wars between France and Germany, the creation of a third force in world politics, and the re-establishment of Western Europe as a world power are frequently mentioned as political goals that would be served by economic integration. Many regard these as primary objectives and relegate economic considerations to second place. No attempt will be made here to evaluate the relative importance of political and economic considerations. This position is taken, partly because this relationship is not quantifiable, partly because a considerable degree of interdependence exists between these factors. Political motives may prompt the first step in economic integration, but economic integration also reacts on the political sphere; similarly, if the initial motives are economic, the need for political unity can arise at a later stage.

From the economic point of view, the basic question is not whether economic or political considerations gave the first impetus to the integration movement, but what the economic effects of integration are likely to be. In some political circles the economic aspects are deliberately minimized and the plan for economic integration is regarded merely as a pawn in the play of political forces. Such a view unduly neglects the economic expediency of the proposal. Even if political motives did have primary importance, this would not mean that the economist could not examine the relevant economic problems without investigating elusive political issues. By way of comparison, although the formation of the United States was primarily the result of political considerations, nobody would deny the economic importance of its establishment.

We shall not disregard the political factors, however. Political *ends* will not be considered, but at certain points of the argument we shall examine various economic problems the solution of which is connected with political *means* and political processes. We shall explore, for example, how the objective of exploiting the potential benefits of economic integration affects the decision-making process. Changes in the decision-making process, on the other hand, become a political problem. Nevertheless, we shall go no further than to state the need for coordinated action in certain fields and will leave it for the political scientist to determine the political implications of such developments.

The "Liberalist" and the "Dirigist" Ideal of Economic Integration

The recent interest in economic integration has prompted various proposals concerning the means and objectives of integration. Two extreme views—an all-out liberalist and a dirigist solution—will be contrasted here. The champions of economic liberalism regard regional integration as a return to the free-trade ideals of the pre–First World War period within the area in question and anticipate the relegation of national economic policy to its pre–1914 dimensions.[15] If this approach is followed, integration simply means the abolition of impediments to commodity movements. At the other extreme, integration could also be achieved through state trading and through the coordination of national economic plans without the lifting of trade barriers. This alternative discards the use of market methods and relies solely on administrative, nonmarket means. It can be found in the integration projects of Soviet-type economies; the operation of the Council of Mutual Economic Assistance, comprising the Soviet Union and her European satellites, is based on the coordination of long-range plans and bilateral trade agreements. A similar method, but one which put more reliance on market means, was used by Germany during the last war. In this study we shall examine problems of economic integration in market economies and shall not deal with Nazi Germany and Soviet-type economies. Nevertheless, we shall see that dirigistic tendencies appear in the writings of some Western authors, too.

Among the proponents of the liberalist solution, Allais, Röpke, and Heilperin may be cited. They regard economic integration as identical with trade (and payments) liberalization. Allais asserts that "practically, the only mutually acceptable rule for close economic cooperation between democratic societies is the rule of the free market."[16] Röpke is of the opinion that European economic integration is nothing else than an attempt to remedy the disintegration of the post–1914 period that destroyed the previous integration of national economies.[17] A less extreme position is taken by Heilperin, who rejects the consideration of regional development plans and subsidies to industries for reconversion purposes but accepts state responsibility for investment decisions in certain areas.[18] To the majority of observers, however, the liberalist ideal of integration is a relic from the

15 Opposition to economic integration comes also from the side of free-trader economists. On this controversy, see my "Towards a Theory of Economic Integration," pp. 11–14.

16 Maurice Allais, "Fondements théoriques, perspectives et conditions d'un marché commun effective," *Revue d'Economie Politique*, January–February, 1958, p. 65. Allais's position does not exclude some degree of harmonization of the fiscal and social security systems in order to avoid distortions in competitive cost relationships. Cf. his *L'Europe unie—route de la prospérité* (Paris: Calmann-Lévy, 1960), pp. 106–7.

17 Wilhelm Röpke. "Integration und Desintegration der internationalen Wirtschaft," in *Wirtschaftsfragen der freien Welt* (Erhard-Festschrift) (Frankfurt, 1957), p. 500.

18 M. A. Heilperin, "Freer Trade and Social Welfare," *International Labour Review*, March, 1957, pp. 173–92.

past, and its application to present-day economic life appears rather anachronistic. As Jean Weiller put it, "It would be a great error to believe that the decision to create a regional union would re-establish the conditions of an economic liberalism, extirpating with one stroke all so-called dirigistic policies."[19]

It can rightly be said that considerations such as the avoidance of depressions, the maintenance of full employment, the problems of regional development, the regulation of cartels and monopolies, and so forth, require state intervention in economic life, and any attempts to integrate national economies would necessarily lead to harmonization in various policy areas. This idea is not new. The need for the coordination of fiscal, monetary, social, and countercyclical policies was stressed in the League of Nations study on customs unions published immediately after the end of the Second World War.[20] In fact, the question is not whether government intervention is needed or not in an integrated area, but whether economic integration results in a more intensive participation of the state in economic affairs or in a more intensive reliance on market methods.

Some authors advocate an intensification of state intervention in economic affairs. The need for economic planning in a union is emphasized, for example, by André Philip and by other French Socialists. In Philip's opinion, "there is no alternative to a directed economy," since "the market can be extended not by liberalising but by organising."[21] Although not an advocate of centralized planning, the stepping-up of state intervention is also recommended by Maurice Byé, who contrasts his "integration theory" with Heilperin's "market theory."[22] Considering the pronouncements of French economists and industrialists, it can be said that, by and large, the French view of economic integration contains more dirigistic elements than, for example, that of most German economists and entrepreneurs.

The defenders of dirigistic tendencies fail to consider, however, the lessening of planning and government intervention—and the beneficial effects thereof—in Europe since the end of the Second World

---

19 Jean Weiller, "Les objectifs économiques d'une coopération durable," *Economie Appliquée*, October–December, 1953, p. 579.

20 *Customs Unions*, pp. 63–74.

21 "Social Aspects of European Economic Co-operation," *International Labour Review*, September, 1957, p. 255.

22 "Freer Trade and Social Welfare, Comments on Mr. Heilperin's Article," *International Labour Review*, January, 1958, pp. 38–47.

War. Although this change does not indicate a return to the pre-1914 situation, it brought about an increased use of the market mechanism and contributed to the spectacular growth of the European economy during the 1950's. It appears, then, that a reintroduction of dirigistic methods would slow down, rather than accelerate, future growth. State intervention may be stepped up in some areas, such as regional development planning, and will also be required to deal with transitional problems, but it is expected that an enlargement of the economic area will intensify competition and lead to less interference with productive activities at the firm level. Therefore, those who regard the European Common Market as a *marché institué*[23] err in the opposite direction from the holders of old-fashioned liberalist views.

It has been widely accepted that a higher degree of government intervention is likely to be necessary in Latin-American integration projects. This reflects the proposition that present-day underdeveloped countries need more state interference in economic affairs than do advanced economies, since, in the former, market incentives are often not conducive to development. Nevertheless, the role of private enterprise is emphasized in most discussions of Latin-American integration,[24] and the sphere of government decision making may well diminish as development proceeds.

Economic Integration and Welfare[25]

It can be said that the ultimate objective of economic activity is an increase in welfare. Thus, in order to assess the desirability of integration, its contribution to welfare needs to be considered. But the concept of welfare is fraught with much obscurity. First, the noneconomic aspects present some ambiguity; second, even restricting the meaning of the concept to "economic welfare" in the Pigovian tradition, we are confronted with the well-known difficulties of interpersonal comparisons if we try to say anything over and above the Pareto condition: an increase in one man's welfare leads to an increase in

[23] Henri Guitton, "L'Europe et la théorie économique," *Revue d'Economie Politique,* January–February, 1958, pp. 324–39.

[24] Cf., e.g., United Nations, Department of Economic and Social Affairs, *The Latin American Common Market* (prepared by the Secretariat of the Economic Commission for Latin America, 1959), pp. 31, 125, and V. L. Urquidi, *Trayectoria del Mercado Común Latinoamericano* (Mexico, D.F.: Centro de Estudios Monetarios Latinoamericanos, 1960), p. 123.

[25] The reader with little background in economic theory should skim this section.

social welfare only if there is no reduction in the welfare of any other members of the group. In the case of integration, economic welfare will be affected by *(a)* a change in the quantity of commodities produced, *(b)* a change in the degree of discrimination between domestic and foreign goods, *(c)* a redistribution of income between the nationals of different countries, and *(d)* income redistribution within individual countries. Accordingly, distinction is made between a real-income component and a distributional component of economic welfare. The former denotes a change in potential welfare (efficiency); the latter refers to the welfare effects of income redistribution (equity).

With regard to potential welfare, separate treatment is allotted to changes in the quantity of goods produced and changes in their distribution. First, there is an increase (decrease) in potential welfare if —owing to the reallocation of resources consequent upon integration —the quantity of goods and services produced with given inputs increases (decreases) or, alternatively, if the production of the same quantity of goods and services requires a smaller (larger) quantity of inputs. If we regard inputs as negative outputs, we may say that a rise in net output leads to an increase in potential welfare. A higher net output entails an increase in potential welfare in the sense that a larger quantity of goods and services can now be distributed among individuals so as to make some people better off without making others worse off. Second, potential welfare is also affected through the impact of economic integration on consumer's choice. Restrictions on commodity movements imply discrimination between domestic and foreign commodities; a tariff causes consumers to buy more of lower-valued domestic and less of higher-valued foreign goods. The removal of intra-union tariffs will do away with discrimination between the commodities of the member countries but will discriminate against foreign goods in favor of the commodities of partner countries. In short, economic efficiency means efficiency in production and efficiency in exchange,[26] and an improvement in one or both constitutes an increase in potential welfare.

Given a change in potential welfare (the real-income component), we also have to consider the distributional component in

---

[26] This distinction corresponds to "production maximization" and "optimization of trade" in J. E. Meade, *Problems of Economic Union* (Chicago: University of Chicago Press, 1953), pp. 9 ff, and to "production effects" and "consumption effects" in H. G. Johnson, "The European Common Market—Risk or Opportunity," *Weltwirtschaftliches Archiv*, Vol. LXXIX, No. 2 (1957), p. 273.

order to determine changes in economic welfare.[27] It can easily be seen that an evaluation of changes in income distribution would require interpersonal comparisons of welfare. The new welfare economics, however, does not admit the possibility of making interpersonal comparisons. As a possible solution, it has then been suggested that changes in welfare could be determined in terms of potential welfare; that is, the *possibility* of making everybody better off (or, at least, no one worse off) would be taken as equivalent to an increase in economic welfare.[28] This proposition can be criticized primarily on the grounds that the hypothetical situation *after* compensation is irrelevant if compensation actually does not take place.[29] Nevertheless, changes in the real-income component give a good approximation of changes in welfare *within a country,* since compensation is politically feasible, and in case of integration this would actually be carried out to some degree in the form of assistance to relocating workers or reconverting firms. In addition, a nation can be regarded as an entity, where a redistribution of income accompanying an increase in real income can be accepted—provided that the redistribution does not run counter to generally accepted ideals of equity.

The distributional component cannot be neglected if economic integration redistributes income between countries, especially between the member states of a union, on the one hand, and the nonparticipating economies, on the other. It is not possible to claim an increase in world welfare in every case when the increase in real income in the participating countries will be greater than the loss to third countries. This proposition would hold true only if international comparisons of welfare could be made or if we disregarded differences in the marginal utility of income between countries. The

27 The distinction between efficiency and equity was first advanced by Cournot, in whose opinion "it is not enough that national income increases and that [some people] gain more than the others lose: the principles of equity . . . do not permit that acts of the public authority should have for their tendency to increase the natural inequality of conditions." See Augustin Cournot, *Researches into the Mathematical Principles of the Theory of Wealth* (New York: Macmillan Co., 1927), p. 170. Similar propositions were advanced by A. C. Pigou and his followers. Cf., e.g., *The Economics of Welfare* (London: Macmillan & Co., Ltd., 1920), *passim.*

28 An excellent review of the controversy about the concept of potential welfare is given in J. de V. Graaf, *Theoretical Welfare Economics* (Cambridge: At the University Press, 1957), chap. v. For a recent application of the concept to trade-induced changes in welfare, see H. G. Johnson, "International Trade, Income Distribution, and the Offer Curve," *Manchester School of Economic and Social Studies,* September, 1959, pp. 241–60.

29 Cf. J. E. Meade, *Trade and Welfare. The Theory of International Economic Policy,* Vol. II (London: Oxford University Press, 1955), p. 78.

first possibility was ruled out above, and the equality of the marginal utility of income is no less implausible. According to some, the marginal utility of income in an underdeveloped economy might be two or three times as high as in the rest of the world.[30] If such a view were accepted, a union of developed economies which would register gains in the real-income component might still reduce world welfare by redistributing income from "poor" to "rich" countries.

In the preceding discussion we have followed the customary exposition of welfare economics in using the concept of potential welfare in a static sense. Thus an increase in potential welfare was taken as equivalent to an improvement in the allocation of resources at a point of time. Static efficiency, however, is only one of the possible success criteria[31] that can be used to appraise the effects of economic integration. Instead of limiting our investigation to a discussion of efficiency in resource allocation under static assumptions, greater attention should be paid to the impact of integration on dynamic efficiency. I have elsewhere defined dynamic efficiency as the hypothetical growth rate of national income achievable with given resource use and saving ratio.[32] In technical terms, whereas static efficiency would require that the economy operate on its production-possibility frontier,[33] dynamic efficiency can be represented by the movement of this frontier in the northeast direction.[34] The concept of dynamic efficiency can be used in intercountry comparisons to indicate which economy is capable of faster growth under identical conditions with regard to resources and saving, or, alternatively, it can be applied for comparing the growth potentialities of an economy at different points of time. In the present context, we wish to compare the hypothetical growth rate attainable *before* and *after* integration, under the assumption of given initial resources and saving ratio.

[30] Cf., e.g., Marcus Fleming, "The Optimal Tariff from an International Standpoint," *Review of Economics and Statistics*, February, 1956, p. 8.

[31] For a discussion of various possible success criteria, cf. Bela Balassa, *The Hungarian Experience in Economic Planning* (New Haven: Yale University Press, 1959), chap. i.

[32] The term "given resource use" is employed here as a shorthand expression for given material resources and the use of given amounts of human labor. Cf. *ibid.*, p. 10.

[33] The production-possibility frontier describes the society's production potential at a point of time with given inputs. If the society is at its production frontier, a reallocation of resources cannot lead to an increase in the output of any desired commodity without reducing the output of another desired commodity. For a full statement of the conditions for static efficiency, see n. 23 in Chapter 3.

[34] Cf. R. Dorfman, P. A. Samuelson, and R. M. Solow, *Linear Programming and Economic Analysis* (New York: McGraw-Hill Book Co., Inc., 1958), chap. xii.

Given the static efficiency of an economy, the main factors affecting its dynamic efficiency are technological progress, the allocation of investment, dynamic interindustry relationships in production and investment, and uncertainty and inconsistency in economic decisions. In addition to these factors, the actual growth of national income would also be affected by an increase in the proportion of national income saved and/or by interference with the individual's choice between work and leisure. Changes in the latter variables will be disregarded here, partly because we assume that they are but rarely affected by economic integration,[35] partly because their effects cannot be evaluated in welfare terms, given the disutility of increased saving and/or work. Under these assumptions an increase in the rate of growth can be considered as equivalent to an improvement in dynamic efficiency and represents a rise in potential welfare.

In evaluating the effects of economic integration, we shall use dynamic efficiency as the primary success indicator, taking into account both changes in the efficiency of resource allocation in the static sense and the dynamic effects of integration. In addition, attention will be paid to the impact of integration on income distribution, on the regional pattern of production and income, and on the stability of the participating economies.

Some Fundamental Problems of Integration

The choice of dynamic efficiency as the main success criterion for evaluating the economic effects of integration entails an examination of the impact of integration on resource allocation and growth. In addition, we also have to consider the policy measures necessary to exploit the potential benefits of integration in the framework of a union. The distinction between problems of resource allocation, growth, and economic policies gives the main breakdown of this study.

The first part of the book examines the impact of economic integration on the allocation of resources within the union and in the nonparticipating countries. First, it is assumed that trade barriers are abolished while restrictions on the movements of factors are maintained within the integrated area. In connection with the freeing of commodity movements, the theory of customs unions and the problems of establishing a free-trade area will be dealt with. In a later chapter the removal of obstacles to factor mobility is postulated. Here we

[35] See, however, p. 181 below.

shall evaluate the economic effects of factor movements in a common market.

Whereas the first part of the study deals with problems of resource allocation in a static sense, in the further chapters dynamic considerations are introduced. These include a general discussion of the interrelationship between market size and economic growth, followed by an examination of theoretical problems and empirical evidence on internal and external economies. The closing chapter of Part II inquires into the impact of integration on market structures, technological change, risk and uncertainty in foreign trade, and investment activity.

The policy aspects of economic integration are the subject of the third part of the study. Separate chapters are devoted to the analysis of regional problems in a union, the harmonization of social policies, fiscal problems, and monetary unification. In connection with the discussion of monetary unification, we will consider balance-of-payments problems and the coordination of policies for stability and growth in an economic union.

APPENDIX

The Sectoral Approach to Integration

In this chapter, distinction has been made between various forms of economic integration, the main characteristics of which will be examined in the subsequent chapters. All these forms require concerted action in the entire field of economic activity, be it the abolition of customs barriers or the coordination of fiscal policies. Another approach to economic integration would be to move from sector to sector, integrating various industries successively. The application of this method had already been commended in the interwar period, and it found many champions in the period following the Second World War. Proposals were made to integrate various sectors such as the iron and steel industry, transportation, and agriculture. The Stikker Plan advocated the integration of national economies by removing barriers, industry by industry.[36] Supporters of this view contended that national governments were more inclined to make limited commitments with

36 Cf. D. U. Stikker, "The Functional Approach to European Integration," *Foreign Affairs*, April, 1951, pp. 436–44.

reasonably clear implications than to integrate all sectors at the same time. The flexibility of this method was also extolled, and it was hoped that integration in one sector would encourage integration on a larger scale.

From the theoretical point of view, various objections can be raised against the sectoral approach. Whereas the simultaneous integration of all sectors allows for compensating changes, integration in one sector will lead to readjustment in this sector alone, the reallocation of resources in other sectors being impeded by the continued existence of tariffs and other trade barriers—hence the losses suffered by countries whose productive activity in the newly integrated sector contracts will not be compensated for until the next phase. More generally, under the sectoral approach every step in integration results in a new and temporary equilibrium of prices, costs, and resource allocation, and this "equilibrium" is disturbed at every further step. Production decisions will then be made on the basis of prices that are relevant only in a certain phase of integration, and shifts in resource allocation will take place which may later prove to be inappropriate. On the other hand, the adjustment of relative prices and the reallocation of resources proceed more smoothly if all sectors are integrated at the same time, since some industries are expanding, others contracting, and unnecessary resource shifts do not take place.

Integration sector by sector puts an additional burden on the external balance also. At various steps, pressures will be imposed on the balance of payments of countries where the newly integrated sector is a high-cost producer. In the absence of exchange-rate flexibility, this process unnecessarily burdens exchange reserves in some, and inflates reserves in other, participating countries. If, on the other hand, exchange rates are left to fluctuate freely, temporary variations in rates of exchange will bring about transitional and unnecessary changes in the international division of labor.

In addition, lack of coordination in monetary, fiscal, and other policies is likely to cause difficulties under the sectoral approach, since differences in economic policies can lead to perverse movements of commodities and factors. For example, if inflationary policies are followed in one country while deflationary policies are pursued in another, an overadjustment will take place in the integrated sector (or sectors), while trade barriers restrict adjustments in other industries. Finally, any joint decisions made with respect to the integrated sector will affect all other branches of the participating economies.

A noneconomic objection of considerable importance should also be mentioned here. The sectoral approach is bound to bring about a conflict between producer and user interests in individual countries. In countries with relatively high production costs, for example, users will welcome integration because of its price-reducing effect; high-cost producers, however, will object to it. Experience suggests that producer interests have greater influence on governmental decision making; hence these pressures are likely to have a restrictive effect on integration if the sectoral approach is followed. The interests of exporting and importing countries being opposed, there can be no "give and take"—the necessary pre-condition for intercountry agreements in most practical instances.

These theoretical objections suggest the inadvisability of integration sector by sector. This conclusion does not mean, however, that integration in one sector may not be beneficial if political obstacles hinder integration in all areas. The European Coal and Steel Community is a case in point. At the time of its inception, the realization of a European Common Market was not yet possible, but the governments of the participating countries were prepared to accept a limited measure of integration. The establishment of the Coal and Steel Community has been conducive to the expansion of production and trade in the partaking industries,[37] and the Community demonstrated the possibility of integration in Europe, thereby contributing to the establishment of the Common Market.

It has also been argued that the difficulties of adjustment in production and trade in the Coal and Steel Community have been less than expected because the considerable increase in the national incomes of every participating country has made adjustment easier.[38] This does not, however, rule out the possibility of maladjustments in other industries which will not be corrected until trade barriers are removed in all sectors. In addition, the Coal and Steel Community has encountered serious difficulties with respect to transportation policies, fiscal and social problems, etc., which have been due—to a great degree—to the fact that integration extends over only one sector.[39]

[37] See below, p. 52.

[38] William Diebold, *The Schuman Plan* (New York: Frederick A. Praeger, 1959), p. 627.

[39] See *ibid.*, chap. viii–x; Louis Lister, *Europe's Coal and Steel Community* (New York: Twentieth Century Fund, 1960), chaps. 12–13; and Maurice Byé, "Les problèmes posés par la Communauté européenne du charbon et de l'acier," *Revue Economique*, November, 1960, pp. 845–53.

PART I

The Statics of Economic Integration

Chapter 2

COMMODITY MOVEMENTS: PRODUCTION ASPECTS

The Community shall be based upon a customs union covering the exchange of all goods and comprising both the prohibition, as between Member States, of customs duties on importation and exportation and all charges with equivalent effect and the adoption of a common customs tariff in their relations with third countries.

—Article 9 of the Treaty establishing the European Economic Community

The Theory of Customs Unions

One of the basic forms of economic integration is the customs union. According to the definition given in the General Agreement on Tariffs and Trade, a customs union must meet the following requirements: (*a*) the elimination of substantially all tariffs and other forms of trade restrictions among the participating countries and (*b*) the establishment of uniform tariffs and other regulations on foreign trade with nonparticipating economies.[1]

The discussion of theoretical problems raised by the formation of a customs union is of recent origin, although we find references to some relevant issues in earlier writings. Augustin Cournot, for example, distinguished between the effects of the removal of tariff barriers on efficiency and equity.[2] Explicit consideration was given to customs unions by Wicksell,[3] and the economic aspects of a customs

---

[1] "A customs union shall be understood to mean the substitution of a single customs territory for two or more customs territories, so that (i) duties and other restrictive regulations of commerce are eliminated with respect to substantially all the trade between the constituent territories of the union . . . and, (ii) substantially the same duties and other regulations of commerce are applied by each of the members of the union to the trade of territories not included in the union." GATT, *Basic Instruments and Selected Documents*, Vol. I (Geneva, 1952), Part III, Article XXIV, Sec. 8(a).

[2] *Researches into the Mathematical Principles of the Theory of Wealth* (New York: Macmillan Co., 1927), chaps. x and xii.

[3] Knut Wicksell, *Lectures on Political Economy* (London: Routledge & Kegan Paul, 1934), Vol. I, p. 133.

union were dealt with in more detail during the 1940's.[4] Neverthe-less, there had been no consistent theoretical analysis of the issues involved until 1950, when the writings of Maurice Byé, Herbert Giersch, and Jacob Viner appeared simultaneously.[5] Among these writers, Viner investigated the impact of a customs union on trade flows and distinguished between the "trade-creating" and the "trade-diverting" effects of a union. Byé also tackled the trade-creation versus trade-diversion issue, although in a looser framework and without the Vinerian terminology; in addition, he dealt with some policy problems originating in a union. The locational aspects of a union were emphasized by Giersch, who applied Weber's and Lösch's location theory to economic integration. The subsequent literature,[6] builds on the theoretical framework provided by Viner and analyzes, under varying assumptions, the welfare gains and losses resulting from the creation of a customs union.

In the following discussion we shall examine the effects of the removal of trade barriers within a union on the two components of world welfare: efficiency in resource allocation (static efficiency) and intercountry income distribution. Throughout the argument it will be assumed that no factor movements take place between countries, and, furthermore, we shall disregard the dynamic effects of integration (increasing returns, external economies, etc.). The assumption of intercountry factor immobility will be removed in Chapter 4, while the discussion of dynamic effects follows in Part II.[7]

The analysis of the impact of a union on resource allocation can be conveniently begun with reference to a hypothetical free-trade

[4] Cf., e.g., K. Heinrich, "Zollunionen und Grosswirtschaftsräume," Schmoller's Jahrbuch, No. 3 (1941), pp. 25–45; J. S. de Beers, "Tariff Aspects of a Federal Union," Quarterly Journal of Economics, November, 1941, pp. 49–92; Customs Unions (Lake Success: United Nations, 1947); C. Westrate, "The Economic and Political Implications of a Customs Union," Quarterly Journal of Economics, May, 1948, pp. 362–80; René Courtin, "Le problème de l'union économique douanière," Revue d'Economie Politique, May–June, 1948, pp. 366–93.

[5] See Byé, "Unions douanières et données nationales," Economie Appliquée, January–March, 1950, pp. 121–58 (the English translation was published in International Economic Papers, No. 3 [London: Macmillan & Co., Ltd., 1953], pp. 208–34); Giersch, "Economic Union between Nations and the Location of Industries," Review of Economic Studies, No. 2 (1949–50), pp. 87–97; and Viner, The Customs Union Issue (New York: Carnegie Endowment for International Peace, 1950).

[6] The main contributors are J. E. Meade, H. Makower and G. Morton, R. G. Lipsey, Tibor Scitovsky, and H. G. Johnson. For references, see below.

[7] The reader will note that, in some formulations, economies of scale are static phenomena. On this problem, see pp. 120–21 below.

situation. In a system of free trade, the prices of individual commodities can vary only by the amount of transportation cost, and any given commodity is produced at the cheapest source (sources) of supply. The institution of tariffs affects resource allocation in two ways: (*a*) the production of some commodities will shift from lower-cost foreign producers to protected home producers operating with higher costs (discrimination against foreign sources of supply of the *same* commodity); (*b*) consumer demand will shift from foreign goods to domestic products in response to the change in relative prices consequent upon the tariff (discrimination against foreign goods that are different in *kind* from domestic goods).

Both these changes will reduce world welfare. The shift from lower-cost to higher-cost sources of supply amounts to a redistribution of productive factors in such a way that less is produced with a given amount of resources than under free trade. In addition, consumers will be restricted in their choice of different commodities designed to fill certain needs and will consume more of lower-valued domestic goods and less of higher-valued foreign goods.

Through abolishing tariffs within the union and maintaining them against third countries, a customs union entails the suppression of discrimination between home-produced goods and goods produced in partner countries, and, at the same time, it gives rise to discrimination between commodities produced in partner and in third countries. Whether the net effect of the union's establishment represents a move in the direction of free trade or, on balance, increases discrimination depends on the relative magnitudes of various factors. These factors will be examined under the different forms in which the impact of the union on welfare becomes apparent. These are the production effects, the consumption effects, the terms-of-trade effects, and administrative economies.

Production effects result from shifting purchases of a given commodity from more expensive domestic to cheaper member-country sources of supply (positive effect) and from shifting sources of supply from lower-cost foreign to higher-cost member-country producers (negative effect). Production effects will be discussed in the present chapter under the assumption that the pattern of consumption remains unchanged, notwithstanding changes in relative prices. This assumption will be removed as we progress to the examination of consumption effects in Chapter 3.

The consumption effects of a union entail the substitution of commodities of the partner countries for domestic goods and foreign goods. As in the case of production effects, consumption effects may be beneficial or detrimental to efficiency in resource allocation. The removal of discrimination against the commodities of partner countries has beneficial effects, whereas the newly created discrimination against foreign products relative to those of the partner countries acts in the opposite direction.[8]

Both production and consumption effects relate to shifts in the demand for commodities produced by member and nonmember countries which modify the world production and trade pattern. Separate consideration will be given to the impact of these changes on the relative prices of exports and imports—the terms of trade. It will be shown that these terms-of-trade effects entail a redistribution of real income among the participating and nonparticipating countries and will thus affect world welfare.

Administrative economies of a customs union emanate from the abolition of customs formalities that constitute additional obstacles to international trade. In connection with administrative economies we shall also discuss disguised protection through the procedural rules of tariff laws. Administrative economies, as well as the terms-of-trade effects, will be considered in Chapter 3. In the same chapter we shall summarize the impact of integration on economic efficiency and discuss its effects on intercountry income distribution.

In a free-trade area, as distinct from the case of a customs union, the freeing of commodity movements between the member countries is not accompanied by the establishment of uniform tariffs on imports from third countries. Consequently, these two forms of economic integration will have identical effects on world welfare only if all participating economies had the same tariffs prior to integration. In examining the economic effects of the removal of intra-area trade restrictions below, identical initial tariff levels will be assumed for each country. By reason of this assumption, our analysis will apply to customs unions and free-trade areas as well, and the expression "customs union" or "union" will refer to both. The existence of disparate

[8] The parallel between the production effects and the consumption effects of a customs union will be apparent at this point: while the former entails substitution between sources of supply of the *same* commodity, the second refers to *intercommodity* substitution. It should be added that intercommodity substitution, too, will lead to changes in the production pattern, since production will respond to shifts in demand.

tariff levels in the participating countries would not materially affect the conclusions in the case of customs unions[9] but would influence the trade and production pattern of a free-trade area. The latter problem will be examined in the Appendix to Chapter 3.

Trade Creation and Trade Diversion

We have referred to the distinction made by Viner between the trade-creating and the trade-diverting effects of a customs union. The former relates to newly created trade between the member countries of the union, the latter to trade diverted from a foreign country to a member country, both consequent upon the abolition of tariffs within the union.

Under the assumption of pure competition, constant costs, and zero transportation costs,[10] the world market price of any commodity will be equal to the cost of production in the lowest-cost country. It follows that countries whose production costs are higher than the sum of the tariff and the world market price will import the commodity in question from the lowest-cost source, while other countries will produce it domestically. Assume, now, that a customs union is formed between countries A and B which excludes country C.[11] Five possible cases can be distinguished here.

1. Both participating countries produced the commodity in question prior to the formation of the customs union, and the union includes the lowest-cost producer. After the union is established, the inefficient producer, e.g., country A, will cease to produce this commodity, and its entire demand will be satisfied through importation from country B (trade creation). The same result would follow if tariffs against all countries were abolished.

2. Both countries produced the commodity in question under protection, and the union does not include the lowest-cost producer. The removal of tariffs between the participating countries will again create new trade, since the exploitation of cost differences, which was previously prevented by the tariff, will now become possible. Nevertheless, the new position is inferior to universal free trade, since under

[9] On the determination of the common tariff and related problems, see pp. 44–49 below.

[10] The latter assumption will be maintained throughout this section; transportation costs will be considered below (pp. 39–44).

[11] In the following, we shall refer to A as the home country, B as the partner country, and C as the foreign (nonmember) country.

free trade neither member country would produce the commodity, but both would import it from the lowest-cost source.

3. Country B is the lowest-cost producer, A did not produce the commodity under tariff protection. No change takes place after the union is formed (same as under free trade).

4. Country B produced the commodity under protection, while country A imported it from country C, the lowest-cost source. Removal of tariffs between A and B shifts A's entire import demand from the lowest-cost producer C to country B, since—under the assumption of uniform tariff levels—production costs in B are less than the sum of the tariff and the cost of production in C (trade diversion).[12] The resulting situation is less efficient than that existing prior to the union's establishment and, a fortiori, less efficient than universal free trade.

5. Neither A nor B produced the commodity under tariff protection. No change takes place after the union is established; both countries will continue to import the commodity from the lowest-cost source, C (same as under free trade).

Trade creation, then, represents a movement toward the free-trade position, since it entails a shift from high-cost to low-cost sources of supply, while trade diversion—a shift of purchases from lower-cost to higher-cost producers—acts in the opposite direction. The beneficial effects of the union will predominate, according to Viner, if trade creation outweighs trade diversion. He also points out, however, that the benefit or loss depends on differences in unit cost.[13] Combining the two elements—changes in the volume of trade and differences in costs—the production effects of a customs union can be estimated as the difference between (*a*) the amount of trade created, each item multiplied by differences in unit costs, and (*b*) the amount of trade diverted, each component multiplied by differences in cost per unit.[14] Consequently, if unit cost differences are considerably greater for commodities in which trade has been created than for goods in which trade has been diverted, a customs union may have a beneficial effect

12 Otherwise B would not have produced the commodity in question prior to integration.

13 Viner, *op. cit.*, pp. 46, 51.

14 Cf. J. E. Meade, *The Theory of Customs Union* (Amsterdam: North Holland Publishing Co., 1955), pp. 35–36. For other methods for measuring gains arising from the formation of a customs union, cf. H. G. Johnson, "The Gains from Freer Trade with Europe: An Estimate," *Manchester School of Economic and Social Studies*, September, 1958, pp. 247–55, and Tibor Scitovsky, *Economic Theory and Western European Integration* (Stanford: University Press, 1958), pp. 52–60.

on world efficiency, even if trade diversion measured as changes in the volume of trade outweighs trade creation.

We can conclude that the expressions "trade creation" and "trade diversion" cover only one aspect of production effects, and, to be more accurate, we should distinguish between positive and negative production effects. Positive production effects can be defined as the saving in cost resulting from a shift of purchases from higher-cost to lower-cost sources of supply. Negative production effects, on the other hand, refer to the extra cost of producing a commodity in the partner country rather than in the foreign country as trade diversion shifts the source of supply from lower-cost (foreign) to higher-cost (partner) producers. The world gains or loses according to whether the positive production effects are larger or smaller than the negative production effects.

The above-described method for estimating gains and losses due to the formation of a customs union—multiplying the amount of trade created (diverted) by differences in unit costs for each commodity—can be applied only under the assumption of infinite supply elasticities; if increasing costs prevail, cost increments will vary along the supply curves. Our formulation of positive and negative production effects included, however, the case of constant costs and increasing costs as well, since the definitions were phrased in terms of "cost saving" and "excess cost" without reference to the method of estimation.[15] We turn now to the discussion of gains and losses in efficiency resulting from the removal of intra-union trade barriers under the assumption of increasing costs.

The reader will recall that, in the case of constant costs, the world market price of a commodity was equal to its production cost at the lowest-cost source. Consequently, countries whose production cost was less than the world market price augmented by the tariff satisfied domestic demand entirely by home production, and the lowest-cost producer was the only exporter of the commodity in question. On the other hand, under the assumption of increasing costs, the world market price of any commodity is determined by world demand and supply, and the condition of producing a commodity in any country

---

[15] The reader is warned that an estimation of cost savings and excess costs for each commodity separately is based on *ceteris paribus* assumptions. Actually, the reshuffling of productive resources will affect prices and costs in all industries, and a consideration of all possible repercussions in a general equilibrium framework may result in a greater or smaller gain (loss) than that calculated by using partial-equilibrium methods.

will be that its production should be profitable, given the sum of the world market price and the tariff. The commodity will be exported by countries whose marginal cost of production equals the world market price at the point where output exceeds domestic demand.

Let us assume that, prior to the union's establishment, the domestic demand for commodity X in country A was satisfied partly by domestic production, partly by imports from countries B and C. If a customs union is formed between A and B, the price of the commodity will fall, and imports from the member country will increase at the expense of home production and of imports from the foreign country. The shift of production from A to B will increase efficiency (trade creation), while the shift in imports from C to B will reduce efficiency (trade diversion). It will become apparent that the higher the elasticity of supply in the home country, the larger will be the reduction in home production and thus the positive production effect. On the other hand, the greater the elasticity of supply in the foreign country, the larger will be the reduction of imports from that country and the negative production effects.[16]

Different considerations become relevant if, prior to the formation of the customs union, country B exported the commodity in question to country D. The removal of tariffs between A and B will now create new trade partly at the expense of B's exports to country D. In other words, while in the case of constant costs the exports of member countries to nonparticipating economies are not affected by the increase in intra-union trade, under increasing costs some of country B's exports will be diverted from foreign countries (country D) to member countries (country A). Again, the gain from trade creation is greater, the higher the elasticity of supply in country B, and the loss from trade diversion is greater, the higher the elasticity of supply in country D.[17]

16 Trade creation will be greater or less than trade diversion, depending on whether a reduction in the price of the commodity in question will cut back domestic production more than it will reduce imports from nonparticipating countries. H. G. Johnson has shown in an ingenious analysis along Marshallian lines that, under the assumption of linear supply and demand curves and specific duties, the relative magnitudes of trade created and diverted indicate the existence of positive or negative production effects (the reader will observe that the conclusion applies only to the partial-equilibrium analysis of the removal of tariffs on one commodity). See his "Discriminating Tariff Reduction: A Marshallian Analysis," *Indian Journal of Economics,* July, 1957, pp. 39–47.

17 For an interesting analysis of this case, see H. G. Johnson, "Marshallian Analysis of Discriminatory Tariff Reduction: An Extension," *Indian Journal of Economics,* October, 1958, pp. 177–82.

In the more general case, countries B and C had been exporters and countries A and D importers of the commodity in question. Consequently, the welfare losses due to the trade-diverting effects of a union between A and B will be partly compensated for by gains resulting from the increased division of labor among nonmember countries: country C may lose some of its markets, country D some of its suppliers, but trade between C and D will expand.

Turning from tariffs to other forms of trade restrictions, we note that while the net production effect of the abolition of tariffs may be positive or negative, the lifting of quantitative restrictions will always have a positive production effect. Provided that quotas had been effective, their removal will increase intra-union trade without causing a reduction in trade with third countries.

We have considered the impact of freeing commodity movements within an area on productive efficiency for the world as a whole. At this point we should also distinguish between production effects within the union and for third countries. The positive production effects arising from trade creation within the union will accrue to the member countries only; so will negative production effects under the assumption of constant costs. If increasing costs prevail, however, the negative production effects will be shared by members and nonmembers alike. Third countries, then, will lose on this count, and the union members may gain, even if negative production effects outweigh the positive production effects for the world as a whole.[18]

As Viner, Meade, and others rightly emphasize, no a priori judgment can be made about the possible production effects of a hypothetical customs union. The consideration of certain factors can be of help, however, in determining the probable impact of a union on productive efficiency. In a static framework, the complementarity or competitiveness of the participating economies, differences in production costs, the size of the union, propinquity and transportation costs, and the height of tariffs can be regarded as the main determinants of production effects. These factors will be discussed in the subsequent sections.

Complementarity and Competitiveness

Jacob Viner writes in his classic *The Customs Union Issue:* "In the literature on customs union, it is almost invariably taken for

18 This possibility was overlooked by Viner, *op. cit.*, p. 44.

granted that rivalry is a disadvantage and complementarity is an advantage in the formation of customs unions."[19] Union between complementary economies had been advocated by protectionists and free-traders alike, but for opposite reasons. Protectionists looked upon complementarity between participating countries as an assurance that the formation of the union would create the possibility for autarkic economic policies.[20] Free-traders, on the other hand, regarded complementarity between union members as beneficial, on the grounds that it gave promise of larger savings in costs, since cost differences between complementary economies were greater than between rival economies.[21] In *The Customs Union Issue*, Viner reached different conclusions. He contended that the less the degree of complementarity —or the greater the degree of rivalry—of the member countries with respect to protected industries prior to customs union, the greater the benefit from a customs union.[22] Viner's somewhat ambiguous formulation stirred up a great deal of controversy about his seemingly paradoxical proposition, but the arguments presented often confused rather than clarified the issue.

In recent writings, the terms "rival" and "complementary" refer to differences in comparative costs,[23] and those economies are regarded as complementary in which production costs, expressed in some common unit, show large disparities for most commodities. If this definition were accepted, we could restate the conclusion reached with regard to the trade-creating and the trade-diverting effects of a customs union as follows: complementarity (i.e., large differences in production costs) will be beneficial if both countries produced the com-

---

19 *Ibid.*, p. 51 n.

20 Complementarity as a prop for autarky appears in its clearest form in the Hitlerite *Grossraum* plans. See Heinrich, *op. cit.*, pp. 25–46.

21 Cf., e.g., Gottfried Haberler, "The Political Economy of Regional or Continental Blocs," *Postwar Economic Problems*, ed. S. E. Harris (New York: McGraw-Hill Book Co., Inc., 1943), p. 334, and Walther Hoffman, "Die Integration der Volkswirtschaften als dynamisches Problem," *Economia Internazionale*, August, 1950, pp. 711–12.

22 P. 51. A similar position had already been taken in 1948 by René Courtin (*op. cit.*, p. 375), whose work apparently escaped Viner's attention.

23 J. E. Meade, "The Removal of Trade Barriers: The Regional versus the Universal Approach," *Economica*, May, 1951, p. 190; and H. Makower and G. Morton, "A Contribution towards a Theory of Customs Unions," *Economic Journal*, March, 1953, pp. 33–49. A different definition is used by F. V. Meyer, who borrows these terms from demand theory and refers to complementarity and substitutability in consumption. See his "Complementarity and the Lowering of Tariffs," *American Economic Review*, June, 1956, pp. 323–35. This formulation will not be discussed in connection with production effects but rather in examining the consumption effects of integration, since it assumes changes in the demand pattern and in the utility of consumer goods.

modity before the formation of the union (in Meade, potential complementarity) and harmful if one participating country was a producer before the union was established and the union excluded the lowest-cost producer (in Meade, actual complementarity).[24]

It will be recalled that this conclusion was based on the assumption of constant costs and zero transportation costs. The argument needs modification if we introduce the possibility of increasing costs. The same commodity can now be produced in more than one country, and differences in the shape of the cost curves will be decisive in determining the production and trade pattern.[25] The above definition of complementarity will then find little application, since the distinction between potential and actual complementarity becomes blurred. And we would evade the issue instead of solving it if we applied Makower's and Morton's formulation to this case, according to which "if two Unions both offer a gain, the one offering the greater gain is, definitionally, the Union between the more complementary pair of countries."[26]

Definitions of complementarity and rivalry based on disparities in comparative costs have the further disadvantage that they do not distinguish between differences in the range of products, on the one hand, and in the unit costs of commodities actually produced, on the other. Recent contributions to the theory of customs unions discuss the standard case of economic theory, where the production possibilities of *all* countries include *every* commodity.[27] Such reasoning is useful in abstract theorizing, but it is far from being realistic. For a great number of commodities, such as cotton, rubber, tropical fruits, and all mineral products, production possibilities are determined by natural advantages, and the production of these commodities in countries without the necessary resource endowments is physically impossible or would involve practically infinite costs. In the case of another group of commodities, the absence of cooperative factors or the existing degree of specialization does not permit manufacturing. Nobody would consider, for example, producing transport airplanes in Nicaragua or setting up an atomic reactor in Tunisia. For other com-

24 Cf. pp. 25–26 above.

25 On transportation costs, cf. pp. 39–44 below.

26 *Op. cit.*, p. 40; see also pp. 45–48.

27 Meade states, for example, that "if there were no international trade [country] A would have to produce her raw materials as well as her finished cloth" ("The Removal of Trade Barriers: The Regional versus the Universal Approach," p. 190). But how can a country produce cotton if its natural endowment is not suitable for cotton production?

modities, production will not take place in the absence of international trade, since there would be no demand for the product at a price sufficient to induce domestic entrepreneurs to undertake their manufacture.[28] In all these cases—as well as in instances when the domestic production of a commodity is not profitable unless tariffs are raised to a level which is regarded as prohibitive—the scope of production in various countries will differ greatly.

In distinction from the interpretation advanced by Meade et al., Viner apparently referred to similarities and dissimilarities in the range of products manufactured in defining complementarity and rivalry. Competitiveness is characterized as "correspondence in kind of products of the range of high-cost industries as between the different parts of the customs union which were protected by tariffs in both of the member countries before customs union was established."[29] Consequently, competitiveness denotes a large degree of overlapping in the range of the commodities produced, and complementarity means substantial differences in the scope of production. It should be added that, in the case of product differentiation, protected commodities may also be exported, or even all countries manufacturing certain commodities may protect *and* export them. Similar results may ensue if increasing costs and transportation costs are introduced. In all these cases efficiency is likely to be improved in a customs union of competitive economies, although the beneficial effects will be impaired if the member countries have strong competitors abroad. Finally, if the participating economies were largely complementary, discrimination against third-country producers would lead to negative production effects.[30]

It is a separate problem that, in a union of competitive economies, productive efficiency will improve in a greater degree if there are substantial differences in the cost of manufacturing the commodities that were actually produced before the union's establishment. Then the reallocation of resources will take place to a larger extent, and the gain per unit of trade created will also increase. Viner, too,

----

[28] This is the so-called corner solution of modern theory, when the marginal rate of transformation between two products is greater than their marginal rate of substitution at zero output for one of the products.

[29] *Op. cit.*, p. 51.

[30] Complementarity is desirable, however, if the union includes the lowest-cost producer.

points out that "the greater the differences in unit costs for protected industries of the same kind as between different parts of the customs union,"[31] the greater will be the gain from the union.

The definitions adopted here re-establish the Vinerian conclusion that a union of competitive economies will be desirable when competitiveness means that the participating countries produce—to a large extent—commodities of the same kind prior to the formation of the union, and complementarity denotes considerable differences in the range of products manufactured. In a union of competitive economies, the gain in productive efficiency will be further augmented if large differences exist in unit costs. On the other hand, complementarity between the economies of the participating countries will result in negative production effects.[32]

The impact of complementarity and rivalry on economic efficiency can, to a certain degree, be forecast for particular integration plans. Even a cursory glance at the industrial and foreign-trade statistics of the European Common Market countries would reveal a considerable degree of rivalry in the economic structure of these economies. In addition, a significant part of this union's imports consists of raw materials which cannot be produced inside the Common Market. Complementarity rather than competitiveness exists, however, in agriculture between the European member countries and their former overseas dependencies. The Common Market is expected to have negative production effects, for example, with regard to certain tropical produce such as coffee, cocoa, and bananas. Under static assumptions, the importation of these products would, in part, shift from nonparticipating economies to the associated overseas countries and territories. Such a change would unfavorably affect certain Latin-American and African producers and reduce world efficiency by diverting trade from lower-cost to higher-cost sources.[33]

Similar developments will occur in industries which have strong

---

31 *Op. cit.*, p. 51.

32 For qualifications, see above.

33 GATT, *The Possible Impact of the European Economic Community, in Particular the Common Market, upon World Trade*, Trade Intelligence Papers, No. 6 (Geneva, 1957), pp. 40–42. The magnitude of trade-diverting effects on this count will depend on how many of the overseas countries and territories listed in Annex IV of the Common Market Treaty will actually be the beneficiaries of tariff reductions. The situation will change, furthermore, if we consider future increases in incomes in the Common Market. On this point, see pp. 185–87 below.

competitors among the nonparticipating countries. The automobile industry is an often used example. Before the Common Market was established, West Germany levied a 14 per cent duty, France 30 per cent, Italy 35–45 per cent, while the Benelux states applied a 24 per cent tariff on imported automobiles. The abolition of duties among the Six and the establishment of a uniform tariff at the level of the arithmetical average of these duties against outsiders is bound to reduce the share of American and British automobile exports in the Common Market. In the manufacture of precision instruments, German industry may benefit at the expense of Swiss producers, whereas in wool fabrics the gain for France and Italy would be a loss for England. American exports of copper, metal-working machinery, machine tools, and organic chemicals are also likely to suffer a certain amount of displacement.[34]

The countries participating in the Free Trade Association of the "Outer Seven" are less competitive and more complementary than the Common Market countries. In intra-area trade, British exports consist mainly of chemicals, machinery, and other manufactures, while —with the exception of Austria and Switzerland—the exports of the other participating countries are heavily weighted with food and raw materials. The trade-diverting effects of the Free Trade Association will then be felt with respect to trade in manufactures, foodstuffs, and raw materials as well.[35]

Latin-American countries are, by and large, complementary with advanced industrial economies. Nevertheless, there will be trade diversion in those cases where domestic production is substituted for imports. At the same time, there appears to be some reluctance to rely on the possibilities of trade creation in nondurable consumer goods in whose manufacture the highly protected industries of these countries are actually competitive. If this were the case, the trade-creating effects of the Latin-American union would be operative mostly in newly created industries, and in existing industries they

[34] Cf. H. S. Piquet, "First Effects of the Common Market: The Impact of Changing Tariffs on U.S. Exports," in *The European Common Market: New Frontier for American Business* (New York: American Management Association, 1958), pp. 124–59, and M. E. Kreinin, "European Integration and American Trade," *American Economic Review*, September, 1959, pp. 615–27.

[35] An interesting attempt has been made for a numerical comparison of the two unions with regard to complementarity and competitiveness in M. E. Kreinin, "The 'Outer Seven' and European Integration," *American Economic Review*, June, 1960, pp. 381–85.

would depend on the need for increased production in response to the growth of incomes.[36]

Size of the Union

There is a divergence of opinion as to the effects of the size of a union on world efficiency. While Jacob Viner, J. E. Meade, and Jan Tinbergen argue that the larger the area of a customs union, the greater will be the positive production effects, G. A. Duncan, R. G. Hawtrey, and Wilhelm Röpke maintain the opposite.[37] However, the differences in these views can be reduced to differences in assumptions with respect to the policies that are likely to be pursued after the union has been established. Those who regard an increase of the integrated area as beneficial assume that economic policies remain unchanged in the union,[38] whereas most proponents of the contrary view base their case on the possibility of protectionist tendencies in trade policies.

Viner and Meade use the common-sense argument that, other things being equal, a larger economic area increases the potential scope for the internal division of labor. While a smaller customs union, so they argue, may lead to useful shifts in some lines of production, the chances for the reallocation of production increase with the extension of the area. At the same time, successive increases in the size of a union are said to reduce the possibility of trade diversion. In the limiting case, a union including the whole world would not lead to any trade diversion. A more rigorous formulation is given by Tinbergen, who uses a simple mathematical model involving countries of equal size that produce one commodity each; he concludes that every extension of the union will increase total production and thereby world welfare.[39]

Duncan and Röpke, on the other hand, envisage modifications

---

36 See also pp. 172–73 below.

37 Viner, *op. cit.*, p. 51; Meade, *The Theory of Customs Unions*, p. 109; Tinbergen, "Customs Unions: Influence of Their Size on Their Effect," *Selected Papers* (Amsterdam: North Holland Publishing Co., 1959), pp. 152–64; Duncan, "The Small State and International Economic Equilibrium," *Economia Internazionale*, November, 1950, pp. 933–43; Hawtrey, *Economic Destiny* (London: Longmans, Green & Co., 1944), pp. 135–36; Röpke, "Gemeinsamer Market und Freihandelszone," *Ordo, Jahrbuch für die Ordnung von Wirtschaft und Gesellschaft*, Vol. X (1958), p. 53.

38 It is also implicitly assumed that enlarging the area does not introduce countries with an economic structure greatly different from that of the countries participating in the union.

39 *Selected Papers*, p. 164. Note that this argument is not based on the assumption of increasing returns of any kind. The interrelationship between market size and increasing returns will be discussed in chap. 5.

in economic policies as the area of the union increases. They maintain that while small nations are interested in the international division of labor, large nations are more inclined toward autarky, since protectionist interests can have greater scope in a large nation. This may or may not be true. The example of the Soviet Union would substantiate this assertion, but there is not much sense in applying the evidence supplied by the Soviet Union to the European Common Market, and recent developments in Europe do not bear out Duncan's and Röpke's pessimism. Nevertheless, protectionist tendencies may have greater scope in Latin-American integration projects.

Among the opponents of regional unions, Hawtrey seems to disregard the possibility of positive production effects in arguing that "the wider the extent of economic activity encircled by a tariff barrier of given height, the greater is its effect in excluding goods of foreign producers."[40] But this is only half the truth: the enlargement of an economic area may increase trade diversion in certain fields, yet, according to Tinbergen's and others' findings, in the absence of a change in economic policies, this would be more than offset by enhanced trade creation.

Accepting the view that an enlargement of the union increases potential benefits for the world as a whole, the question is how the size of the area can be measured. Various definitions of market size have been given. Some authors maintain that the size of the market should be measured by population.[41] Such a concept would not reveal, however, the possibilities of the division of labor in an area and would falsely intimate that, for instance, the economic area of China or India was greater than that of the United States. Objections can also be raised against the use of geographical extension as an indicator of market size. A more appropriate yardstick—the volume of production—was advocated first by Allyn Young.[42] Under this definition, the size of the market for a national economy or for a union would be measured by its gross national product. Further qualifications are introduced if we consider differences in tastes and transportation costs within the area. For a given gross national product, the greater the

40 *Op. cit.*, pp. 135–36.
41 Cf., e.g., Simon Kuznets, "Economic Growth of Small Nations," *Economic Consequences of the Size of Nations*, ed. E. A. G. Robinson (London: Macmillan & Co., Ltd., 1960), p. 14.
42 "Increasing Returns and Economic Progress," *Economic Journal*, December, 1928, p. 533.

costs of transportation and the more diversified the tastes of the population, the smaller is the effective size of the market.

The effects of transportation costs on intra-union trade will be discussed in the following section; hence this qualification will be disregarded here. Differences in tastes are relevant within a country and, in the case of a union, between member countries as well. It has often been argued, for example, that the European market is more heterogeneous than the American; consumption habits are highly correlated with social position, and economic integration is not likely to change this situation. Nevertheless, although consumption habits between various social classes seem to differ more in Europe than in the United States, integration may result in a "horizontal" change, even in the absence of a "vertical" change. In other words, granted the correlation between social position and consumption habits, the consumption of the same social strata in the countries participating in a union can become more uniform and would allow for the standardization of consumer goods. Similar conclusions may apply to Latin America.

This "horizontal" change may be impeded in the case of differentiated products if domestically produced goods are better suited to domestic tastes. For example, French consumers may not like the style of Dutch furniture or the lines of the German Volkswagen. Reluctance to purchase foreign products is strengthened by imperfect information and inadequate maintenance and repair facilities for imported consumer durables. These tendencies may be counteracted, however, by dissemination of market information and also by consumers' preferences—often irrational—for foreign goods that have snob appeal. And there seems to be no reason why adequate repair facilities could not be provided in the member countries.

Similar problems arise from the diversity of systems of weights and measures and differences in specifications, standards, and usages which affect especially trade in steel, metal manufactures, electrical engineering products, railway vehicles, and building materials. Note that the less developed countries of Latin America possess an advantage over Europe in this regard, inasmuch as in the former area the development of standards and specifications proceeds *pari passu* with integration.

Differences in tastes and specifications are hardly quantifiable. Thus, with these qualifications in mind, we shall rely on national income figures as a rough approximation to the size of the market. Two propositions will be advanced in this connection: *ceteris paribus,* the larger the size of the union, the greater are the potential gains from integration for the world as a whole, and the greater the increase in the market of the participating economies, the more will the world and the member countries benefit.

As to the size of the union, the beneficial effects of the European Common Market for world efficiency will be considerably larger than those of the Benelux union, given that the gross national product of the former amounts to 42 per cent, while that of the latter only 6 per cent, of the United States GNP.[43] The corresponding figure for the European Free Trade Association is approximately 27 per cent.[44]

Estimates on the national income of Latin-American countries are less reliable, partly because the error possibilities of national income data are significantly greater in Latin America than in advanced industrial economies, partly because the conversion to United States dollars at rates allegedly approximating purchasing-power parities is admittedly imperfect. In 1955 the gross national product of Latin America as a whole totaled $50 billion measured in 1950 prices, amounting to approximately 14 per cent of GNP in the United States. The corresponding figures for the two union projects under implementation are about 10 per cent for the Latin American Free Trade Association and one-third of 1 per cent for Central America.[45] Thus, using the size of the union's market as an indicator, the free-trade area of the larger Latin-American countries would seem to offer smaller benefits for the world as a whole than the European integration projects, and the beneficial effects of the Central American union appear to be negligible.

In view of our second proposition, productive efficiency is also affected by the size of the member countries. Given the size of the union, the association of a number of small countries is likely to bring

[43] Milton Gilbert and Associates, *Comparative National Products and Price Levels* (Paris: Organisation for European Economic Co-operation, 1958), p. 87. The GNP figures used here are geometric averages of gross national products calculated at United States and European relative price weights. This method avoids the distortions inherent in comparisons at exchange rates. For a methodological note, see *ibid.*, pp. 21-24. Data refer to 1955.

[44] Estimated from *ibid.*, p. 87, and United Nations, *Per Capita National Product of Fifty-five Countries, 1952–54* (New York, 1957), p. 9.

[45] Estimates based on United Nations, *Economic Survey of Latin America, 1957* (New York, 1959), p. 83; *Per Capita National Product in Fifty-five Countries,* p. 8; and B. F. Hoselitz, "Economic Development in Central America," *Weltwirtschaftliches Archiv,* Vol. LXXVI, No. 2 (1956), p. 276.

a greater improvement in world efficiency than the integration of two large economies, and the gain for individual member countries will also be positively correlated with the relative increase in market size. Therefore, in relative terms, the potential gains for Latin-American economies may well be greater than for France or Germany. The latter conclusion is strengthened if the possibilities of future development are taken into account. As a result of the operation of dynamic factors, the enlargement of the market through integration will raise productivity to a greater extent if the initial size of the market was small. We shall return to the examination of the latter problem in Chapter 5.

Propinquity and Transportation Costs

In traditional trade theory it is customarily assumed that trade takes place between countries which have no spatial dimensions. Correspondingly, locational problems have also been neglected in the theory of customs unions. This neglect could be defended if we assumed that, in an intercountry comparison, the cost of transportation was included in the cost of production. But it is questionable what the explanatory value of such a theory is. Grouping together production and transportation costs indiscriminately, one tends to overlook the advantages of propinquity in judging the desirability of customs unions. Jacob Viner, for example, maintains that "it is not evident that contiguity or proximity has sufficient economic significance of itself to justify special sanction for tariff preferences on that score."[46] The disregard of locational factors may also provide an explanation why R. G. Hawtrey regarded the breakup of the Austro-Hungarian monarchy as advantageous for economic efficiency.[47]

Introducing the spatial element into the theory of customs unions, we have to consider how the propinquity of the countries participating in a union bears upon the economic effects of integration. Given the existing tariff barriers, economic integration will remedy distortions in the location of productive activity caused by the decomposition of an economic area into national units. In this context, a customs union will have beneficial effects to the extent that it establishes (or re-establishes) the continuity of economic flows disturbed by national boundaries.[48] If we take into consideration noneconomic

[46] *Op. cit.*, p. 122.
[47] *Op. cit.*, pp. 135–36.
[48] For a good discussion of some of the relevant issues, see Giersch, *op. cit.*, pp. 87–97.

factors, too, the advantages of propinquity can be enumerated as follows: (*a*) the distances to be traversed are shorter in the case of neighboring countries; (*b*) tastes are more likely to be similar, and distribution channels can be more easily established in adjacent economies; and (*c*) neighboring countries may have a common history, awareness of common interests, etc., and hence be more willing to coordinate policies.[49]

To begin with the second proposition, propinquity will often be accompanied by similarities in tastes. It can also be argued that it is easier for a firm to establish distribution channels in adjacent countries, since the cost of supervision and communication increases with distance. The same considerations apply to the case of repair facilities. The latter have special importance in regard to durable consumer goods, machinery, and equipment. In addition, awareness of common traditions and common interests may facilitate the coordination of economic policies in a union comprising the countries of a particular area and may alleviate the task of settling disputes and undertaking common responsibilities. This consideration has been given emphasis with regard to the European Common Market and has lately been stressed in Latin America, where common interests are regarded as a cohesive force of primary importance. Traditional enmities and aversions of neighboring countries, however, may also obstruct the way toward integration.[50] But these feelings may undergo changes in a relatively short time—witness the amelioration of Franco-German relations during the 1950's.

These propositions may be of importance for some present-day integration projects; yet one encounters serious obstacles in attempting to assess their actual significance, especially in cases when subjective factors play an important role. Another major advantage of propinquity—low transportation costs—can be evaluated in objective terms and will therefore be discussed in greater detail.

Empirical studies indicate that geographical distance has a con-

---

[49] Savings in the cost of administering tariffs is an additional issue (cf. pp. 65–67 below).

[50] In the economic literature we often find reference to the "unneighborly" feelings of neighbors. Adam Smith writes, for example: "[France and England] being neighbours, they are necessarily enemies, and the wealth and power of each becomes, upon that account, more formidable to the other; and what would increase the advantage of national friendship serves only to inflame the violence of national animosity." *An Inquiry into the Nature and Causes of the Wealth of Nations* (Modern Library ed.; New York: Random House, 1937), p. 463.

siderable effect on economic intercourse. The findings of the German National Bureau of Statistics, for example, show fairly high negative correlation between distance measured in miles and the flow of goods via water between 23 areas of the world.[51] Similar results have been reached in studies on internal trade in the United States by Rutledge Vining and by Isard and Peck.[52] It should be noted, however, that these studies consider a homogeneous means of transportation (e.g., rail or sea), and the results require modification if alternative means of conveyance and natural obstacles to transportation are taken into account. In considering alternative transportation possibilities, the lower cost of sea transport will influence the results, and the experience of the United States cannot be immediately applied to Africa, Asia, or Latin America, where topographical difficulties and the paucity of roads and railroads hinder the intracontinental transfer of commodities.

For the purposes of evaluating the relative advantages of customs unions comprising different combinations of countries, the cost of traversing the distance rather than actual mileage is relevant. We can then distinguish between geographical distance and economic distance when the latter is determined by geographical distance, the cost of rail, truck, and sea transport, and existing railway and port facilities. For example, the economic distance between London and Copenhagen is less than between Frankfurt and Copenhagen, although the geographical distance is shorter in the latter case. Also in Latin America poor transportation facilities and the separation of inhabited areas often make for greater economic distances between near-situated points on the mainland than between faraway seaports.

To circumvent the difficulties inherent in the direct measurement of economic distances, an ingenious method has been advocated by W. Beckerman. He suggests that economic distances between countries should be measured as the markup between (a) the f.o.b. average value of exports of certain specific goods as they appear in the export statistics of individual countries, accompanied by specification of the destination of these exports, and (b) the c.i.f. average value of those quantities of the same goods which are specified as being imported

---

[51] Cited in W. Isard and M. J. Peck, "Location Theory and International and Interregional Trade Theory," *Quarterly Journal of Economics*, February, 1954, p. 103.

[52] *Ibid.*, pp. 100–102, and Vining, "Delimitation of Economic Areas: Statistical Conceptions in the Study of the Spatial Structure of an Economic System," *Journal of the American Statistical Association*, March, 1953, pp. 44–64.

from the corresponding countries in the import statistics of the relevant importing countries.[53] This markup would roughly indicate the relative costs of transfer, including insurance. Although this method has certain limitations—the time period is not identical in exporting and importing countries, product classification differs, correction cannot be made for transit trade, etc.—it can be commended as a first approximation to indicate economic distance.

Beckerman's results reveal that a high degree of correlation exists within the European area between the ranking of economic distances of countries from a given country and the ranking of the same countries with respect to their relative importance in the trade of that country.[54] As a general proposition it can be stated that, other things being equal, the shorter the economic distance between any two countries, the greater are the potentialities of economic intercourse between them, and the more will the world benefit from their integration. Low transportation costs associated with short economic distances will increase the positive production effects through the low degree of geographical protection and are likely to cause less trade diversion between the union and third countries. This proposition can be used in evaluating actual integration projects.

The ranking of certain European countries[55] according to the economic distances between them makes it possible to assess the desirability of the Common Market on the basis of propinquity. This can be done by summing up the ordinal values indicating economic distances between various countries.[56] If we consider only Belgium and Luxemburg (taken as a unit), France, Germany, and the Netherlands, the composite index of economic distances between these countries would be 12, which is the absolute minimum for the combination of any four countries.[57] The inclusion of Italy increases the index

[53] "Distance and the Pattern of Intra-European Trade," *Review of Economics and Statistics,* February, 1956, p. 34.

[54] *Ibid.,* pp. 36–37. Such relative distances are not necessarily symmetrical, since the export pull and the import pull between any two countries may differ considerably in multilateral trade.

[55] Belgium-Luxemburg, Denmark, France, Germany, Italy, Netherlands, Norway, Sweden, United Kingdom. Unfortunately, only partial information is available in regard to Austria, Portugal, Spain, and Switzerland; hence these countries will not be included in the calculation that follows.

[56] Actually, economic distance between every pair of countries is designated by two numbers which give the ranking from the point of view of each country separately. In our discussion, the arithmetical average of the two values is used.

[57] The inclusion of Austria and Switzerland in the estimate would change the figures slightly, but the above combination would still be more advantageous than the exclusion of any of these countries and the inclusion of Austria or Switzerland.

to 32, in contrast with the possible minimum of 25 for five countries. Including Denmark and excluding Italy, the index will rise to 34, whereas the substitution of Great Britain for Italy would result in a value of 28. If Switzerland and Austria were also included in the estimate, the consideration of economic distances would suggest that the participation of Great Britain, Switzerland, and Austria in the Common Market would be more advantageous than the participation of Italy.

If economic distance is taken as an indicator, the Free Trade Association of the "Outer Seven" is not much to be commended, since these countries are located on the periphery of the Common Market. Denmark, Norway, and Sweden constitute a natural unit, but the economic distance between the United Kingdom and three of the Common Market countries (Belgium, the Netherlands, and France) is shorter than between the United Kingdom and any of the participants in the Free Trade Association. Similarly, Austria, Switzerland, and (to a lesser degree) Portugal are not natural trading partners of the other Free Trade Area countries.

We noted above that the lack of adequate transportation facilities and the absence of continuous economic activity across national frontiers indicate large disparities between economic distances and geographical distances in Latin America. Because of undeveloped land transport and inland waterways, about 90 per cent of the existing trade between South American countries uses the sea route.[58] In addition, the use of ocean transportation for the future expansion of trade between these countries is hampered by the insufficiency of present Latin-American fleets and harbor facilities and the inadequacies of the land and water approaches that link the ports with their hinterlands.

Given the existing transportation facilities, objections can be raised against the formation of a customs union including all Latin-American economies. This conclusion, in turn, might be challenged on the grounds that new developments in transportation may change the picture in a few decades. For example, around the 1840's the economic distance between New York and London was considerably shorter than between New York and Pittsburgh, and this situation has since changed drastically as a result of the rapid development of rail-

[58] For data on South American trade, see United Nations, Department of Economic and Social Affairs, *Study of Inter-Latin American Trade* (New York, 1957), p. 11. The percentage for Latin America as a whole may differ only to an insignificant degree.

roads and other means of transportation. It could also be contended that the lack of overhead capital in the form of transportation equipment ought not to be used as an argument against the integration of all Latin America, since the existence of these facilities provides developed countries with an artificial advantage. Nevertheless, one should realize that the construction of new transportation facilities has an opportunity cost in the form of alternative investments forgone, which has to be taken into account in evaluating any integration scheme. Furthermore, in the case of Latin America, natural barriers to economic intercourse are more formidable than in the United States.[59]

The picture becomes brighter if we consider the locational advantages and disadvantages of establishing regional unions within this area. The distance factor would speak for the integration of a group of countries in the Southern Zone (Argentina, Bolivia, Brazil, Chile, Paraguay, and Uruguay), in the Northern Zone (Colombia, Ecuador, and Venezuela), and also in Central America.[60] The consideration of economic distances does not, however, warrant the inclusion of Mexico in the free-trade area of the Southern Zone.

Height of Tariffs

The height of tariff levels affects the economic desirability of a union in three principal ways. The production effects will be more advantageous (*a*) the higher the average level of initial tariffs on trade between the participating countries; (*b*) the lower the tariff level of the union against the outside world; (*c*) the lower the tariff level in export markets outside of the union.[61] However, these propositions become meaningful only if we can indicate what the expression "the height of tariff levels" means in this context. This will be our concern in what follows.

It is customary to distinguish between the restrictive and the

---

59 For a detailed discussion of this problem cf. R. F. Mikesell, *Liberalization of Inter-Latin American Trade* (Washington: Pan American Union, 1957), pp. 29–31.

60 In the first-mentioned areas, trade could be expanded considerably with existing transportation facilities, while in Central America an improvement in the highway network would greatly increase economic intercourse.

61 Cf. Viner, *op. cit.*, pp. 51–52, and Meade, *The Theory of Customs Unions*, pp. 108–9. On point (*c*) Meade's position was accepted rather than Viner's. Viner believed that high tariff levels in export markets were more advantageous, because in the case of high tariffs there was not much trade to be diverted in the first place. On the other hand, the amount of export trade diverted from third countries to partner countries would be less if third countries had lower tariffs. We believe that the latter argument is likely to carry greater weight.

protective effect of a tariff when the former refers to a reduction in the importation and the latter to an increase in the domestic production of a given commodity consequent upon the imposition of the tariff. Actually, the restrictive effect is composed of two elements: reduction in the consumption of the commodity and increase in its domestic production. The reader will recall that in the present chapter we disregard changes in the pattern of consumption; consequently, for the purposes of examining the effects of tariff reductions on productive efficiency, the restrictive and the protective effect of a tariff can be regarded as identical.

A distinction between "low-tariff" and "high-tariff" countries can now be interpreted to refer to the restrictive (or protective) effect of the tariff. In Viner's opinion, "there is no way in which the 'height' of a tariff as an index of its restrictive effect can be even approximately measured, or, for that matter, even defined with any degree of significant precision."[62] Nevertheless, although no unambiguous measure can be found for this purpose, indicators can be devised for comparing the restrictive effect of tariff levels in different countries with some degree of accuracy.

One possible yardstick is the unweighted average of ad valorem duties. If the number of tariff positions is sufficiently large, the unweighted average of duties will give some indication of the height of tariff levels. This measure is greatly affected by differences in the tariff nomenclatures, however, and can be useful in the comparison of tariff levels of different countries only if identical classification of tariffs is used. This has been done by Raymond Bertrand, who compared average unweighted tariff levels calculated from 1910 tariff positions for the countries participating in the European Common Market. The estimates obtained for the period 1953–55 (See Table 1) lend support to the generally accepted view that the Benelux states are low-tariff countries, while protectionist tendencies are strong in France and in Italy.

For measuring the "effectiveness" of tariffs, the unweighted average of duties is far superior to their weighted average.[63] The weighted average will give distorted results, since high levels of duties that keep imports out would be given little weight (in the case of prohibitive

---

[62] *Op. cit.*, pp. 66–67.

[63] In the latter case, duties are weighted by the amount imported of each commodity.

tariffs, the weight would be zero), while low duties associated with high levels of imports would have large weight and zero duties would not figure in the computation at all. The unreliability of the latter measure can be seen from the comparison of estimates referring to the countries of the Common Market (Table 1). France, for example,

TABLE 1

AVERAGE TARIFF LEVELS IN THE COMMON MARKET COUNTRIES, 1955*

Country	Unweighted Average (1)	Weighted Average (2)	Difference as a Percentage of the Unweighted Average $\dfrac{(1)-(2)}{(1)} \times 100$
Belgium-Luxemburg......	9.5	4.3	55
Netherlands.............	9.5	5.5	49
Germany...............	15.5	5.6	64
Italy..................	17.3	7.1	59
France.................	18.1	5.1	72

*SOURCE: On unweighted averages of duties, Raymond Bertrand, "Comparaison du niveau des tarifs douaniers des pays du marché commun," *Cahiers de l'Institut de Science Economique Appliquée*, Série R, No. 2, February, 1958, p. 7. On weighted averages, H. C. Binswanger, "Der Zollschutz in den Ländern der europäischen Wirtschaftsgemeinschaft und in der Schweiz," *Aussenwirtschaft*, March–June, 1959, p. 131. Fiscal duties (duties assessed for revenue purposes on cacao, coffee, tea, wine, etc.) were not included in calculating the weighted average.

would appear as a low-tariff country on the basis of the weighted average of duties; yet, in reality, low import levels associated with high duties are responsible for this outcome. More meaning can be attached to differences between the unweighted and weighted averages. The higher the protective effect of particular duties, the smaller will be the amounts imported, and thus the lower is the weighted average. Therefore, the percentage difference between the unweighted and the weighted average of duties provides another indicator for the comparison of the restrictive effect of tariffs in different countries. For the countries of the European Common Market this measure gives similar results as the unweighted averages of duties, with the exception of the relative position of Germany and Italy.[64]

The protective effect of a given tariff structure depends not only on the arithmetical averages of duties but also on their frequency distribution. Bertrand rightly notes that uniformly higher rates of duties may be less protective than a lower average tariff with widely differing

[64] The reader will note the differences in the weighted average of duties for Belgium-Luxemburg and for the Netherlands. This result shows that the restrictive effect of identical tariffs will differ, depending on the economic structure of the countries in question.

rates.[65] To obtain more accurate results, however, we would have to examine the protective effect of tariffs, industry by industry. For example, for a given average tariff level, the protective effect of the tariff would be greater if duties on manufactured products were high and on raw materials low than if equal duties were levied on all commodities. Yet a more detailed investigation along these lines cannot be attempted within the scope of this study.[66]

Our next problem is how the common tariff of the countries participating in a customs union should be determined. According to Article XXIV of the GATT, "the duties and other regulations of commerce imposed . . . in respect of trade with contracting parties not parties to such union . . . shall not on the whole be higher or more restrictive than the general incidence of the duties and regulations of commerce applicable in the constituent territories prior to the formation of such union." This ambiguous formulation offers little help, however, in the calculation of the new tariff level, since no explanation is offered as to what is meant by the height of the tariff or by its restrictive effect.[67]

In the case of the Common Market, the choice was made for an unweighted average of duties effective on January 1, 1957, in the Benelux countries, France, Germany, and Italy. It has often been argued that this procedure imparts an upward bias to the new tariff level, since the high French and Italian tariffs receive the same weight as the lower German and Benelux duties, although the volume of trade in France and Italy is smaller than in the latter countries.[68] A

[65] "Comparaison du niveau des tarifs douaniers des pays du marché commun," *Cahiers de l'Institut de Science Economique Appliquée*, Série R, No. 2, February, 1958, p. 13. Bertrand seems to underemphasize, however, the restrictive effect of high average tariffs. In doing so, he implicitly assumes that every industry is import-competing and that, therefore, the protection of all is the protection of none. Actually, a uniform increase in duties would harm industries producing nontraded goods and exports and benefit those that are import-competing.

[66] If dispersion is measured by the quartile coefficient (the difference between the two quartiles expressed in the percentage of the median and divided by 2), the relatively high dispersion of duties in the Benelux countries and the low degree of dispersion in France indicate that the range of the unweighted averages of duties is likely somewhat to overstate differences in the protective effect of tariffs within the Common Market. (The quartile coefficients are: Benelux, 0.93; Germany, 0.54; Italy, 0.35; France, 0.38. See H. C. Binswanger, "Der Zollschutz in den Ländern der europäischen Wirtschaftsgemeinschaft und in der Schweiz," *Aussenwirtschaft*, March–June, 1959, p. 131).

[67] For a good discussion of this problem, see A. Loveday, "Article XXIV of the GATT Rules," *Economia Internazionale*, February, 1958, pp. 1–16.

[68] Cf., e.g., F. Hellwig, "Un point de vue allemand sur les problèmes du marché commun," *Politique Etrangère*, No. 1 (1957), pp. 5–16, and H. Giersch, "Einige Probleme der kleineuropäischen Zollunion," *Zeitschrift für die gesamte Staatswissenschaft*, Vol. CXIII, No. 4 (1957), p. 604.

crude calculation can be made to check the validity of this assertion. The unweighted arithmetical average of the average tariff levels of these countries is 15.1 per cent, while, using the countries' 1957 import trade (after deducting intergroup trade)[69] as weights, the new tariff level would be 15.0 per cent. As an alternative method of measurement, aggregate expenditure figures could be used to base the estimate on "import capacity" (assumed to be approximated by data on aggregate expenditure) rather than on actual imports.[70] The latter method of estimation gives an average level of duties of 15.8 per cent.[71]

Our results suggest that the procedure employed in calculating the new Common Market tariff does not have an upward bias. Nevertheless, the new tariff appears to be higher than the average of duties actually applied by the participating countries in 1957, since the 25 per cent reduction of the German tariffs in 1957 and the Italian 10 per cent temporary tariff reduction have not been taken into account in calculating the common tariff.[72] On the other hand, according to the decision reached by the Six in May, 1960, the calculated average tariff *minus* 20 per cent is used as a basis for the first step in the equalization of tariffs.[73] In addition, the Germans have to restore but half of the 25 per cent tariff reduction that was accomplished in 1957. The last-mentioned changes would certainly reduce the Common Market tariff below the average level of duties applied in 1957, but the 20 per cent cut in tariff levels may not be maintained, since this has been made dependent on reciprocity on the part of other members of GATT.

Finally, we should note the differential impact of the averaging of tariffs on participating and nonparticipating countries. Within the union, low-tariff countries (in the Common Market, the Benelux

69 The import figures for 1957, given in *Commodity Trade Statistics* (United Nations, Statistical Papers, Ser. D, Vol. VII, No. 4) are: Benelux, 4,363; France, 4,807; Germany, 5,736; and Italy, 2,841 millions of dollars.

70 The amount of imports actually reflects the protective effect of the tariff. A fortiori, it would be a serious error to calculate the new level of every individual duty as the average of duties weighted by the amount imported of the commodity in the different countries.

71 National expenditure figures are for 1955 (Gilbert and Associates, *op. cit.*, p. 87).

72 Deviations from the averaging rule can also be mentioned. These cut both ways: for a number of tropical products (e.g., bananas, cacao, coffee, sugar) the new tariff is higher than the unweighted average; for commodities on the so-called G list, comprising about 18 per cent of the Common Market's imports, it is slightly lower. See Henri Corson, "L'établissement de la liste G," *Revue du Marché Commun*, April, 1960, pp. 136–42.

73 This provisional cut in the common tariff is fully applicable when it comes to raising the tariff of a particular country but is not applied in the case of countries whose tariffs are reduced in the equalization process.

countries and, considering the reduction of duties undertaken in 1957, Germany) will find it easier to encroach upon the markets of high-tariff member states (e.g., France and Italy) than vice-versa. On the other hand, among nonparticipating economies, those will suffer more from trade diversion who have been trading mostly with the low-tariff members of the union. This refers, for example, to the suppliers of tropical products to the Benelux states and Germany.

Reallocation of Production in a European Union

It was often assumed that the main effects of economic integration would arise from the reallocation of production. This view has been challenged by Tibor Scitovsky, in whose opinion the gain from production effects is likely to be of little consequence, at least in Europe. Scitovsky argues that among European countries differences in transportation costs, natural endowments, and productivity are not sufficiently large to bring about a substantial shift in the allocation of resources.[74] A different position is taken by Gehrels and Johnston. In their view, "general knowledge of the economic composition of the area is sufficient to suggest that quite considerable relative cost differences do exist."[75] They also add that, because of the high degree of protection, individual countries have engaged in productive activities unsuited to their natural endowments, capital stock, and manpower.

Statistical measurement of production effects in a European union has been attempted by P. J. Verdoorn. He estimated the amount of possible trade creation and trade diversion for a hypothetical customs union consisting of the present Common Market countries, Great Britain, and the three Scandinavian countries, on the basis of the 1952 trade matrix.[76] Verdoorn assumes an elasticity of substitution between imports and domestic production of −0.5, and an elasticity of substitution between different countries' exports of −2.0, uniform for all countries within each of the three-digit Standard International Trade Classification commodity groups which give the

[74] *Op. cit.*, pp. 32–40. A similar view is expressed by H. G. Johnson with regard to the projected European free-trade area in "The Gains from Freer Trade with Europe: An Estimate," *Manchester School of Economic and Social Studies*, September, 1958, pp. 247–55.

[75] Franz Gehrels and B. F. Johnston, "The Economic Gains of European Integration," *Journal of Political Economy*, August, 1955, pp. 279–80.

[76] "Two Notes on Tariff Reductions," Appendix III, in International Labour Office, *Social Aspects of European Economic Co-operation*, Report by a Group of Experts (*Ohlin Report*) (Geneva, 1956), pp. 160–69.

breakdown of the estimate. Verdoorn's results show a 19 per cent primary increase in intra-European trade, 60 per cent of which would be due to trade diversion from other areas. Taking into account the realignment of exchange rates which is assumed to be necessary for balance-of-payments equilibrium, trade creation would amount to 15 per cent of intra-European trade ($750 million), 20 per cent of which would be diverted from outside sources. At the same time, $611 million of European overseas exports would be diverted. On the basis of these figures, Scitovsky puts the potential gain from the reallocation of production at $0.8 million (the difference between $68.8 million gain due to trade creation and $68 million loss due to trade diversion).[77] These estimates, if realistic, would indicate that little benefit could be expected from production effects in an integrated Europe. Their reliability is open to doubt, however.

Verdoorn himself notes some of the limitations of his analysis: trade in coal and steel, the impact of the abolition of quantitative restrictions on trade, as well as secondary repercussions, are disregarded, and the method used has a downward bias in regard to gains forthcoming in effectively protected industries. Further deficiencies of the procedure employed are more serious, however. In the first place, on the basis of statistical measurements in the immediate postwar years, Verdoorn significantly underestimates the relevant elasticities.[78] This becomes conspicuous if we cite Verdoorn's subsequent results for the Benelux union. Examining changes in the trade pattern after the establishment of this union, he estimated the elasticity of substitution between imports and domestic production as -2.5 to -3.4 and indicated that the elasticity of substitution between different countries' exports may assume values between -4 and -4.5.[79] Second, short-run estimates are inappropriate in measuring gains from trade, even in the absence of a downward bias in the coefficients. Over a longer period, existing contracts will run out, political and psychological obstacles are overcome, new investments can be made, etc., and

[77] *Op. cit.*, pp. 65–66.

[78] The downward bias in these estimates has been ably discussed in G. H. Orcutt, "Measurement of Price Elasticities in International Trade," *Review of Economics and Statistics*, May, 1950, pp. 117–32.

[79] P. J. Verdoorn, "The Intra-Bloc Trade of Benelux," *Economic Consequences of the Size of Nations*, pp. 293, 314–15. Note that, *ceteris paribus*, a higher elasticity of substitution between exports means that not only trade creation but also trade diversion will increase.

the responsiveness of trade flows to price changes will be correspondingly higher. The diversion of European exports from third countries to union members might be negligible, for example, since the reconversion of existing factories and new investments will take place *pari passu* with the reduction of tariffs and, after the necessary adjustments have been made, individual commodities may be regarded as being supplied at constant costs. Finally, calculations based on data grouped according to the three-digit Standard International Trade Classification conceal the possibility of specialization within industries and commodity groups.[80] In view of these limitations, the downward bias in Verdoorn's estimate appears to be so large that his figures can be of no use in evaluating the production effects of economic integration in Europe.

A different method was used by H. H. Liesner for ascertaining the probable gains from the reallocation of production in the framework of a European union. Liesner examined absolute export figures and indices of the growth of exports in Britain and in certain European countries for sixty commodity groups. If the export performance of these industries is used as an indicator, it appears that substantial differences exist with regard to the efficiency of various industries as between the above countries. The results led Liesner to conclude that economic integration could bring considerable gains in Europe.[81]

Another way to assess the probable production effects would be to use the evidence provided by trade developments in existing regional unions and preferential agreements. A comparison of changes in incomes and imports can be instructive in this regard. Nevertheless, changes in import/GNP ratios indicate only general trends rather than giving accurate expression to trade creation and trade diversion, since there is no reason to assume that the (money) income elasticity of import demand would be unity or that this would be equal with respect to imports from member and nonmember countries. Raw-material imports, for example, may expand more than proportionately as income rises. Note also that data on the past performance of a customs

---

[80] Again in regard to the Benelux union, Verdoorn found that, for the 121 commodity groups examined, there has been a tendency for specialization *within* rather than *between* the different categories of products after the lifting of tariff barriers ("The Intra-Bloc Trade of Benelux," pp. 291–318).

[81] "The European Common Market and British Industry," *Economic Journal*, June, 1958, pp. 302–16.

union include the effects of dynamic changes; hence it cannot be ascertained to what extent production effects contributed to an expansion of trade.

In the Benelux union, both trade inside the union and that with third countries has increased considerably. Between 1948 and 1957 the increase in the over-all trade of Benelux was 111 per cent, comprising a 182 per cent rise in interunion trade and a 100 per cent increase in trade with third countries. Given the approximately 45 per cent increase in gross national product, it appears that the establishment of the union contributed to an expansion of trade between the participating countries, and there is little evidence of trade diversion.[82] The European Coal and Steel Community offers another example. Between 1952 and 1957 crude steel production increased by 43 per cent, intracommunity trade in steel by 171, and exports to third countries by 51 per cent.[83]

The experience of the Benelux countries and the Coal and Steel Community would imply that beneficial production effects result from integration. The expansion of OEEC trade after the partial removal of quantitative trade restrictions on intra-OEEC trade also deserves consideration. In Scitovsky's opinion, trade liberalization has had little effect on intra-European trade. To substantiate this proposition, Scitovsky points out that the share of intra-European trade in the total trade of the OEEC countries has risen from 42 per cent in 1938 to only 47 per cent in 1956.[84] But the legitimacy of this comparison is open to doubt. Changes between 1938 and 1956 are not relevant for judging the issue, since in many European countries quantitative restrictions were not significant in 1938. And the total effect of the removal of quantitative restrictions cannot be gauged simply by measuring changes in the percentage of intra-European trade, but rather by comparing changes in imports and income. Actually, between 1949 and 1956, intra-OEEC trade expanded by 144 per cent, trade with other countries rose by 56 per cent, while the gross na-

---

[82] Data on trade are from United Nations, *Yearbook of International Trade Statistics, 1957* (New York, 1958); estimates on the gross national product of the Benelux countries are based on data of the UN *Statistical Yearbook* and *Demographic Yearbook* (1957).

[83] W. Diebold, *The Schuman Plan* (New York: Frederick A. Praeger, 1959), p. 577. For various reasons, discussed by Diebold, the increase in trade in coal was considerably smaller.

[84] *Op. cit.*, p. 32.

tional product of the OEEC countries increased by 51 per cent.[85] The effects of trade liberalization, then, appear to be much larger than Scitovsky suggests.

With regard to production effects in the two European integration projects, the reader is referred to our previous considerations on complementarity versus competitiveness, cost differences, market size, propinquity, and tariffs. Some indication of the possible magnitude and direction of production effects in a union can further be given by considering the existing degree of trade relations between the participating countries.[86]

Possibilities of further specialization are indicated by the high degree of economic intercourse between the Common Market countries. In 1957, 36 per cent of the foreign trade of these countries was carried out with the partner countries, including the associated overseas countries and territories participating in the Common Market. A considerable degree of trade diversion is implied, however, by the figures referring to the Free Trade Association of the "Outer Seven." In the same period, only 17 per cent of the member countries' trade was with each other, while they had 24 per cent of their trade with the Common Market countries. Only two countries (Denmark and Norway) had more intensive trade relations with other economies participating in the Free Trade Association than with the Common Market, and two others (Austria and Switzerland) had four times as much trade with the Common Market countries as with those of the Free Trade Association.[87] The formation of the two separate blocs, then, is likely to have an adverse effect on the economies of the latter countries.

Production Effects in a Latin-American Union

In contrast with the extensive economic intercourse between European economies, trade among Latin-American countries is of

[85] *Statistics of National Product and Expenditure,* 1938 and 1947 to 1955 (Paris: OEEC, 1957), p. 39; OEEC, *Statistical Bulletin,* Ser. IV, September, 1959, p. 7, and 9th Report of the OEEC, *A Decade of Co-operation, Achievements and Perspectives* (Paris, 1958), p. 159.

[86] The reader will note that the volume of existing trade itself depends, among other things, on complementarity, propinquity, tariffs, etc.

[87] *Direction of International Trade* (United Nations Statistical Papers, Ser. T, Vol. X, No. 8). Note that the proportion of intra-area trade in the Common Market decreases to 30 per cent if trade with the associated overseas countries and territories is not regarded as intra-union commerce.

little importance. For Latin America as a whole, intra-area trade amounts only to about 9 per cent of total trade. The extent of intra-area trade is somewhat greater in the Southern Zone, but not even here does it exceed 11 per cent. The inclusion of Mexico in the free-trade area of the Southern Zone reduces the latter percentage to 9, since Mexico carries on less than 0.5 per cent of her trade with the countries of the Southern Zone. Finally, trade among the Central American republics amounts to about 4 per cent of their total trade.[88]

While the relative importance of intra-area trade implies the possibilities of further specialization in the European Common Market, it is often argued that the low degree of economic intercourse between Latin-American countries indicates the inherent limitations of the reallocation of productive activity in a Latin-American union.[89] This argument, however, takes the existing structure of these economies and their institutional arrangements as given and fails to consider the causes of the present low level of inter-Latin-American trade or the possibilities of future developments.

The extent of intra-area trade in Europe and in Latin America reflects the degree of economic development in the two areas. In Europe, far-reaching specialization has evolved among highly developed industrial economies; in Latin America, trade is necessarily limited between the underdeveloped countries of the area. For the most part, Latin-American economies export raw materials, liquid fuels, and unprocessed food to industrialized countries, from which they import heavy and light industrial products. The export commodities of the area are also the principal items of inter-Latin-American trade. Trade in food amounts to about 45–50 per cent, in liquid fuels 20–25 per cent, in raw materials 20 per cent of total intra-area trade, while trade in industrial products is insignificant.[90]

The concentration of trade in primary products is typical of countries on a low level of economic development. There are further factors, however, that have impeded economic intercourse between Latin-American countries. We have discussed the inadequacy of

88 Data refer to 1957 and are taken from *Direction of International Trade* (United Nations, Statistical Papers, Ser. T, Vol. X, No. 8).

89 Cf., e.g., C. P. Kindleberger's testimony before Congress in *Foreign Economic Policy: Hearings before the Subcommittee on Foreign Economic Policy of the Joint Economic Committee on the Economic Report* (84th Cong., 1st sess.), p. 521.

90 United Nations, Department of Economic and Social Affairs, *Inter-Latin American Trade: Current Problems* (1957), pp. 86–88.

transportation facilities in the Latin-American area, the adverse effects of which are augmented by the virtual absence of market information and distribution channels. Import quotas and multiple exchange rates have had a similar effect, since in these schemes the lowest priorities were assigned to commodities produced domestically (or desired to be produced domestically), and thus consumer goods and other industrial products manufactured on a small scale in some of these countries have rarely become objects of exchange. Finally, bilateral trade-and-payments agreements also discriminate against inter-Latin-American trade. While multilateral payments agreements have been reached between several countries of this area and Western Europe, intra-area specialization has been restricted by the inflexibilities and uncertainties associated with bilateral trade.

These considerations imply that, by dispensing with bilateral agreements, exchange practices, tariffs, and quotas, inter-Latin-American trade has possibilities for future growth. In the Latin American Free Trade Association the existence of excess capacity in various industries of the member countries gives promise of an enlargement of trade. Brazil is reported to have unused capacity in automobile production, both Brazil and Argentina in the manufacturing of various kinds of machine tools, household electric appliances, electric motors, chemicals—although not necessarily in the same products.[91] Mexico claims to have excess capacity in sixteen industries.[92] Trade is expected to expand in raw materials and fuels and especially in the newly created branches of heavy industry and durable consumer goods.[93]

In Central America, food and raw materials account for most of the existing trade, while the exchange of manufactured products is insignificant. Developing industries like textiles and cement are protected behind high tariff walls and work mostly with excess capacity. The expansion of trade is encouraged through the creation of so-called

[91] For this information, I am indebted to Nuno Fidelino de Figueiredo, Research Director of the UN Economic Commission for Latin America.

[92] These include, among others, most of the textile industry, artificial fibers, chinaware and porcelain, cement, glass, plastic articles, the shoe industry, etc. Cf. Plácido García Reynoso, "Problemas de integración industrial latinoamericana," *Comercio Exterior*, October, 1959, p. 594.

[93] Victor L. Urquidi, "El mercado común y el desarrollo económico nacional," *Comercio Exterior*, November, 1959, p. 650, and Plácido García Reynoso, "Probables efectos del Tratado de Montevideo en la industrialización de América Latina," *El Trimestre Económico*, April–June, 1960, pp. 193–202.

"integration industries," whose products are freely exchanged. Pulp and paper, tires and inner tubes, insecticides, and petroleum derivatives belong to this category.[94]

In most discussions of Latin-American integration, it is emphasized that the greater part of the expansion in trade would come about in newly created industries, in raw materials, and in fuels.[95] The trade-creating effects of the Latin-American integration projects would be restricted, however, if the application of liberalization measures to trade in nondurable consumer goods was unduly delayed.[96] Finally, the possibilities of trade diversion exist in all these projects. But in countries where integration and economic development are expected to proceed *pari passu,* this problem can hardly be discussed in a meaningful way under static assumptions; therefore, its discussion will be postponed to Chapter 8.

[94] United Nations Department of Economic and Social Affairs, *La integración económica de Centroamerica* (1956), chaps. v–vi.

[95] Cf., e.g., Plácido García Reynoso, "Dos conferencias sobre el mercado común latinoamericano," *El Trimestre Económico,* October–December, 1959, p. 542, and UN Department of Economic and Social Affairs, *The Latin American Common Market* (1959), pp. 18, 46, 86.

[96] It has often been suggested that difficulties of readjustment and existing large disparities in the production costs of these industries warrant their preferential treatment (cf., e.g., *The Latin American Common Market,* p. 86). On the defects of this argument and the need for intensified competition, see pp. 172–73 below.

Chapter 3

COMMODITY MOVEMENTS: CONSUMPTION AND WELFARE ASPECTS

> The effect of tariffs is to make the apparent price of imports to the consumer higher than the actual cost of imports to the country . . . whereas for domestically produced goods the price reflects the true cost.
> —Harry G. Johnson, "The European Common Market—Risk or Opportunity?" *Weltwirtschaftliches Archiv*, Vol. LXXIX, No. 2, p. 273

Consumption Effects

In the preceding chapter we examined the production effects of a customs union under the assumption that commodities are consumed in the same proportions before and after integration. Having postulated a fixed pattern of consumption, we disregarded the consumption effects of the union. In the present chapter, we remove this assumption; thus any judgment on the desirability or undesirability of a union will depend on its effects on efficiency in production *and* in exchange.

The reader will recall that, whereas productive efficiency is affected by substitution between sources of supply of the *same* commodity, efficiency in exchange relates to substitution between consumer goods that are different in *kind.* Tariffs created intercountry differences between the price ratios of traded commodities; hence their removal will improve the efficiency of exchange through the equalization of these ratios. In common-sense terms, the domestic consumers were restricted in their demand for imported goods by the tariff, and, after tariffs have been eliminated, they can adjust consumption by purchasing more of higher-valued imported, and less of lower-valued domestic, goods.[1]

[1] The impact of tariffs on efficiency in exchange will become apparent if we consider that, from the viewpoint of the consumers in any country, a tariff can be regarded as an excise tax. It is a generally accepted proposition that an excise tax is a less efficient form of taxation than an income tax. (For a different view, see Milton Friedman, "The 'Welfare' Effects of an Income Tax and an Excise Tax," *Essays in Positive Economics* [Chicago: University of Chicago Press, 1953], pp. 100–16.) The removal of tariffs will then

Since the effects of a customs union on world efficiency depend on the ensuing changes in the pattern of production and consumption, world real income can increase even in the absence of any improvement in productive efficiency, provided that efficiency in exchange improves. It is also possible that a customs union will result in negative production effects, but this loss in welfare will be more than outweighed by the gain in consumer satisfaction derived from the abolition of discrimination between domestic commodities and the products of the partner countries. The application of the theory of the second-best shows that, under such circumstances, a less efficient production solution would provide a more efficient welfare solution.[2]

This separation of production effects and consumption effects should not imply the absence of interaction between the two. Changes in the production pattern will affect consumption, and intercommodity substitution will, in turn, lead to modifications in the production pattern. Furthermore, as in the case of production effects, efficiency in exchange may improve or deteriorate in a union. Whereas the abolition of discrimination between domestic goods and the commodities of partner countries constitutes an improvement (positive consumption effects), the newly created discrimination between the commodities of partner countries and the products of foreign countries on the market of the home country (negative consumption effects) will be detrimental to efficiency.

At this point we should indicate the similarity in the logic applied to production effects and consumption effects. Production effects tend to be favorable if increased purchases of a given commodity from a member country take place at the expense of domestic rather than foreign sources of supply and if cost differences are greater for commodities in which trade has been created than for commodities in

---

lead to an increase in consumer welfare, provided that the loss in tariff revenue is remedied by an income tax. This will not necessarily be the case if another excise tax is substituted for the tariff. Finally, consumer welfare might decrease rather than increase if tariffs were reduced below the rate of a general excise tax levied on domestic products, since thereby home-produced goods would be discriminated against. Nevertheless, this possibility is of little practical interest under present-day conditions, given that a general excise tax usually applies to all commodities, irrespective of their origin, domestic or foreign.

2 Cf. R. G. Lipsey and K. J. Lancaster, "The General Theory of the Second Best," *Review of Economic Studies*, No. 1 (1956–57), pp. 11–32, and R. G. Lipsey, "The Theory of Customs Unions: Trade Diversion and Welfare," *Economica*, February, 1957, p. 43. The reader is reminded here that the consideration of the distributional issue follows in a later section.

which trade has been diverted. Similarly, positive consumption effects are likely to predominate if consumers substitute the commodities of partner countries for domestic goods rather than for foreign products; and, given the changes in the trade pattern, the positive consumption effects will be larger, the greater are the initial differences in the price ratios of traded commodities between the member countries,[3] whereas the negative consumption effects will be small if the price ratios of traded goods differ little between participating and nonparticipating countries.[4]

The possibility of a deterioration in the efficiency of exchange was denied by Franz Gehrels, who suggested that consumption effects were always positive and would lead to an improvement in welfare.[5] Gehrels' conclusions, however, were based on the examination of the case of two commodities, one domestic and one foreign. In criticism of Gehrels' argument, R. G. Lipsey used a model containing three commodities and concluded that a customs union may lead to an improvement, as well as to a deterioration, in the efficiency of exchange. Lipsey's reasoning can be summarized as follows: if, before the formation of the union, country A produced commodity Z domestically and imported X (from country B) and Y (from country C), both imported goods being subjected to the same ad valorem tariff, the optimum conditions in exchange (the equality of the price ratios) were fulfilled between X and Y, but not between Z and X or between Z and Y. After the establishment of the customs union between countries A and B, the tariff on commodity X is removed. The optimum conditions are now fulfilled between Z and X (which constitutes an improvement), but not between Z and Y or between X and Y, although the latter condition was fulfilled before the union was established. Lipsey concludes that the same "number" of optimum conditions are fulfilled as before; thus it is uncertain whether there is any net effect on welfare.[6]

[3] Differences in intercountry price ratios give expression to the distortion in the prices of consumer goods caused by the tariffs. See also p. 60 below.

[4] The analogy can be pursued further if we regard commodities as different ways of "producing" utility. E.g., the consumer can choose between domestic and imported fruits or between home-produced wine and imported whisky. Then the choice between sources of supply (production effects) will find its parallel in the choice between different sources of utility (consumption effects), when in both cases the tariff interferes with the satisfaction of needs from the lowest-cost source.

[5] "Customs Unions from a Single Country Viewpoint," *Review of Economic Studies*, No. 1 (1956–57), pp. 61–64.

[6] "Mr. Gehrels on Customs Unions," *Review of Economic Studies*, No. 3 (1956–57), pp. 211–14.

This argument can be objected to on the grounds that we cannot reach meaningful conclusions simply by "counting" optimum conditions. Nevertheless, a reinterpretation of the argument would throw some light on the possible outcome of consumption effects. If we assume excise taxes to be zero, there is a presumption that the larger the share of internal trade (domestic goods plus commodities imported from member countries) in the union's consumption, the greater will be the positive consumption effects, since the optimum conditions of exchange will be fulfilled for a larger part of the domestically consumed commodities. Expressed differently, the larger the amount of trade conducted with partner countries in comparison to trade with nonparticipating economies, the more likely it is that consumption effects will be positive; and the lower the volume of pre-union foreign trade conducted by the prospective member countries, the smaller will be the possibility of negative consumption effects.[7] The qualifications to this argument are many: one should consider absolute changes instead of marginal adjustments, data on pre-union trade do not sufficiently indicate changes in trade patterns, etc. Still, information on existing trade relations provides at least some indication of the probable consumption effects of a union. Given the volume of intra-area trade, one can suggest, for example, that the European Common Market is more likely to lead to positive consumption effects than is the Free Trade Association of the "Outer Seven" or the Latin-American integration projects.

The consumption effects of a union also depend on the rate of the duties applied. The higher the initial tariff on trade between the participating countries, the greater is the distortion in the consumption pattern, which is remedied through the removal of duties, i.e., the more new trade will be created and the larger will be the gain in consumer satisfaction per unit of trade. On the other hand, the maintenance of high tariffs against third countries will contribute to the substitution of the commodities of partner countries for foreign goods and will increase the loss in welfare resulting from this shift in imports.

Another factor to be considered is the competitiveness and complementarity of the participating economies. The more competitive

7 After the manuscript of this chapter was completed, I found essentially the same argument used in a survey article on the theory of customs unions by Mr. Lipsey. See his "The Theory of Customs Unions: A General Survey," *Economic Journal*, September, 1960, pp. 508–09.

the production structure of the countries that form a union, the better substitutes are the commodities of the member countries, hence the greater will be the increase in trade and the positive consumption effects. On the other hand, complementarity between member countries and third countries is equivalent to a low degree of substitutability between the commodities of the two groups of countries and leads to little reduction in imports from foreign countries. Further repercussions occur in the form of changes in the exportation or importation of commodities that are substitutes or complements to goods whose trade is directly affected by the removal of intra-union tariffs.[8]

Following Meade, we have considered here the possibilities of substitution between the commodities of the countries participating in a union after the removal of tariff barriers. A different aspect of substitutability is studied by F. V. Meyer, who examines the effects of the importation of substitutes and complementary goods on the utility of domestic commodities. Meyer argues that the welfare gain from integration increases if the newly imported goods are complementary to domestic commodities and decreases if they are substitutes.[9] The example given by Meyer can be used as an illustration. If the duty on imported gasoline is removed, the utility of home-produced automobiles and the welfare of the consumers will increase thereby (complementarity); while the importation of green cars may not result in increased welfare, since the benefit to owners of green cars might be more than counterbalanced by the loss of utility to the envious owners of home-produced blue cars. The latter is a clear case of external effects in consumption, with Meyer's green cars substituted for Veblen's diamonds. There is one deficiency in the argument, however; it is relevant only in a situation immediately following integration because it takes the existing stock of goods as given and disregards future changes in the production pattern. In the complementary relationship of car and gasoline, the gain in utility will be maintained and even increased after modifications in the pattern of production have taken place, since car production is likely to expand. On the other hand, in the case where substitutes are imported, the disutility of the blue-car owners is likely to be temporary, considering that, as demand shifts,

8 For a discussion of secondary and tertiary repercussions cf. J. E. Meade, *The Theory of Customs Unions* (Amsterdam: North Holland Publishing Co., 1955), chaps. v–vi.

9 "Complementarity and the Lowering of Tariffs," *American Economic Review*, June, 1956, p. 325.

the production (and price) of blue cars will be cut. In addition, although the importation of competitive goods may reduce the utility of the existing stock of some commodities, it will have a lasting effect on consumer welfare by increasing the range of choices available. The Italian car buyer, for example, will be better off if he has a choice between Fiat, Renault, and Volkswagen instead of Fiat only. This applies even if he ends up choosing the Fiat, since an increase in the possibilities of choice can be said to provide a nonquantifiable element of welfare.

One can conclude that the consumption effects of a union may be positive or negative, depending primarily on the extent of trade relations between the member countries, the complementarity and competitiveness of the participating economies, and the height of tariff levels. In addition, as the reader will no doubt realize, considerations regarding the influence of propinquity and the size of the union on production effects find application in the case of consumption effects, too. Finally, we should note that, even if the establishment of the union leads to an improvement of efficiency in exchange for the world as a whole, the nonparticipating countries will lose, since their commodities will be discriminated against.

Terms-of-Trade Effects

The changes in the pattern of trade consequent upon the removal of intra-union tariffs will also affect the net commodity terms of trade (for short, terms of trade), defined as the ratio of export and import prices. In the following we shall distinguish between short-run and long-run changes in the terms of trade. Factors that become operative in the short run comprise trade diversion, exchange-rate adjustments, and bargaining power, while changes in productivity and real income are listed as long-run determinants. One may object to this classification on the basis that income effects will make their appearance from the first day of integration and therefore should be classified among short-run factors. But the approach followed in this study regards increases in income as a result of changes, mostly dynamic, which might need considerable time for their full operation. Balance-of-payments repercussions, however, are listed among the short-run determinants, since trade diversion may necessitate adjustments in exchange rates even in the absence of income effects.

Using Marshallian terminology, the trade-diverting effects of a customs union can be characterized as a shift in the union members' reciprocal demand for foreign goods.[10] This shift will improve the union's terms of trade, and, other things being equal, a greater shift in reciprocal demand will bring about a larger improvement in the terms of trade. In addition, changes in the terms of trade will also depend on the elasticity of reciprocal demand.

The elasticity of reciprocal demand is determined by the elasticities of supply and demand of the traded commodities. In the limiting case, when the union is so small that it cannot influence world market prices, the elasticity of demand for its exports and the elasticity of supply of its imports can be regarded as infinite; therefore, the formation of the union does not affect the terms of trade. Although these conditions are not likely to be fulfilled in the real world, this constellation might be approximated in the Central American Common Market. On the other hand, an increase in the size of the union will have the tendency to improve its terms of trade. This conclusion can be derived from the proposition that, *ceteris paribus*, the larger the economic area, the greater the elasticity of its reciprocal demand for outside products is likely to be, and the smaller will be the elasticity of reciprocal demand on the part of third countries for the union's products.[11]

Arguing in terms of Marshallian reciprocal demand curves, we implicitly assumed that the balance of payments of participating and nonparticipating countries would be equilibrated through price and wage flexibility; i.e., the described changes in the terms of trade referred to a comparison of the situation before *and* after integration, with the balance of payments continually in equilibrium. The possible need for a realignment of exchange rates can be considered if we distinguish two steps in the adjustment process. To begin with, trade diversion has an immediate effect on the terms of trade by increasing export prices and reducing import prices for the union. At the same time, the union's balance of payments will be affected as a result of these primary price changes and the ensuing increases and decreases in the volume of exports and imports. Aside from the rather unlikely case when integration would reduce the union's exports by

[10] Marshall defines the reciprocal demand of country A as the demand in country A for the "representative" import commodity from country B in terms of the "representative" goods exported by A.

[11] See Jacob Viner, *The Customs Union Issue* (New York: Carnegie Endowment for International Peace, 1950), p. 55.

so much more than it reduced its imports that the surplus due to the advantageous developments of the terms of trade was wiped out, the union will experience a balance-of-payments surplus. Consequently, the terms of trade of the union will further improve *either* through secondary price changes *or* via an appreciation of the union members' currencies designed to equilibrate the balance of payments.[12] The first of these alternatives corresponds to the previous use of the Marshallian reciprocal demand curves when the final equilibrium reflected both primary and secondary price changes; the second will be used at this point in order to shed light on possible changes in the value of the currencies of individual union members.

Within the union, the modification of exchange rates necessary to equilibrate the balance of payments of the member countries will largely depend on the height of pre-union tariffs in the individual countries. The currency of a participating country with high initial duties may even depreciate, since member-country producers may encroach upon its markets. On the basis of 1952 data, P. J. Verdoorn concluded that this would not be the case in a Western European union. According to his findings, the absolute increase in the value of exports would exceed that of imports for each participating country. As a result, depending on the height of the original tariffs, the exchange rates of the countries participating in the union would appreciate by 1.9 to 10.0 per cent.[13]

The terms of trade will also be affected by the bargaining strength of the union in negotiating tariff concessions. Meade notes that "the larger the trading area which is negotiating as a single unit the better the commercial policy treatment which it can hope to exact

12 The opposite result is reached if the product of the domestic and foreign elasticities of demand is greater than the product of the domestic and foreign elasticities of supply.
13 "Two Notes on Tariff Reductions," *Social Aspects of European Economic Cooperation* (Geneva: International Labour Office, 1956), p. 167.

	Average Tariffs Prior to Liberalization (Per Cent)	Possible Appreciation in Exchange Rates (Per Cent)
Germany	33.5	1.9
Italy	24.9	3.8
France	21.9	2.3
United Kingdom	12.4	3.4
Netherlands	11.0	9.7
Belgium and Luxemburg	10.2	5.7
Scandinavia	9.7	10.0

The results would change if the more recent estimate of tariff levels by R. Bertrand were taken into account (see above, p. 46).

in its bargains from other countries, and the better therefore its terms of trade with the rest of the world are likely to be."[14] The recent history of tariff negotiations seems to bear out Meade's contention, and no one would deny that the bargaining strength of the Common Market, for example, is significantly greater than that of the Benelux countries. This factor, then, would contribute to an improvement in the terms of trade as the size of the union increased.

Changes in productivity and real incomes have been listed as long-run factors affecting the terms of trade. Actually, if we ignore the growth of population, any rise in real income results from increased productivity. Increased real income will deteriorate the terms of trade of the union even in the absence of price changes (income effect). The union's terms of trade will deteriorate further if the rise in productivity leads to a general reduction in the price level (substitution effect). Price reductions, however, will favorably affect the terms of trade if the increase in productivity is concentrated in the import-competing sectors.[15]

The income and substitution effects, besides acting on the terms of trade directly, will also affect these indirectly, via the balance of payments. An increase in real income will deteriorate the balance of payments of the union through increased imports, whereas price reductions will improve it. An improvement (deterioration) in the balance of payments, in turn, will bring about an appreciation (depreciation) of the union's currency, accompanied by a probable amelioration (worsening) of the terms of trade.

Administrative Economies

The suppression of tariffs between the union members leads to administrative economies in the form of cost saving in the state fiscal apparatus.[16] But this is not the only gain that results from the abolition of customs formalities. The expense and time required for com-

---

[14] *The Theory of Customs Union*, p. 96; cf. also Viner, *op. cit.*, pp. 55–56, and Maurice Byé, "Customs Unions and National Interest," *International Economic Papers*, No. 3 (London: Macmillan & Co., Ltd., 1953), pp. 221–22.

[15] For an analysis along similar lines see Tibor Scitovsky, *Economic Theory and Western European Integration* (Stanford: Stanford University Press, 1958), pp. 70–76. On this problem the *locus classicus* is J. R. Hicks, "An Inaugural Lecture," *Oxford Economic Papers*, June, 1953, pp. 117–35.

[16] See Viner, *op. cit.*, pp. 58 ff. However, administrative economies will be reaped only in a customs union but not in a free-trade area. In the latter case, the cost of administration is likely to increase rather than decrease. Cf. p. 74 below.

plying with customs formalities, as well as the cost of additional transportation necessary for transboundary traffic to pass through a port of entry, constitute additional charges in international trade that not only burden the trader but can result in the loss of marginal transactions, too.

The complexity of tariff laws in most countries is another obstacle to foreign trade. In the United States, for example, it is said that the intricacies of customs procedures and the best and safest ways to comply with the regulations are known only to a group of highly specialized customs brokers and lawyers, and the cost of their services increases the cost of importation. Yet, according to some, American customs procedures are not so burdensome as the corresponding practices of some other countries.[17]

In addition to procedural hurdles and consequent costs encountered by importers in general, administrative regulations on importation also provide indirect protection to special groups of domestic producers. Indirect protection may supplement or supplant direct protection through tariffs. The importance of administrative regulations in restricting imports has been expressed in an often quoted passage from B. A. Levett's *Through the Customs Maze:* "Let me write the Administrative Act and I care not who fixes the rates of duty."[18] Procedural rules on importation often assume a protective character in connection with the classification of commodities for tariff purposes, procedures for assessing and collecting customs duties, and rules on sanitation, preservation of health, maintenance of standards, prevention of misleading or fraudulent labeling, packaging, advertising, protection of copyright, patents, trade marks, etc. In the United States, for instance, regulations on the imports of animals and animal products, plants and plant products, foods, drugs, and cosmetics provide indirect protection to domestic industries.[19]

While the abolition of tariffs results in cost saving for the state and for the transactors, the additional burden of negotiation, coordination of codes, mutual supervision, and tax problems will act in the opposite direction. The latter appear most formidable since—if the destination principle is applied—the existence of different tax systems

17 Cf. P. W. Bidwell, *The Invisible Tariff* (New York: Council on Foreign Relations, 1939), p. 6.

18 (New York, 1923), p. 11.

19 Bidwell, *op. cit.*, Part II. Cf. also G. A. Elliott, *Tariff Procedures and Trade Barriers* (Toronto: University of Toronto Press, 1955), chap. i.

will make the payment of compensating taxes and subsidies necessary, and the formalities involved would greatly burden the traders.[20] Also, the experience of the United States indicates that the member states may attempt to hinder trade by the use of means other than tariffs, such as discriminatory taxes, highway regulations, inspection requirements, "buy domestic" rules for state institutions, or labeling requirements.[21]

Changes in Welfare[22]

Our findings on the production and consumption effects of a customs union can be reformulated in terms of welfare economics. Efficiency in resource allocation requires, among other things, (*a*) the equality of the marginal rates of transformation in the production of any two products for all producers, (*b*) the equality of the marginal rates of substitution of any two commodities for all consumers, and (*c*) the equality of the marginal rates of transformation and substitution.[23] These conditions are not fulfilled if tariffs discriminate against commodities produced in foreign countries.

In the absence of monopolistic elements and excise taxes, the removal of tariffs will equalize the marginal rates of transformation (positive production effects) and the marginal rates of substitution (positive consumption effects), and will also restore the equality of the marginal rates of transformation and the marginal rates of substitution within the union. At the same time, the maintenance of tariffs

[20] Under the destination principle, taxes are paid according to the rates applied at the place of destination. More will be said on this problem in Chap. 11.

[21] Cf. F. E. Melder, "State and Local Barriers to Interstate Commerce in the United States—A Study in Economic Isolationism," *Maine Bulletin*, November, 1937.

[22] The reader with little background in economic theory should skim this section.

[23] The marginal conditions for an optimum (efficient) allocation in a static situation are: (1) the marginal rates of substitution of any two commodities should be the same for all consumers; (2) the marginal rates of transformation in the production of any two products should be the same for all producers; (3) the marginal physical productivity of a given factor for a given product should be the same for any two producers; (4) the marginal rates of equal-product substitution should be the same for any pair of producers; (5) the marginal rate of substitution of any consumer for any pair of commodities should be equal to the marginal rate of transformation of these commodities in production; (6) the marginal reward of a factor should equal the marginal rate of substitution of reward for use.

For a detailed exposition, cf. K. E. Boulding, "Welfare Economics," in *Survey of Contemporary Economics*, Vol. II, ed. B. F. Haley (Homewood, Ill.: Richard D. Irwin, Inc., 1952), pp. 19–23. A more rigorous formulation is achieved if not only marginal equivalencies but also inequalities are included in the formulation. See T. C. Koopmans, *Three Essays on the State of Economic Science* (New York: McGraw-Hill Book Co., Inc., 1957), pp. 1–126.

against third countries results in discrimination between the commodities produced in member countries and in third countries and
leads away from the optimum.

The final outcome will depend on whether the movement toward the optimum or away from the optimum carries greater weight.[24]
On the basis of the arguments presented in the last two chapters we
can conclude that, *ceteris paribus,* a union is more likely to have beneficial effects on world efficiency (*a*) the more competitive the structure
of the participating economies; (*b*) the greater the differences in the
cost of commodities actually produced prior to the establishment of
the union; (*c*) the larger the size of the union; (*d*) the shorter the economic distances between the member countries; (*e*) the higher the
level of the pre-union tariff; and (*f*) the greater the degree of pre-union
economic intercourse between the participating countries. In addition, administrative economies will also contribute to an increase in
real income, while the terms-of-trade effects represent a redistribution
of world real income.

So far we have considered only the real-income component of
welfare and neglected the distributional component.[25] We have seen
that, under static conditions, the real income of the union members
may rise or fall,[26] while nonparticipating countries stand to lose by
reason of the negative production, consumption, and terms-of-trade
effects.[27] If production effects, consumption effects, and administrative economies, taken together, are positive, world real income will
rise, i.e., the increase in the member countries' real income will be
greater than the reduction in the real income of nonparticipating
countries. Yet, in the case when some countries gain and others lose,
a rise in world real income would represent an equivalent increase in
world welfare only if international compensation were made or if we
disregarded differences in the marginal utility of income. Both these

[24] An ingenious attempt was made to combine production and consumption ef-
fects in examining the conditions for a favorable outcome by H. G. Johnson who applied
Marshallian producer and consumer surplus analysis to the case of a single commodity.
See his "Discriminatory Tariff Reduction: A Marshallian Analysis," *Indian Journal of
Economics,* July, 1957, pp. 39–47, and October, 1958, pp. 177–82.

[25] On the terminology used, cf. Chap. 1, pp. 10–12.

[26] The production and consumption effects may be positive or negative, whereas
the terms-of-trade effects and administrative economies will benefit the union.

[27] Note, however, that income effects will benefit third countries if world efficiency
improved since, *ceteris paribus,* the rise in the union members' real income will lead to
increased imports.

alternatives have been discarded above. Thus an increase in world real income may be associated with a deterioration in welfare and vice-versa. In addition, the terms-of-trade effects cannot be regarded as "neutral" from the point of view of world welfare; although a change in the terms of trade does not affect real income for the world as a whole, there will be a change in world welfare through the redistribution of real income.

It is suggested here that the marginal utility of income is likely to be higher in underdeveloped countries than in the rest of the world. If this proposition were accepted, the distributional component of welfare would appear to be negative for a union of developed economies, while the opposite result would hold if underdeveloped countries were integrated. Making use of this proposition, no clear conclusion emerges with regard to the European Common Market. Economic integration among the Six will hurt some countries with higher per capita income (United States, Switzerland), others with similar standards of living (England, Denmark), and also underdeveloped countries in Latin America and Africa. It would be difficult to estimate the redistributional component in world welfare, partly because the magnitude and distribution of negative effects on real income are not known, partly because the marginal utility of income cannot be measured. We can only venture a guess that, under static assumptions, the redistribution of real income between member and nonmember states might have a slight negative effect on world welfare through its impact on underdeveloped countries. The same argument can possibly be applied to the Free Trade Association of the "Outer Seven."

The redistributional effect on world welfare is likely to be more favorable in the case of a Latin-American union, since trade diversion and changes in the terms of trade would have an adverse effect mostly on more-developed economies. Nevertheless, the adverse repercussions emanating from regional unions in Latin America might also reduce welfare in those Latin-American countries which do not participate in such projects.

APPENDIX

Problems of a Free-Trade Area

In a free-trade area, as distinct from a customs union, the suppression of intra-area trade restrictions is not accompanied by the establishment of uniform duties and other regulations on commerce with third countries, but rather the member countries maintain their individual tariffs and the freedom of determining and modifying their commercial policies.[28] In the preceding analysis of the economic effects of freeing commodity movements within an area, we assumed identical initial tariffs (and other forms of trade restrictions) in all participating countries; hence—given these assumptions—our conclusions applied to customs unions and free-trade areas as well. Presently we shall remove the above assumptions and shall consider various problems arising from the existence of disparate tariff levels and diverse commercial policies in the countries participating in a free-trade area.

To begin with, the maintenance of differing rates of duties in trade with nonparticipating economies will create possibilities for deflection of trade, production, and investment. Deflection of trade will occur if the trade barriers of high-tariff member countries are circumvented through the importation of products originating outside the area from low-tariff members. If no precautionary measures were taken and tariff differentials exceeded the additional cost of transportation, imports would enter the free-trade area via the country which applies the lowest tariff on the commodity in question. Thus, implicitly, tariffs would be equalized at the level of the lowest common denominator. From the point of view of world welfare, this development cannot be objected to, since the resulting reduction of tariffs in trade with third countries would diminish the trade-diverting effects of the union. On the other hand, such an arrangement would run counter to the established principles of free-trade areas: the freedom of individual countries to set their own tariffs.

Besides causing deflection of trade, the establishment of a free-trade area may bring about an uneconomic structure of production. The manufacture of products which contain a high percentage of foreign-made materials and semifinished products will shift to low-tariff countries if differences in tariffs outweigh differences in production costs. It should be added that we can distinguish between low-tariff and high-tariff countries only as a first approximation. Actually, duties

[28] According to the definition given by GATT: "A free trade area shall be understood to mean a group of two or more customs territories in which the duties and other restrictive regulations on commerce are eliminated on substantially all the trade between the constituent territories in products originating in such territories." GATT, *Basic Instruments and Selected Documents*, Vol. I, Part III, Article XXIV, Sec. 8(b).

on some commodities may be higher in country A, while higher tariffs may be levied on others in B. Production of some commodities will then shift from country A to B, others from B to A. The participation of more countries adds to the complexity of the problem. The ensuing reallocation of resources will have detrimental effects on world efficiency, since the pattern of productive activity will not follow the lines of comparative advantage but rather the differences in duties.

Deflection of production may also be accompanied by undesirable movements of investment funds. The establishment of so-called tariff factories is a case in point; other things being equal, foreign investors will move funds to countries with lower tariffs on raw materials and semimanufactured products. Similarly, factories will be set up to assemble parts produced in third countries with low labor costs if tariff advantages make this operation profitable.

Various methods have been recommended to avoid deflection of trade, production, and investment.[29] Among the alternatives suggested, three will be examined here: the percentage rule, the rule of transformation, and the use of compensating taxes in intra-area trade. Both the percentage rule and the rule of transformation are designed to determine whether a product can be regarded as originating within the area or from outside the area. Commodities that are considered area products do not bear any tariff in intra-union trade, whereas each country applies its existing duties on nonarea products. Compensating taxes, on the other hand, are used to eliminate tariff differences on traded goods.

The percentage rule for the determination of origin is based on the calculation of value added for every product. Goods whose prices contain a predetermined percentage of value added inside the union would be traded duty-free under this rule.[30] The first problem that arises in regard to this procedure is that of determining the "cutoff point." Two considerations will act in opposite directions here: on the one hand, a low percentage will increase the possibility of trade deflection; on the other, a high cutoff point will restrict the possible trade-creating effects of the union. The percentage rule adopted should thus be the one that maximizes the gains from the union; this

29 For an interesting discussion, see Hans Bachmann, "Die Verhinderung von Handelsumlenkungen in einer Freihandelszone," *Aussenwirtschaft*, March–June, 1958, pp. 1–24.

30 In the calculation of value added, materials that are imported duty-free by every member country are also considered as originating within the area.

would require the equalization of the marginal advantages of trade creation and the marginal disadvantages of trade and production deflection.[31]

In the course of the negotiations about the establishment of a European free-trade area embracing all OEEC countries, it was recommended that goods whose prices contain at least 50 per cent value added inside the union should be regarded as area products. Subsequently, this rule has been adopted in the Free Trade Association of the "Outer Seven." In the absence of sufficient evidence, no a priori judgment can be made whether the 50 per cent rule is "optimal" or whether another percentage should have been adopted instead. Because of difficulties in determining the possible repercussions of various alternatives on resource allocation, the choice can be narrowed down to a range of percentage values, but within this range the final judgment is likely to be arbitrary.[32]

Aside from the obstacles encountered in ascertaining the percentage rule that would lead to the maximization of gains in a free-trade area, further problems arise in the practical application of this rule. First, accounting procedures vary between countries, although the calculation of the percentages of value added would require uniformity. Second, fluctuations in the world market prices of raw materials will bring about changes in the percentage share of value added in the price of a number of products and may necessitate the frequent reclassification of these commodities. Third, the same material may represent differing percentages of the value of the product, depending on quality. Fourth, producers will have an inducement to raise prices in order to qualify under the percentage rule and may, at the same time, give discounts to buyers. Finally, the implementation of this procedure requires considerable administration, and administrative control is difficult to achieve because the producer (as well as his home country) is materially interested in evading the payment of compensating duties.

In view of these deficiencies of the percentage rule, it has been proposed that this be supplemented by the rule of transformation. In the latter case, a list of production processes is drawn up, and that

[31] The reader will note that the percentage rule most favorable to the union will not necessarily be the one most favorable for the world as a whole.

[32] It can be suggested that "rounding" played an important role in the determination of the 50 per cent rule.

country is regarded as the country of origin where the relevant process of transformation is performed. This procedure avoids some of the pitfalls of the value-added method but has a few disadvantages of its own. Obstacles will be encountered in attempting to draw up the common lists, and protectionist interests may have considerable influence on the outcome. In addition, although the application of the transformation rule would be relatively simple in some industries such as textile or shoe manufacturing, unambiguous results would not be obtained in others (e.g., the machine-tool and chemical industries) where the technological process is more complex and a great part of the industry's output is used as input by the industry itself. Finally, the administrative difficulties of the percentage rule persist in the application of this method also.

The third procedure discussed here is that advocated by the former Italian Foreign Minister, Guido Carli, for application in the proposed all-European free-trade area. According to the Carli plan, compensating taxes are to be paid automatically in intra-area trade in cases when differences in duties between the exporter and the importer member countries exceed certain limits. These limits, as well as the level of tariff chosen as a norm, were proposed to be negotiated separately sector by sector. The application of this plan would have been accompanied by some degree of harmonization in tariffs within the union.

Aside from the difficulties encountered in arriving at a decision with regard to the relevant limits and the tariff norms applied, the most conspicuous shortcoming of the Carli plan lies in its disregard of deflections in production. Through the payment of compensating taxes, trade deflection would be avoided, but, in the absence of compensation for differences in tariffs on raw materials and intermediate products, countries that levied low duties on these commodities would continue to have differential advantages in lines of production where these were used as inputs. It could be suggested that, in order to avoid the resulting inefficiencies in the allocation of productive activity, duties paid on all inputs should be considered in calculating the amount of compensating tax. However, under the latter alternative, the cost of administration—and the possibility of falsifications— would greatly increase, and the feasibility of this solution is open to doubt.

We have examined three alternatives suggested for remedying

deflections in trade, production, and investment. Actually, various combinations of these can be applied; in the Free Trade Association of the "Outer Seven," for example, the percentage rule is supplemented by the rule of transformation. Combining various procedures, the deficiencies of each can be reduced, but at least some of these shortcomings will not be eliminated. A comparison of customs unions and free-trade areas will be useful at this point.

From the economic point of view, customs unions are superior to free-trade areas by reason of the deflection of production and investment and the higher costs of administration in the latter. Deflection of production (and investment) will occur, no matter whether the percentage rule or the rule of transformation is applied. Under the first alternative, tariff differences on the inputs utilized provide a differential advantage in the manufacturing of commodities that qualify as area products—excepting the unlikely occurrence when no inputs contain elements originating from outside the area. Similarly, the list of transformation processes is necessarily limited; hence the possibility of deflections in production remains. Another important difference between a customs union and a free-trade area lies in the cost of administration. The reader will recall that the removal of tariff barriers between countries participating in a customs union results in administrative economies. In a free-trade area, on the other hand, any procedure used to avoid deflections in trade and production will require considerable administration, so that the additional cost of administration can be expected to outweigh the cost saving in the fiscal apparatus that results from the suppression of intra-area tariff barriers. Thus, other things being equal, a free-trade area will lead to a less efficient resource allocation than a customs union, and unproductive expenditures will also be higher.

We have reviewed various reasons for deflection of trade, production, and investment in a free-trade area. The experience of the free-trade area between Norway and Sweden in the nineteenth century showed some of these difficulties in practice. At that time, Sweden protected her iron and textile production, whereas duties on these products were considerably lower in Norway. As a League of Nations study notes: "It proved . . . to be extremely difficult to control the origin of goods and to prevent 'foreign' goods from being imported into the country with the lower tariff and re-exported as duty-free 'domestic' goods into the country with the higher tariff."[33] This was true especially for imported textiles, which were subjected to some minor working-up process in Norway and then exported duty-free into Sweden.

With regard to the proposed European free-trade area, a report prepared for the Council of the OEEC by a special working party is rather optimistic. In its conclusions, the report asserts that "real danger would be limited," since (a) a significant proportion of the manufactured goods included in trade within the area is produced from raw materials and even more so from semimanufactures which themselves originate in the area; (b) tariffs on raw materials are negligible; and (c) high-tariff countries are often offered lower prices than low-tariff countries.[34]

Less optimistic conclusions have been reached by other authors,[35] who have pointed out that the establishment of a free-trade area in Europe would increase the flow of semimanufactures into countries with lower tariffs. Japanese cloth, they allege, would be imported for finishing into Denmark and Sweden at low tariff rates, whereas gray cloth from India and Hong Kong might enter Britain duty-free. Some also fear that factories might be established to assemble machine parts imported from Japan at a low rate of duty. Possibilities of deflection of production have further been noted with regard to organic chemicals, pharmaceuticals, plastics, and building machinery. Finally, in the case when a country produces and imports the same commodity, it may be difficult to determine whether goods of home or of foreign origin have been re-exported or utilized as inputs by various producers. Substitution of area and nonarea products may be of some importance, e.g., in the case of some nonferrous metals (lead, zinc, aluminum oxide, ferroalloys).

Britain's special advantages in a European free-trade area are another matter of controversy. The abolition of tariffs within the free-trade area and her preferential status with Commonwealth countries

[33] Customs Unions: A League of Nations Contribution to the Study of Customs Union Problems (Lake Success, N.Y.: United Nations, 1947), p. 61.
[34] Organisation for European Economic Co-operation, Report on the Possibility of Creating a Free Trade Area in Europe (Paris, 1957), p. 38.
[35] Cf., e.g., A. Hummler, "Das Problem des Warenursprungs in einer europäischen Freihandelszone," Aussenwirtschaft, December, 1957, pp. 247–53; Pierre Uri, "La zone de libre-échange," Revue d'Economie Politique, January–February, 1958, pp. 310–23; Bachmann, op. cit., pp. 1–24.

would create an advantageous position for Britain. The market for British products will be larger than for commodities originating in countries participating in the free-trade area or in member countries of the Commonwealth; Britain would enjoy advantages of a discriminatory character in comparison with Commonwealth countries in Europe and maintain her discriminatory advantages with respect to other European economies in the Commonwealth.[36] The French also fear that Britain's differential advantage over other European countries would induce American investors to shift their European establishments to England.

Many of the objections raised against the creation of an all-European free-trade area find their origin in the possibility of deflections in trade, production, and investment. Nevertheless, these considerations did not deter the "Outer Seven" from establishing a free-trade area. In Miriam Camps's opinion, "the underlying thesis of the Stockholm plan is that a free trade area is a valid concept and that origin controls can effectively prevent important deflections of trade without unduly restricting the scope of the area."[37] This does not mean, however, that there would be no trade, production, or investment deflection in the area but rather that other advantages are expected to outweigh any possible detrimental effects. These advantages include the granting of tariff preferences to counter the trade-diverting effects of the Common Market and the increased bargaining power of the Seven for future negotiations with the Six.[38] In addition, the danger of deflections in production may be less in the Free Trade Association of the Seven than in a free-trade area embracing all OEEC countries, since the degree of competitiveness appears to be less in the former than in the latter.[39]

In the absence of some degree of harmonization, the existing large differences in tariffs would result in a considerable degree of

[36] At the same time, Commonwealth countries would be discriminated against in the British market in favor of member countries of a European free-trade area, since the latter would pay no tariffs in Britain.

[37] *The European Free Trade Association: A Preliminary Appraisal* (London: Political and Economic Planning, 1958), p. 16.

[38] According to Miriam Camps, "it seems clear that in most of the countries concerned the determining factor was not the prospect of economic advantage, but the belief that the formation of the new association would improve materially the chances of an accommodation with the Six" (*ibid.*, p. 27). See also R. Rogé, "Perspectives d'une petite zone de libre échange," *Etudes et Conjoncture*, October, 1959, pp. 961 ff.

[39] On the complementarity of the economies participating in the Free Trade Association of the "Outer Seven," see p. 34 above.

trade and production deflection in a Latin-American free-trade area, too. For example, while Brazil levies an ad valorem duty of 70 per cent on industrial machinery, the same goods can be imported duty-free in Argentina, and the tariff rates are low in Chile and Mexico; on iron, steel, and chemical products, high duties are levied in Argentina, Brazil, and Mexico, and low rates are applied in Chile and Peru.[40] However, the establishment of a free-trade area in Latin America is not regarded as an end in itself but rather as a step toward a customs union, and the need for the reduction of tariff differentials on commodities procured from third countries has long been recognized. Also, the Montevideo Treaty expressly states that the creation of the Free Trade Association is to be accompanied by the harmonization of tariffs and the coordination of trade policies.[41] These moves toward harmonization will then reduce the possibilities for deflections in trade and production.

Besides the problems of trade, production, and investment deflection, the formation of a free-trade area also raises the question of coordinating commercial policies.[42] Two considerations are relevant here; freedom to modify tariffs, subsidies, etc., unilaterally would (a) create new possibilities for deflection of trade and production and (b) upset the balance of mutual advantage built into the agreement. In the course of the negotiations on the European free-trade area, widely different views were held on the scope of the necessary coordination of trade policies. It is interesting to note that the Convention establishing the Free Trade Association of the "Outer Seven" appears to go further in this matter than the original British position and endeavors to achieve some degree of coordination of commercial poli-

---

[40] Cf. Octaviano Campos Salas, "Comercio interlatinoamericano e integración regional," *Comercio Exterior*, October, 1959, p. 598.

[41] "In order to ensure fair competitive conditions among the Contracting Parties . . . the Contracting Parties shall make every effort . . . to reconcile their import and export regimes, as well as the treatment they accord to capital, goods and services from outside the area" (Article 15).

[42] A memorandum from the countries of the European Common Market (October 20, 1958) notes in regard to the creation of a European free-trade area: "The Community considers that although a common trade policy should not be regarded as one of the objectives of the Association, it is nevertheless essential that Member States . . . should proceed to coordinate their trade policies in regard to third countries. The Community attaches the same importance to solving this problem as it attaches to solving problems due to disparities between external tariffs" (*Negotiations for a European Free Trade Area: Documents Relating to the Negotiations from July, 1956, to December, 1958, Presented to Parliament by the Paymaster General by Command of Her Majesty* [London, 1959], p. 98).

cies in directing member states to give advance notification of changes in tariffs and in forbidding the use of direct and indirect export subsidies by the participating countries.[43]

On the other hand, it has been claimed that, from the point of view of liberal tariff policies, a free-trade area will have an advantage over a customs union, inasmuch as, "if all nations are forced into the strait jacket of having a single tariff common to them all against each article from the outside world, the general tariff level [will be] higher than if the several nations retain the liberty to proceed with their own policies in regard to external tariffs."[44] It is questionable, however, whether single nations would be more inclined to carry out liberal trade policies than a customs union, considering that sectional protectionist interests might have a stronger voice in the determination of commercial policies in the former case than in the latter. Nevertheless, it is conceivable that tariff differences between countries participating in a free-trade area would have beneficial effects, since their self-interest might encourage member countries to reduce tariffs in order to avoid deflection of trade and production, provided that the loss to producers resulting from lower tariffs against the outside world were not greater than the loss due to trade (and production) deflection within the union at a higher tariff level. There is no way to determine a priori which result would occur, but the author believes that administrative regulations have a greater chance to be used to avoid trade deflection than competitive tariff reductions.

We come, finally, to the question of the coordination of economic policies in a free-trade area. The OEEC report notes that the removal of trade barriers between countries participating in a free-trade area would increase the interdependence of these economies and that the objective of avoiding fluctuations in employment and production would necessitate closer coordination in economic and financial policies.[45] The negotiations on a European free-trade area again displayed differences in views with respect to the degree of coordination, the countries of the Common Market arguing for more, Great Britain and others for less. Also in this regard, the Convention establishing the Free Trade Association of the "Outer Seven" seems to go

[43] Articles 6.4 and 13.1.

[44] Roy Harrod, "Britain and the Common Market," *Foreign Affairs*, January, 1957, p. 232.

[45] *Op. cit.*, p. 19. See also M. Ouin, *The OEEC and the Common Market* (Paris: Organisation for European Economic Co-operation, 1958).

further than the original British position, and the formulation used resembles that in the Common Market treaty.[46] Some observers believe that this implies a similar degree of coordination of economic policies by the Seven as will supposedly be done by the Six.[47] Nevertheless, the implementation of these provisions may greatly differ in the two unions, and if a high degree of coordination in commercial and economic policies was actually accomplished by the Seven, this would represent a great step toward the transformation of the free-trade area into a higher form of integration.

[46] "Member States recognize that the economic and fiscal policies of each of them affect the economies of other Member States and intend to pursue these policies in a manner which serves to promote the objectives of the Association. They shall periodically exchange views on all aspects of these policies. . . . The Council may make recommendations to Member States on matters relating to these policies to the extent necessary to ensure the attainment of the objectives and the smooth operation of the Association" (Article 30).

[47] Cf., e.g., Pierre Languetin, "L'association européenne de libre-échange," *Revue Economique et Sociale*, January, 1960, p. 10.

Chapter 4

FACTOR MOVEMENTS

It appears evidently from experience, that a man is of all sorts of luggage the most difficult to be transported.

—Adam Smith

Commodity Movements and Factor-Price Equalization[1]

In the previous chapter we indicated that one of the conditions of efficiency in resource allocation is the equalization of the marginal rates of transformation for any two commodities. Under conditions of pure competition, this equality is achieved in a customs union through the equalization of price ratios between the participating countries. This result does not necessarily involve, however, the equalization of the marginal products of factors within the union. Such an outcome would require—in addition to equal product prices—the equality of the prices of productive factors. In the absence of equal factor prices, some of the optimum conditions will not be fulfilled, and hence a fully efficient solution is not reached.[2] Within a national economy, it is usually assumed that factors of production are mobile and that their prices are equalized via factor movements. In traditional trade theory, on the other hand, factor immobility is postulated as between countries. The question arises whether, in the absence of factor movements, commodity movements would bring about, or might contribute to, the equalization of factor prices in the trading countries.

The problem was first tackled by Heckscher and Ohlin,[3] who

---

[1] Readers with little background in economic theory should skim this section.

[2] For an enumeration of the optimum conditions, cf. n. 23 in the previous chapter. Note that the equality of prices refers to prices expressed in some common unit after appropriate conversion at equilibrium exchange rates.

[3] Eli Heckscher, "The Effect of Foreign Trade on the Distribution of Income," *Readings in the Theory of International Trade*, ed. H. S. Ellis and L. A. Metzler (Philadelphia: Blakiston Co., 1949), pp. 272–300; Bertil Ohlin, *Interregional and International Trade* (Cambridge, Mass.: Harvard University Press, 1933).

reached the conclusion that factor prices tend to be equalized as a result of trade. In Heckscher's and Ohlin's view, under the assumption of identical production functions and qualitatively identical factors, differences in factor endowments are the primary causes of trade. In the absence of trade, differences in factor endowments result in relatively lower prices of the abundant, and higher prices of the scarce, factors, whereas trade will mitigate divergences in factor-price ratios, since the trading countries will export (import) products which use the abundant (scarce) factors more intensively. In Ohlin's words, "the mobility of goods to some extent compensates the lack of interregional mobility of the factors," and the "tendency towards equalisation also of the prices of the factors of production . . . means a better use of them and thus a reduction of the disadvantages arising from the unsuitable geographical distribution of the productive factors."[4]

The Heckscher-Ohlin analysis has been further developed by P. A. Samuelson, who specified the conditions of complete factor-price equalization through commodity trade for the case of two countries, two commodities, and two factors, and later extended the analysis for a more general framework.[5] In the ensuing controversy,[6] the conclusion has been reached that the conditions for the equalization of factor prices through commodity movements are so restrictive that they are not likely to be fulfilled, even approximately, in the real world. Nevertheless, even though the prices of productive factors are not equalized, the question remains: Will trade lead to less inequality in regard to factor prices?

It cannot be decided a priori whether such a result is obtained, since some of the qualifications to the Samuelson theorem only mitigate the tendency toward the equalization of factor prices, while others imply an intensification of the disparities. The findings of

4 Ohlin, *op. cit.*, pp. 42, 49. Ohlin points out that by "abundance" or "scarcity" of the factors of production, relative rather than absolute abundance (scarcity) is meant when correction should be made also for differences in demand patterns.

5 "International Trade and the Equalization of Factor Prices," *Economic Journal*, June, 1948, pp. 163–84; "International Factor-Price Equalization Once Again," same *Journal*, June, 1949, pp. 181–97; "Prices of Factors and Goods in General Equilibrium," *Review of Economic Studies*, No. 1 (1953–54), pp. 1–20. An elegant geometrical treatment was given to the problem in the early 1930's by A. P. Lerner. Cf. his "Factor Prices and International Trade," *Economica*, February, 1952, pp. 1–15.

6 For a discussion of the contributions and further references, see Bela Balassa, "The Factor-Price Equalization Controversy," *Weltwirtschaftliches Archiv*, Vol. LXXXVII, No. 1 (1961); also R. E. Caves, *Trade and Economic Structure* (Cambridge, Mass.: Harvard University Press, 1960), chap. iii.

Wassily Leontief, which, against all expectations, have shown the United States to export labor-intensive and import capital-intensive commodities, did not help to clarify the issue.[7] Neither did the interpretations and explanations[8] given to the Leontief paradox present sufficient evidence to determine whether trade acts in the direction of factor-price equalization between the United States and her trading partners. Japanese exports and imports have recently been examined by applying the procedure followed by Leontief. The results show Japanese exports, on balance, to be relatively more capital-intensive than imports. More detailed figures indicate that, in trade with the United States, Japanese exports tend to be labor-intensive, and this is more than counterbalanced by the capital intensity of exports to underdeveloped Asiatic countries.[9] These findings, by and large, conform to the Heckscher-Ohlin theorem if we consider that Japan occupies an intermediate position in economic development between the United States and underdeveloped countries.

The empirical results do not provide conclusive evidence for or against the equalizing effect of commodity trade on factor prices. But it can be argued that, between countries with similar environmental conditions and production functions and with small differences in the quality of the factors of production, trade is liable to reduce inequalities in the prices of productive factors.[10] Thus, in the European Common Market and possibly also in other present-day integration projects, the equalizing effect of commodity movements on factor prices is likely to be operative. The liberalization of trade will then contribute to efficiency in production also by reducing differences in

---

[7] "Domestic Production and Foreign Trade: The American Capital Position Reexamined," *Economia Internazionale*, February, 1954, pp. 9–38; "Factor Proportions and the Structure of American Trade: Further Theoretical and Empirical Analysis," *Review of Economics and Statistics*, November, 1956, pp. 386–407.

[8] Differences in environment, production functions, effectiveness of labor and capital, impact of entrepreneurship, natural resources, etc., are some of the variables considered. Cf. P. T. Ellsworth, "The Structure of American Foreign Trade: A New View Examined," *Review of Economics and Statistics*, August, 1954, pp. 279–85; Stefan Valavanis Vail, "Leontief's Scarce Factor Paradox," *Journal of Political Economy*, December, 1954, pp. 523–28; N. S. Buchanan, "Lines on the Leontief Paradox," *Economia Internazionale*, November, 1955, pp. 791–94; and the discussion in the supplement to the February, 1958, issue of the *Review of Economics and Statistics*, by Stefan Valavanis Vail, Romney Robinson, G. A. Elliott, Beatrice Vaccara, and W. W. Leontief, pp. 111–22.

[9] Masahiro Tatemoto and Shinichi Ichimura, "Factor Proportions and Foreign Trade: The Case of Japan," *Review of Economics and Statistics*, November, 1959, pp. 442–46.

[10] On this point, see my "The Factor-Price Equalization Controversy."

factor prices. Nevertheless, it is certainly true that the equalization process would stop far short of complete equalization.

This analysis is of a strictly static character. Its validity depends on the assumption of unchanged technology and demand conditions. If dynamic variables such as technological change, creation of new goods, etc., are introduced, our conclusions need serious modification. The static and the dynamic problem should be clearly distinguished, however. It is one question whether trade contributes to the equalization of factor prices under *ceteris paribus* assumptions; and it is another how technological progress and other dynamic changes affect the prices of factors. The two aspects seem to be confused by Gunnar Myrdal, who argues that trade, instead of equalizing factor prices, increases the differences.[11] Since in a dynamic setting commodity trade is only one of the variables affecting factor prices, the empirical proposition according to which, during the past hundred years, real wages in the United States and other developed economies have increased at a higher rate than elsewhere cannot lead us to the conclusion that *trade* increases the inequalities in the prices of factors.

We conclude that, other things being equal, trade will reduce differences in factor prices within a customs union, provided that the conditions of production show no great dissimilarities among the participating countries. However, dynamic changes such as disparate rates of productivity growth and changes in tastes, may reverse the tendency toward factor-price equalization. The latter possibility will be considered in more detail in Chapter 9.

Economic Effects of Factor Movements

We have noted that the liberalization of commodity movements is not sufficient to bring about the equalization of factor prices in a union. It has also been indicated that factor-price equalization is necessary for efficient resource allocation, since the marginal products of factors will not be equated as long as factor prices differ. The effects of factor movements on efficiency can be demonstrated by a simple example. Let us assume that production conditions in countries A and B can be described by a Cobb-Douglas function of the form $O = b\,L^k\,C^{1-k}$, where O is output (problems connected with the com-

---

[11] *Economic Theory and Under-Developed Regions* (London: Duckworth, 1957), chap. 11.

position of output are disregarded here), L is labor, C is capital (both factors are homogeneous and of identical quality in the two countries), and $k = 1 - k = 0.5$. Country A has 400 units of capital and 200 units of labor, whereas B's factor endowment consists of 200 units of capital and 400 units of labor. Output will amount to 141 units in both countries, the marginal productivity of labor being 0.352 in country A and 0.176 in country B, and the marginal productivity of capital 0.176 in A and 0.352 in B. Marginal returns to factors differ because of differences in factor endowments (the impact of commodity trade on factor prices is disregarded here). By introducing free movement of capital and/or labor, marginal returns to factors will be equalized at 0.25, and the joint output of the two countries will increase from 282 to 300 units. Factor movements will then improve efficiency by removing relative scarcities.

In the foregoing, we have concluded that, between countries with similar conditions of production, commodity movements are partial substitutes for movements of factors by reason of their effect on factor prices. Similarly, factor migration can be regarded as a substitute for trade. Factor movements will reduce quantitative differences in the endowments of qualitatively identical factors and will increase the relative importance of natural resources, transportation facilities, and the pull of the markets in their effect on trade. As a result of the equalizing effect of migration on factor prices, differences in production costs will diminish, and, other things being equal, commodity trade will decrease.

Nevertheless, although under *ceteris paribus* assumptions the liberalization of factor movements results in less intra-union trade, various elements pull in the other direction. Migration will result in more trade if the immigrants are inclined to buy various commodities from the "old" country or if new goods are introduced in the country of immigration. The international movement of labor may also bring about an exchange of technical skill and experience and thus contribute to more trade via increased productivity. Similar results can follow from the migration of capital to less developed countries. Finally, under realistic assumptions, any trade-reducing effect of factor movements is likely to be insignificant compared with the trade-creating effect of the formation of the union.

In the above discussion we endeavored to demonstrate the desirability of factor movements in an integrated area. It is another question whether the desired factor movements will be brought about by the free-market mechanism after barriers to migration have been lifted. In a world of perfect information, differences in factor returns will induce factors to move from places with low returns to those with high returns. In the actual world, imperfect information about possible returns, uncertainty, etc., act as a brake on the migration of factors. Guarantees to investors, information services on the prospective situation of wage earners, etc., might help to overcome these obstacles and could contribute to the desirable migration of factors. It should be added that inertia due to sociological and psychological obstacles causes factors to be more mobile in the long run than in the short run. This short-run immobility may also be eased by the intervention of state authorities.

A further consideration is that, similar to the case of commodity movements, the economic effects of the migration of factors may be detrimental to efficiency under certain circumstances. Adverse effects predominate if a union between countries A and B diverts factor movements from third countries, although the latter alternative would have been more desirable from the point of view of world welfare. Yet it is unlikely that the net effect of factor movements would be of this character. Most restrictions on factor movements take the form of quantitative controls, such as immigration quotas, prohibition of capital movements or exchange controls, and the abolition of these restrictions within the union will not divert factor movements from nonparticipating countries.

Greater importance can be attributed to adverse factor movements that are connected with agglomerative tendencies. In a common market, free factor migration will be directed, in part, to those regions where the existence of social and economic overhead and other forms of agglomeration economies contributes to higher factor returns. The movement of labor and capital would then proceed from "poor" to "rich" countries and regions. We shall argue at a later point that, in such a case, an absolute deterioration of living standards may result at the place of emigration if skilled workers emigrate from the depressed area, the age structure deteriorates, and the per capita burden of taxation increases.

It can also be maintained that, from the standpoint of welfare, not only the absolute level of living standards but also their relative level counts. Stagnating real incomes in one region, coupled with soaring incomes in others, may be interpreted in the same way as an absolute decline in depressed areas. For example, although living standards in Southern Italy are certainly not lower now than they were before the unification of Italy, the relative stagnation of this region is often interpreted as a sign of adverse consequences of the union with the North. If a backward region or country could have achieved a higher rate of growth in the absence of economic integration, factor movements would not contribute to the equalization of factor prices but rather have a perverse effect.

Perverse factor movements can find their origin in differences in wage policies, government-financed social benefits, and monetary and fiscal policies, too. For example, income redistributional measures may induce the movement of capital to countries with a less equalitarian tax structure, whereas labor movements might proceed in the opposite direction. Finally, undesirable factor movements may follow if uncertainty exists with regard to future changes in policies. Some of these and related problems will be discussed in the remaining part of the present chapter. But a more detailed examination of perverse factor movements originating in agglomeration economies or in disparate economic policies within a union is postponed to the policy chapters of this study.[12]

Labor Movements

J. E. Meade explains that wage earners will have an incentive to move if the difference between earnings at the place of immigration and that of emigration is greater than the sum of (a) interest on the direct cost of movement and (b) the intangible costs of migration.[13] In other words, if the intangible costs of migration are regarded as disutility for the workers, wage differentials should cover not only the cost of movement but also differences in disutilities. Arguing from this presupposition, Meade concludes that labor will necessarily migrate if its movement contributes to productive efficiency, and private incentives will thus correspond to social requirements.[14]

This conclusion is valid for the case of perfect rationality and foresight, but it needs modification if irrationality and imperfect foresight are introduced. The previously mentioned short-run immobility

12 Chaps. 9–12.
13 *Trade and Welfare. The Theory of International Economic Policy*, Vol. II (London: Oxford University Press, 1955), p. 358.
14 *Ibid.*, p. 372.

of factors suggests that wage earners are inclined to overestimate the intangible costs of migration. Lack of sufficient knowledge on the possibilities of assimilation, on cultural and social facilities, uncertainty about job security, etc., all contribute to this result. Irrational motives, such as national, religious, and racial prejudices, the "propensity to stick to the birth place," pull in the same direction. An additional consideration is that even if workers are willing to move, borrowing facilities may not be available to them for financing the cost of migration. It is rather unlikely, then, that private incentives would correspond to social needs with respect to labor migration, and an efficient solution would require state intervention which can take the form of compensation for the cost of movement, information on available facilities, etc.

Besides irrationality and lack of necessary information on jobs and working conditions, disparate policies of income redistribution followed by union members can also contribute to a divergence between private incentives and social needs. Redistributional measures can take the form of social benefits (free medical services, old-age pensions, unemployment compensation, etc.) financed from general taxes, for example. Workers may move to a country where the marginal product of labor is lower than in the home country, if in the country of immigration the state provides various kinds of social benefits the sum of which is sufficiently larger than the wage differential that is assumed to reflect differences in marginal products. In this case, the movement of labor will reduce rather than increase world efficiency. On the other hand, as we shall show in Chapter 10, differences in social benefits provided by entrepreneurs (directly or indirectly through state social funds) do not interfere with labor movements, inasmuch as these items constitute a form of wages to the worker, as well as an element of wage cost to the entrepreneur.

At this point we should also consider the impact of labor migration on the distribution of income. Other things being equal, the free movement of labor in a common market will reduce intercountry wage differentials in some occupations.[15] Although the ensuing improve-

---

[15] Under certain restrictive assumptions, this result would follow also if intraunion trade barriers were removed with restrictions on factor movements maintained. Cf. W. F. Stolper and P. A. Samuelson, "Protection and Real Wages," in *Readings in the Theory of International Trade* (Philadelphia: Blakiston Co., 1950), pp. 333–57; L. A. Metzler, "Tariffs, International Demand, and Domestic Prices," *Journal of Political Economy*, February, 1948, pp. 1–28; and K. Lancaster, "Protection and Real Wages: A Restatement," *Economic Journal*, June, 1957, pp. 199–210.

ment in efficiency will permit a rise in average living standards, in a
static situation some worker groups will gain, others lose. Dynamic
changes may annul any tendency toward downward adjustments, however. It will be argued at a later point that economic integration is
likely to accelerate growth; thus, instead of upward and downward adjustments of absolute levels of income, integration may result in differential rates of growth of the standard of living. And even if dynamic
changes are left out of consideration, controls on migration for the
sake of maintaining the present income distribution in certain countries is an inferior solution to free factor movements coupled with
some, necessarily transitional and limited, redistributional measures.[16]

The latter conclusion needs serious modification if consideration
is given to the Malthusian case. In our analysis so far, we implicitly
assumed that the long-run supply of labor in the labor-abundant country was relatively inelastic, i.e., it was surmised that the growth of
population did not respond in any significant degree to the rise of
wages due to emigration. On the other hand, if the labor supply in the
country of emigration was highly elastic, the equalization of labor
returns might not take place at a level intermediate between that of
the low-wage and that of the high-wage country, but on the wage level
of the former, or at least at a level near to it. In this case, the free movement of labor could depress average living standards.[17] Need may
arise, therefore, for controlling the free movement of labor in the event
of considerable differences in the rate of population growth. Such a
situation is not likely to materialize in the European Common Market
but would be relevant in the case of integration between certain Asiatic countries.

Numerous studies have dealt with the present state and the possibilities of labor migration in Europe. It is noted that, while labor
movements had been largely unrestricted up to the First World War,
since then the employment of foreign workers has been strictly regu-
lated in all European countries. Although the equality of treatment
between nationals and foreign workers in regard to wages, social security, and conditions of employment is legally guaranteed, the prac-

16 Cf. Meade, *op. cit.*, pp. 454–57. For the possible undesirable effects of disparate
redistributional measures within the union see, however, pp. 227–28 below.

17 The outcome will depend on various factors, such as the optimum size and the
rate of growth of the population. On some of these problems, see M. Gottlieb, "Optimum
Population, Foreign Trade, and the World Economy," *Population Studies*, September,
1949, pp. 151–69.

tice of issuing permits for limited periods greatly restricts migration. Permits are generally issued for a year and are often valid for a stated place, area, and occupation only. The reconsideration of working permits after a year makes it possible that, in case of a slackening in business, the foreign workers will be dismissed first. The employment of foreigners on a "last in, first out" basis certainly does not give an inducement to labor migration.[18]

In the European Common Market, Italy and the Netherlands have experienced labor surpluses, while France and Belgium face shortages in various areas. Estimates on population growth project a continuation of these trends. Between 1950 and 1980, the population of the Netherlands is expected to grow by 40 per cent and that of Italy by 13 per cent, whereas population growth in the other participating countries is estimated to range between 3 and 8 per cent.[19] Some observers believe that European labor imbalances can be solved by development programs. Such a view appears to be exaggerated, however, since it does not take into account that manpower shortages in labor-scarce areas will not be remedied by development programs elsewhere, and this solution would impart a certain rigidity to the European economy, with a possibly high price paid in the form of subsidization of inefficient industries. A more desirable solution is likely to lie in the middle: development programs in backward areas and the encouragement of migration to assure the flexibility of the European economy.[20]

The Treaty establishing the European Economic Community provides for the free movement of workers "not later than at the date of the expiry of the transitional period."[21] Fears have been expressed, however, that this provision would unnecessarily postpone the liberal-

18 For a good factual account of migration problems in Europe, see "Features of Post-War European Migration," *International Labour Review*, July, 1954, pp. 1–15, and Xavier Lannes, "International Mobility of Manpower in Western Europe," *International Labour Review*, January, 1956, pp. 1–24, February, 1956, pp. 135–51.

19 A. Sauvy and J. Bourgeois-Pichat, "Les problèmes de population européenne," *Population*, January–March, 1953, p. 45. It should be noted that such forecasts have a considerable margin of error and not only can population growth take unexpected turns (as it did after the Second World War), but economic growth in some of the overpopulated countries may also lead to the easing of the situation. A good example is West Germany, where the estimated 1.5 million surplus population in 1951 has been soaked up as the spectacular German recovery proceeded. See J. Isaac, "International Migration and European Population Trends," *International Labour Review*, September, 1952, pp. 185–206.

20 More will be said on this problem in Chap. 9.

21 Article 48, Sec. 1.

ization of labor movements, since the transitional period is expected to last for 12–15 years. Nevertheless, administrative discrimination against foreign workers will probably subside in the first years of implementing the treaty.

National restrictions to migration hinder the movement of labor in Latin America, too.[22] At the same time, with the exception of the Central American Common Market, the integration projects do not deal with the freeing of labor movements. However, the need for intercountry labor mobility is also smaller here, since population imbalances can be found to a lesser extent in Latin America than in Europe.

The abolition of national restrictions is a necessary, but not a sufficient, condition for achieving desirable labor movements. As we pointed out above, migration is also hindered by various sociological, psychological, and economic obstacles. These are operative on the side of the migrants and on the side of the local population as well. Among the sociological and psychological factors restricting emigration, differences in language, customs, religion, climate, educational, medical, and shopping facilities, cooking habits, and, in general, the loss of the accustomed environment deserve mentioning. Economic factors include job and wage insecurity, loss of seniority, and inadequate housing facilities at the place of immigration.

Social, cultural, and language differences inhibit the demand for foreign workers, too. In a number of countries national and racial prejudices stand in the way of migration. Economic motives, such as preoccupation with the security of employment and fear of a reduction of wages in the case of mass migration, have similar effects. In this regard, the trade unions often appear as a powerful force opposing immigration.

The lack of correspondence in skills demanded and supplied is another factor of great importance in restricting migration. In overpopulated areas, the level of education is frequently very low and the would-be migrants not only lack the skills demanded in industrialized areas but often have not even had a minimum elementary education. In Italy, for example, almost half the unemployed are either illiterate (10 per cent) or semiilliterate (32 per cent).[23] The low educational

22 With regard to Brazil, see Estanislau Fischlowitz, "Manpower Problems in Brazil," *International Labour Review*, April, 1959, p. 413.

23 Alessandro Molinari, "Manpower and the Common Market," *Banca Nazionale del Lavoro, Quarterly Review*, December, 1958, p. 493.

standards offer a serious obstacle to the unemployed in the way of acquiring higher skills and give rise to imbalances between the demand for and supply of various skills in intercountry relationships and also within a national economy (for example, between Northern and Southern Italy).

Various measures have been advocated to remedy the inefficiencies stemming from lack of information, irrational overestimation of the intangible advantages of home employment, and imbalance between skills. These measures include the establishment of central agencies to deal with problems of migration which could serve as international clearing houses for placement and would supply information with regard to demand for manpower and on educational, cultural, and social facilities.[24] The previously noted imbalances in skills would make necessary the expansion of elementary and secondary education and vocational training, too. Mobility could be further facilitated if the central agency contributed to the cost of transfer and training of workers.

It is questionable, however, to what degree governmental or intergovernmental measures can overcome the sociological or psychological obstacles to migration in an integrated area. Experience suggests that better results can often be attained by facilitating individual migration through information and labor-market clearing services than by organized group movements.[25] The reason is likely to be that, whereas in the first case the initiative is that of the migrant, in the second the movement is originated by the government. The strength of the workers' resistance to migration can well be seen in the experience of the European Coal and Steel Community.

Although there has been individual migration, especially from Italy to Belgium, the Community's projects to move groups of miners did not meet with success. And the two noted attempts at group migration were not even designed to move workers from one country to another but within individual countries. In March, 1953, the High Authority of the Community authorized a nonrepayable grant toward financing a program of resettlement from the Central Midi of France to the Lorraine and expected about 5,000 miners to move. Actually,

24 The setting-up of appropriate machinery for the fulfillment of these tasks is provided for in the Common Market treaty (Article 49d).
25 Cf. J. Stoetzel, and A. Girard, "Problèmes psychologiques de l'immigration en France," *Population*, January–March, 1953, pp. 73–76.

only 215 miners volunteered, and, of these, 136 had arrived in Lorraine by the end of September of the same year, and 258 had moved by 1955.[26] Similarly, miners were not willing to move from the Borinage in Belgium to the Campine area; in this case differences in language (Walloon-Flemish) and religion were the main obstacles to migration.

The practical difficulties of migration shown by recent experience and the findings of various studies sponsored by the European Coal and Steel Community[27] indicate the problems faced with regard to labor movements. The conclusion emerges that, although the desirability of the movement of manpower is established, there is not much chance for large-scale labor migration in a European or in a Latin-American union. Thus, even though the lifting of administrative obstacles and intergovernmental encouragement to labor movements are likely to increase the flow of wage earners inside a union, inter-country differences in wage rates will persist, primarily as a result of inertia and the high valuation of intangibles on the part of the workers.

Capital Movements[28]

We have argued above that factor mobility is necessary for efficient resource allocation, since the prices of productive factors will not be equalized in the absence of factor movements. With regard to capital, this condition means that all enterprises throughout an integrated area should have access to credit on equal terms and that both loan capital and equity capital should be able to move to places where higher returns can be obtained. Intra-union capital movements are also necessary to facilitate the shifts in resource allocation consequent upon the liberalization of trade. These considerations suggest that the liberalization of capital movements would be a precondition of the optimal operation of a union.

26 M. T. Florinsky, *Integrated Europe* (New York: Macmillan Co., 1955), p. 69; D. C. Bok, *The First Three Years of the Schuman Plan* (Princeton: International Finance Section, Princeton University, 1955), p. 54.

27 A. Girard and P. Mentey, *Développement économique et mobilité des travailleurs* (Paris: Institut National d'Etudes Démographiques, 1956); *Migrations provoquées et problèmes sociaux de mobilité ouvrière* (Liege: H. Vaillant-Carmanne, 1956); and European Coal and Steel Community, *Obstacles à la mobilité des travailleurs et problèmes sociaux de réadaptation: Etudes et Documents* (Luxemburg, 1956).

28 Capital as a factor of production is considered here; hence problems connected with the liberalization of long-term capital movements will be discussed under this heading. The examination of short-term capital flows and balance-of-payments problems in general will follow in Chap. 12.

The Treaty establishing the European Economic Community provides for the abolition of restrictions on capital flows during the transitional period "to the extent necessary for the proper functioning of the Common Market."[29] Subsequently, directives issued by the Council of the Community dealt with the implementation of this provision. Restrictions on direct investment (including the proceeds of liquidation), personal capital movements,[30] and capital movements relating to short-term and medium-term financing of commercial transactions have been abolished unconditionally, while the participating countries are directed to give general authorization to dealings in securities quoted on stock exchanges. Member countries are allowed to maintain or to establish exchange restrictions with regard to capital transactions relating to the flotation of new security issues on foreign capital markets, dealings in securities not quoted on stock exchanges, long-term commercial credits, and medium-term and long-term credits of a purely financial character.[31] On the other hand, the Convention of the Free Trade Association of the "Outer Seven" does not allow for the liberalization of capital movements beyond the provisions of the OEEC Code of Capital Liberalization, which applies primarily to direct investments. Controls on exchange transactions pertain to capital flows in most Latin-American countries, although attempts at liberalization have been made in Central America.

In the absence of exchange restrictions, the movement of capital will be governed by differences in earning possibilities and by the estimated degree of risk and uncertainty. The latter is conditioned by fear of the future imposition of exchange restrictions, political and monetary instability, changes in taxation and in regulations on dividends, price and wage fixing, and nationalization. With the exception of political risk proper, all these elements of uncertainty are connected with the increased role of state intervention in economic life and have greatly contributed to the decline of the international mobility of capital as compared with the pre–First World War situation. Allowance for risk and uncertainty in estimating the expected return on capital is, for the most part, an imputed private cost that cannot be considered as a social cost. The lessening of risk and uncertainty in a common market will then reduce the discrepancy between private and

---

[29] Article 67.
[30] Gifts and endowments, inheritances, dowries, etc.
[31] Liberalization of short-term financial transactions is optional.

social profitability and will lead to a more efficient allocation of resources.

It can be argued that the establishment of a common market will change the valuation of intangibles in regard to capital movements to a much greater degree than with respect to the migration of labor. Whereas in the absence of a conscious policy encouraging migration, the psychological and sociological obstacles to labor movements are likely to be but slightly affected by economic integration, risk and uncertainty associated with capital export will be greatly reduced if a common market is established. Nevertheless, as long as economic policies are not integrated, some elements of uncertainty will persist. An exchange risk will be present in the event of freely fluctuating exchange rates or if fixed exchange rates are expected to change. Uncertainty will further be created by the possibility of modifications in the fiscal, monetary, or social policies of one country unmatched by other countries. Finally, expectations in regard to general changes in economic policy will add another element of uncertainty. Victory of a labor party in the parliamentary elections of one of the member states, for example, may result in capital movements to countries where the attitude toward business is regarded as more favorable.

The above-mentioned causes of uncertainty have a dual effect on the movement of capital between countries participating in a common market. On the one hand, uncertainty reduces the mobility of capital, since the compensating charges added in the profit calculations of the private investor obstruct the exploitation of small differences in the earnings of capital; on the other, it may bring about perverse movements of capital. But undesirable capital movements can find their origin not only in *expected* changes in policies but also in *differences* regarding monetary, fiscal, or social policies. In fact, perverse movements of capital will probably have greater importance than perverse labor movements. Although differences in taxation and social policies influence labor movements in undesirable directions, such differences are likely to have but a small effect because of the great weight attached to intangibles which restrict migration. On the other hand, capital being more sensitive to differences in yields, actual differences and expected changes in monetary, fiscal, and other policies could lead to sizable shifts of capital funds that would deteriorate rather than improve the efficiency of resource allocation. The previously mentioned agglomerative tendencies may have similar effects.[32]

The possibility of perverse capital flows of a considerable magnitude appears to contradict our previous assertion, according to which the liberalization of capital movements is desirable in an integrated area. Actually, the consideration of capital movements responding to differences in economic policies and to agglomeration economies induced some observers to advocate the maintenance of existing restrictions or the slow and cautious removal of controls.[33] Yet the harmonization of economic policies will remove these imperfections and also the need for restrictions on capital movements on this count. In addition, exchange restrictions will not be the appropriate policy in the case of agglomerative tendencies, since it would be absurd to control intercountry movements of capital and let capital move freely between the regions of the same country when—as in the case of the European Common Market—interregional differences in income levels are often more pronounced than international disparities. Agglomerative tendencies would be counteracted by providing social and economic overhead for backward regions. This latter objective can be served by establishing a development bank without giving all-pervading rights and responsibilities to this institution in regard to capital movements.[34]

Lastly, we should also note the practical difficulties in restricting the intra-union flow of capital. As long as the convertibility of currencies is accepted as a general rule, a considerable part of intended private capital movements will actually take place despite any regulations and controls on these transactions. Thus another source of inefficiency is added: the migration of capital, instead of being determined by differences in the rate of return, will be determined partly by the individual investor's ability to circumvent regulations.

The above arguments speak for the removal of restrictions on capital movements, coupled with the coordination of economic policies and assistance given to backward areas. These measures should be

[32] The various causes of perverse capital movements and possible remedies will be discussed in the policy chapters.

[33] International Labour Office, *Social Aspects of European Economic Co-operation* (*Ohlin Report*) (Geneva, 1956), pp. 25–26, 108–9, and André Philip, "Social Aspects of European Economic Co-operation," *International Labour Review*, September, 1957, p. 254.

[34] For a different opinion, cf. A. Philip, "Social Aspects of European Economic Co-operation," *ibid.*, p. 254, and Maurice Byé's note to the *Ohlin Report*, pp. 131–37.

implemented, however, by further actions aimed at facilitating the international flow of capital. Guarantees given in the case of investments in underdeveloped areas, information regarding economic conditions and the possibilities of private investment, avoidance of double taxation and of every form of discrimination would be especially helpful in achieving this objective.[35] Finally, a common market in securities presupposes the harmonization of regulations on the flotation of new security issues, trading in securities, the organization of stock exchanges, etc.[36] In all these matters, there is need for concerted action on the part of the countries participating in a union, in order to create a healthy atmosphere for capital migration.

Movements of Entrepreneurial Resources[37]

The importance of the movement of entrepreneurial resources has often been overlooked. Nevertheless, as there are differences in natural endowments or in the quantity of labor and capital available, there exist considerable differences in the availability of entrepreneurial services, too. Social rigidities, the cultural outlook, disinclination toward risk taking, lack of business education, etc., are mentioned as the main causes of the often observed scarcity of entrepreneurship. The migration of technically and professionally trained persons would relieve these scarcities and would also make it possible to get the best results from international capital movements.

With the outstanding exception of Schumpeter, who placed the figure of the entrepreneur in the center of his theoretical structure, most economic theorists have attached relatively little importance to the role of the entrepreneur. The main reason for this neglect seems to lie in the emphasis given to static equilibrium positions in most of our theory. In a Walrasian general equilibrium system, the entrepreneurial function is reduced to routine, and profits over the compensation of the manager-entrepreneur disappear. The entrepreneurial function assumes greater importance, however, in the process of innovation and decision making under conditions of uncertainty.

In the following discussion, two forms of entrepreneurial ac-

---

35 For a good discussion of these problems, cf. Organisation for European Economic Co-operation, *Intra-European Investments* (Paris, 1951), pp. 62–67.

36 The measures necessary to remove all obstacles to a unified securities market are examined in R. L. Larcier, "Le placement mobilier dans le marché commun," *La Revue de la Banque*, No. 1 (1959), pp. 62–72 and No. 2 (1959), pp. 125–41.

37 In the discussion of this problem, dynamic considerations cannot be avoided. Thus this section also serves as a transition to Part II.

tivity will be distinguished: "routinizable" managerial functions and decision making under uncertainty. Entrepreneurial resources include, then, managerial ability to coordinate the other factors of production and to organize and supervise the operation of a firm (the Walrasian entrepreneur) and a "non-delegable, non-routinizable residual"[38] activity (the Schumpeterian entrepreneur). The efficient use of existing resources and economic development requires both the manager-entrepreneur and the innovator-entrepreneur; hence the desirability of the migration of both kinds of entrepreneurial resources.

It should be pointed out here that the need for both types of entrepreneurial resources varies from industry to industry, as well as between different stages of economic development. Professional personnel appear to be relatively more important in industries characterized by rapid technological and organizational changes and also in multiproduct industries. Chemicals and metallurgical and electrical equipment industries are frequently used examples.[39] The importance of entrepreneurial resources can also become greater at higher stages of development where the operation of production units of increased size makes the task of management more complex. Nevertheless, as is well known, the scarcity of entrepreneurial resources is generally more pronounced in underdeveloped areas; thus the movement of these resources should proceed from more advanced to less developed economies.

In Jacob Viner's opinion, managerial know-how is one of the internationally most mobile resources, and rigidities on the demand side rather than its unavailability obstruct its movement.[40] Others also note obstacles on the supply side in the form of a high differential return required to compensate for the loss of the accustomed environment, the risk associated with problems of adaptation, and the possible disadvantages encountered if returning to the home country. Some of these difficulties and the various ways of transmitting managerial skills have been well described in J. S. Fforde's *An International Trade in Managerial Skills*.[41]

---

[38] Cf. Eberhard Fels and Rudolf Richter, "Entrepreneurship as a Productive Factor," *Weltwirtschaftliches Archiv*, Vol. LXXVIII, No. 2 (1957), p. 219.

[39] Cf., e.g., G. E. McLaughlin, "Management" in *Industrial Location and National Resources* (Washington: National Resources Planning Board, 1943), p. 239.

[40] *International Trade and Economic Development* (Glencoe, Ill.: Free Press, 1952), p. 132.

[41] Oxford: Basil Blackwell, 1957.

The unwillingness to admit independent entrepreneurs is even stronger than the reluctance to accept the inflow of managerial skills. National and racial differences should be emphasized here. Fears of admitting foreign entrepreneurs are often expressed because of their effect on the social structure.[42] At the same time, the uncertainty encountered in setting up a new business in foreign countries acts as a powerful deterrent on the supply side. The possibility of government intervention, the fear of nationalization, and other obstacles mentioned with regard to the migration of capital are all relevant considerations.

Removing discrimination against foreign entrepreneurs, the increase in welfare can be served through the movement of entrepreneurial resources in an integrated area. The abolition of restrictions on the freedom of establishment is, for example, one of the provisions of the Treaty establishing the European Economic Community. The observance of similar rules may also be helpful in the case of Latin-American regional unions. Since psychological and sociological obstacles play a considerably smaller part in the movement of entrepreneurial resources than in labor migration, a greater mobility of entrepreneurs and managerial personnel can be expected than will probably come about in regard to the labor force.

Similar to the movements of labor and capital, perverse movements of entrepreneurial resources may also occur under conditions of economic integration. The establishment of tariff factories mentioned in connection with the creation of a free-trade area is a case in point. Undesirable movements of entrepreneurial resources may, furthermore, result from disparities in income redistributional measures, as well as from expected changes in policies. Nevertheless, also in this case, perverse movements can be counteracted by the harmonization of monetary, fiscal, and other policies. The general conclusion remains: if the necessary actions are taken in order to avoid the perverse movements of productive factors, the mobility of labor, capital, and entrepreneurial resources leads to a more efficient use of economic resources.

42 The case against the free movement of entrepreneurs in a European free-trade area found expression in Max Holzer, "Die Freizügigkeit der Unternehmungen und der Arbeit," *Aussenwirtschaft*, September, 1959, pp. 250–65.

PART II

The Dynamics of Economic Integration

Chapter
5

NATIONAL FRONTIERS AND
ECONOMIC GROWTH

The division of labour is limited by the extent of the market.

—Adam Smith

Growth Models and Technological Change

The recent interest in economic growth has given rise to a number of growth models. Most of these models, admittedly or unadmittedly, appear to have been influenced by the works of Harrod and Domar.[1] In growth models of the Harrod-Domar type the rise in output depends primarily on the rate of capital formation, while the role of technological improvements in the growth process receives little attention.[2] Empirical studies indicate a misplaced emphasis in these models and reveal that, under the assumption of unchanged technology, the increase in the capital stock would have brought about only a fraction of the actual rise in income levels—at least for the United States.

Moses Abramovitz has estimated that, in the absence of technological improvements, the growth of the capital stock explains, at most, 14 per cent of the increase in per capita national income of the United States between 1879 and 1950.[3] In order to exclude from the estimates the rise in productivity originating in a shift from agricultural to industrial employments, R. M. Solow restricted his investigation to the nonfarm sectors. Using an aggregate production function

[1] Roy Harrod, "An Essay in Dynamic Theory," *Economic Journal,* March, 1939, pp. 14–33, and E. D. Domar, "Expansion and Employment," *American Economic Review,* March, 1947, pp. 34–55.

[2] See, however, William Fellner, *Trends and Cycles in Economic Activity* (New York: Henry Holt & Co., 1956), chap. 8, and, more recently, Arthur Smithies, "Productivity, Real Wages, and Economic Growth," *Quarterly Journal of Economics,* May, 1960, pp. 189–205.

[3] *Resources and Output Trends in the United States since 1870,* Occasional Papers of the National Bureau of Economic Research, No. 52 (1956), p. 11.

of the Cobb-Douglas type, Solow reached the conclusion that about nine-tenths of the rise in GNP per man-hour from 1909 to 1949 can be attributed to technological change and the remaining one-tenth to the increased use of capital.[4] More recently, B. F. Massell inquired into the causes of the increase in output per man-hour in United States manufacturing between 1919 and 1955 and, using a method similar to Solow's, found that improved technology had been responsible for a 190 per cent rise in output per man-hour out of a total increase of 220 per cent.[5] Massell's results, like those of Abramovitz and Solow, indicate that, in the absence of technological change, the growth of the capital stock would have caused labor productivity to increase by little more than 10 per cent.

The reader is warned, however, that these results should not be interpreted to mean that capital formation has little to do with the growth of productivity. Capital formation plays a small role in the rise of GNP per man-hour *if* the level of technology is assumed to be constant, but an increase in both variables entails an interconnection between the two. Not only is investment needed to finance research expenditures which contribute to technological change, but the rate of capital formation also serves as a restraint to the application of new production methods; in the absence of positive net investment, new equipment utilizing advanced technology could be used only to replace worn-out machinery. Therefore, although capital formation *by itself* is only a minor determinant of productivity growth, the invention and application of new technological methods would be hampered if the capital stock did not increase.

The concept "technological change" has been used above in a loose sense, subsuming every factor other than the increase in the capital stock under this category. As a first qualification we should note that the rise in labor productivity can be due partly to the interindustry shift of labor from lower- to higher-productivity sectors. In the limiting case, it is conceivable that productivity is unchanged within sectors and that its increase in a group of industries is caused simply by a change in the composition of output. The contribution of interindustry shifts in employment to "technological change" will be of less

4 "Technical Change and the Aggregate Production Function," *Review of Economics and Statistics*, August, 1957, pp. 312–20; Comment by W. P. Hogan and Reply by R. M. Solow, *ibid.*, November, 1958, pp. 407–13.

5 "Capital Formation and Technological Change in United States Manufacturing," *Review of Economics and Statistics*, May, 1960, pp. 182–88.

importance, however, if agriculture is excluded from the estimates.

Making allowance for shifts in the composition of output, we still have to face the question of what is meant by "technological change" in this context. Formally, Solow and Massell represent technological change as an upward shift of the aggregate production function, which is equivalent to saying that a larger output can be produced with the same quantity of inputs. Therefore, the concept of technological change as used by these authors actually corresponds to our definition of dynamic efficiency. In Chapter 1 we referred to various factors that affect the dynamic efficiency of an economy. These factors will now be classified under two headings: (a) large-scale economies and (b) autonomous technological change.

Large-scale economies, as understood here, mean reductions in input coefficients that result from an increase in the size of the market. These improvements may take the form of economies of scale and external economies or may be associated with intensified competition, lessened uncertainty, and a reallocation of investment funds. Large-scale economies will thus include technological improvements, the introduction of which follows an enlargement of the market. If, on the other hand, the use of improved technological methods is not consequent upon an increase in the size of the market, we shall speak about autonomous, as distinct from induced, technological change.

This distinction between large-scale economies and autonomous technological change is admittedly imperfect. It is difficult to classify, for example, the introduction of assembly-line production in the Ford factory, where the expectation of a future increase in demand motivated large-scale manufacturing. There is also an indirect relationship between market size and autonomous technological change through research expenditures. Large-scale economies in research, for example, would speed up the discovery and application of new technology. Finally, not only does an increase in the size of the market evoke technological improvements, but in most instances autonomous technological change also enlarges the market by reducing costs.

Notwithstanding these qualifications, the distinction made above appears to be a useful one, particularly in discussing problems of economic integration, since it focuses attention on the relationship of market size and growth. Economic integration can be regarded as a fusion of national markets; in a customs union, commodity markets are integrated, in a common market also the markets of productive factors. The fusion of national markets is further strengthened through the harmonization of monetary, fiscal, and other policies in an economic union. The dynamic aspects of integration can be explored by examining the impact of an enlargement of the market on growth.

Views on the Interrelationship of Market Size and Growth

The possible effects of market size on productivity growth have long been discussed in the economic literature. According to Adam Smith, "the greatest improvement in the productive powers of labour . . . seem to have been the effects of the division of labour."[6] The division of labor, according to Smith, gives rise to (*a*) an improvement of the dexterity of the worker, (*b*) saving of time lost in passing from one part of work to another, and (*c*) application of machinery. The division of labor is said to be limited, however, by the extent of the market, and, consequently, an increase in the size of the market would contribute to the rise in productivity. Similar arguments were used by J. S. Mill[7] to foster the case of free commodity and factor movements between different territories. Subsequently, Knut Wicksell argued that "the law of 'increasing returns' also applies to some extent to society as a whole."[8]

In Alfred Marshall's writings we also find an awareness of the interrelationship between market size and economic growth. Marshall is of the opinion that an increase in the aggregate volume of production gives rise to internal and external economies, resulting in increasing returns for the economy as a whole, and he emphasizes that "the Statical theory of equilibrium is only an introduction . . . to the study of the progress and development of industries which show a tendency to increasing return."[9] Marshall, however, went no further in devising a theory of growth, and his followers did not build on his scattered remarks concerning the problems of economic progress but rather extended his theory of static equilibrium. No wonder that, in the otherwise excellent contributions to the problem of increasing returns, these economists—with one notable exception—concentrated their attention on proving the compatibility of increasing returns with com-

[6] *An Inquiry into the Nature and Causes of the Wealth of Nations* (Modern Library ed.; New York: Random House, 1937), p. 3.

[7] *Principles of Political Economy* (Ashley ed.; London: Longmans, Green & Co., 1923), p. 701.

[8] *Lectures on Political Economy* (London: Routledge & Kegan Paul, 1934), Vol. I, p. 133.

[9] *Principles of Economics* (8th ed.; London: Macmillan & Co., Ltd., 1956), p. 382; see also pp. 265–68.

petitive long-run equilibrium and disregarded the interrelationships between increasing returns and growth.[10]

Among Marshall's successors, Allyn Young was the only exception who did not share his contemporaries' concern about static long-run equilibrium but made important contributions to the problem of "Increasing Returns and Economic Progress."[11] Having defined the size of the market by the volume of production, Young develops Adam Smith's dictum that the division of labor is limited by the extent of the market and maintains that "taking a country's economic endowment as given . . . the most important single factor in determining the effectiveness of its industry appears to be the size of the market."[12] Young's penetrative analysis contains most of the basic elements of the market size–growth relationship. He examines the interrelationship of industries in the process of growth, the emergence of new industries as a result of specialization concomitant with an enlargement of the market, the importance of simplification and standardization in a large market, and the impact of an increase in market size on technological change—although he realized that the causation between the last two variables runs in both directions.

The leads contained in Young's contribution were not followed until relatively recently, when problems of underdeveloped economies captured the attention of economists. Paul Rosenstein-Rodan's famous article[13] was the prelude to the revival of interest in the relationship of market size and economic growth. Later contributions include writings by Ragnar Nurkse, Tibor Scitovsky, and W. A. Lewis.[14] These authors, however, consider the interrelations between market size and productivity only in regard to underdeveloped coun-

10 Cf. Piero Sraffa, "The Laws of Returns under Competitive Conditions," *Economic Journal*, 1926, pp. 535–50. Reprinted in *Readings in Price Theory* (Homewood, Ill.: Richard D. Irwin, Inc., 1952), pp. 180–97; A. C. Pigou, "The Laws of Diminishing and Increasing Cost," *Economic Journal*, June, 1927, pp. 188–97; Lionel Robbins, "The Representative Firm," *ibid.*, September, 1928, pp. 387–404; D. H. Robertson, G. F. Shove, and Piero Sraffa, "Increasing Returns and the Representative Firm: A Symposium," *ibid.*, March, 1930, pp. 79–116; Nicholas Kaldor, "The Equilibrium of the Firm," *ibid.*, March, 1934, pp. 60–76; Austin Robinson, "The Problem of Management and the Size of Firms," *ibid.*, June, 1934, pp. 242–57.

11 *Economic Journal*, December, 1928, pp. 527–42.

12 *Ibid.*, p. 532. Also, pp. 532–39.

13 "Problems of Industrialisation of Eastern and South-Eastern Europe," *Economic Journal*, June–September, 1943, pp. 202–11.

14 See, for example, Ragnar Nurkse, *Problems of Capital Formation in Underdeveloped Countries* (Oxford: Basil Blackwell, 1953), chap. 1; Tibor Scitovsky, "Two Concepts of External Economies," *Journal of Political Economy*, April, 1954, pp. 143–51; W. A. Lewis, *Theory of Economic Growth* (Homewood, Ill.: Richard D. Irwin, Inc., 1955), chap. 6.

tries and, explicitly or implicitly, assume that this relationship loses its importance at higher stages of development.

The impact of market size on growth has also been neglected or de-emphasized in some of the literature on customs unions. Viner deals only with economies of scale for plants or firms and maintains that these are likely to be negligible.[15] Meade, too, neglects the dynamic effects of a customs union and gives no more than a short reference to the possibilities of economies of scale.[16] The Vinerian tradition is followed by some American and British economists, who have considered the case of European integration and contended that the fusion of the national markets would not lead to increasing returns in a European framework.[17]

Continental writers are, by and large, more optimistic. The possibility of internal and external economies in a customs union was first noted by Maurice Byé in his "Customs Unions and National Interests" in 1950.[18] Increasing returns associated with an enlarged market have been emphasized in the *Ohlin Report* and in some other writings on European economic integration.[19] The dynamic aspects of economic integration have also been stressed in the literature on integration in Latin America.[20] These contributions, however, did not go much beyond the assertion that increasing returns would be forth-

[15] *The Customs Union Issue* (New York: Carnegie Endowment for International Peace, 1950), p. 46.

[16] *The Theory of Customs Unions* (Amsterdam: North Holland Publishing Co., 1955), p. 94.

[17] Cf., e.g., H. S. Ellis, *The Economics of Freedom* (New York: Harper & Bros., 1950), p. 393; H. G. Johnson, "The European Common Market—Risk or Opportunity?," *Weltwirtschaftliches Archiv*, Vol. LXXIX, No. 2 (1957), pp. 267–78, and "The Gains from Freer Trade with Europe: An Estimate," *Manchester School of Economic and Social Studies*, September, 1958, pp. 247–55.

[18] Originally published in French in *Economie Appliquée*, January–March, 1950, pp. 121–58; the English translation appeared in *International Economic Papers*, No. 3 (London: Macmillan & Co., Ltd., 1953), pp. 208–34.

[19] International Labour Office, *Social Aspects of European Economic Co-operation* (Geneva, 1956), pp. 11 ff. See also Walther Hoffman, "Die Integration der Volkswirtschaften als dynamisches Problem," *Economia Internazionale*, August, 1950, pp. 695–714; W. E. Rappard, "Le secret de la prospérité américaine," *Revue d'Economie Politique*, May–June, 1954, pp. 389–432; André Marchal, "Mercato comune europeo, zona di libero scambio e differenze nel grado di sviluppo economico, *Rivista di Politica Economica*, August–September, 1958, pp. 815–31.

[20] Cf., e.g., UN Department of Economic and Social Affairs, *The Latin American Common Market* (1959), pp. 5 ff.; S. S. Dell, *Problemas de un mercado común en America Latina* (Mexico, D.F.: Centro de Estudios Monetarios Latinoamericanos, 1959), p. 29; Plácido García Reynoso, "Probables efectos del Tratado del Montevideo en la industrialización de América Latina," *El Trimestre Económico*, April–June, 1960, pp. 195–97.

coming as a result of integration and failed to indicate the forms and conditions of such a development.[21] In this and subsequent chapters of the present study we shall endeavor to explore the interrelationship of market size and economic growth in a systematic way.

Market Size and Productivity: Conceptual Problems

In Chapter 2, the size of the market for an economy as a whole was defined by its gross national product, and this definition was qualified by introducing additional variables: economic distances within a country and differences in tastes. In discussing the dynamic effects of integration, separate consideration should also be given to per capita incomes. This becomes necessary because, in the present context, the size of the market is relevant for those commodities in whose production increasing returns are obtained (mostly manufactured goods), and the consumption of this category of products can be shown to increase more than proportionately with a rise in income per head.[22] Thus, for a given gross national product, the higher the per capita incomes, the larger will be the effective size of the market for the products of those sectors which experience increasing returns. Finally, in determining the size of the market for individual products, the national market can also be broken down into regional markets, and account can be taken of the differentiation of commodities.

The outlined procedure might be criticized on the grounds that, with its emphasis on national boundaries, it tends to underestimate trade possibilities. Nevertheless, we have to distinguish between domestic and foreign markets, since tariffs and trade and exchange restrictions, as well as uncertainty associated with foreign sales, discriminate against imports in favor of domestic output. This discrimination between domestic and foreign products is also largely responsible for the fact that a considerable part of interindustry relationships in production (provision of components, parts and accessories, vertical specialization, etc.), which have an important bearing on productivity

---

[21] A notable exception is Tibor Scitovsky, who gave a searching analysis to the possibility of increased competition in an integrated area. See his *Economic Theory and Western European Integration* (Stanford: Stanford University Press, 1958), chap. 3. See also the *Proceedings* of the 1957 Lisbon Conference of the International Economic Association, published in the volume, *Economic Consequences of the Size of Nations*, ed. E. A. G. Robinson (London: Macmillan & Co., Ltd., 1960).

[22] On the income elasticity of demand for manufactured goods, cf. H. B. Chenery, "Patterns of Industrial Growth," *American Economic Review*, September, 1960, pp. 624–54.

are, on the whole, organized within national boundaries rather than internationally. In addition, in industries which sell a large part of their output on foreign markets, diversified export requirements often hold down productivity levels. Economic integration is equivalent to the removal of various forms of discrimination between the economic units of the participating countries; hence the size of the domestic market and its enlargement in a union becomes a relevant variable.

The hypothesis is advanced here that, with given natural resources and capital, a higher level of manufacturing productivity can be attained in a wider market. The testing of this hypothesis would require comparing productivity levels between countries with identical natural endowments and capital stock. In actual comparisons, however, the existing quantity of natural resources and capital will differ from country to country. Therefore, unit cost rather than labor productivity is the relevant variable. Nevertheless, by reason of the difficulties arising in the international comparison of the cost of capital and the remuneration of natural resources, the productivity measure is generally used as an approximation. This procedure is followed also in this study, although we shall make use of data on unit costs, if available. It will be shown below that, in the cases investigated, the error committed by using labor productivity instead of unit cost figures appears to be rather small.

If the level of productivity depends on the size of the market,[23] a widening of the market through integration will contribute to productivity growth. In terms of the definitions introduced in Chapter 1, this would mean that economic integration leads to an improvement in the dynamic efficiency of the economies participating in the union. Establishing the above relationship between market size and productivity does not imply, however, that integration is necessarily followed by a *sustained* increase in the rate of growth of productivity. It is conceivable that the fusion of national markets results in a once-for-all increase in productivity levels, when, after the end of a transitional period, the rate of increase in productivity (expressed in percentage terms) may return to its former level. Nevertheless, a transitional acceleration of productivity growth will take place also in this instance, and integration will permit a continuously higher yearly *absolute* increase in the standard of living as compared with the pre-integration period.

[23] On the interaction of these variables, see pp. 113–14.

With respect to the alleged impact of integration on productivity, it is often argued that the advantages derived from the larger market in the United States could also be captured in the framework of an integrated Europe. In some cases, comparison is made not only with the United States but also with the Soviet Union.[24] Other authors contend that the analogy between the United States and the European integration projects "is a dangerous one and may be highly misleading," and they also maintain that a comparison between the Common Market and Russia simply does not make sense.[25] To begin with the latter proposition, the level of productivity is considerably lower in the Soviet Union than in most Western European countries, so that, on this count, not much can be said for the larger size of the Soviet economy. On the other hand, it is certainly true that the possibilities of specialization and long production runs in the Soviet economy have given significant help to the achievement of a high rate of growth of productivity. Nevertheless, it would be foolish to neglect the differences in political and economic structure, and not much would be gained were we to pursue this analogy here.

As to the comparison of the United States and European or Latin-American integration projects, two questions should be asked: Can higher productivity levels in the United States be attributed (at least partially) to the larger size of the market? And, what difficulties do the European and Latin-American countries face in capturing the advantages of a large market as they appear in the United States?

Productivity Levels and Market Size

A detailed analysis of productivity levels in American and British industries was made by L. Rostas in his pathbreaking study, *Comparative Productivity Levels in British and American Industry*.[26] Rostas found that in 1935–39, physical output per worker in 31 manufacturing industries was 2.2 times higher in the United States than in Great Britain. The United States had productivity advantages in all but two industries (cement and fish curing).[27] Inquiring into the causes of

---

24 Cf., e.g., W. E. Rappard, "Le secret de la prospérité américaine," pp. 404–9; Maurice Allais, *L'Europe unie—route de la prospérité* (Paris: Calmann-Lévy, 1960), chap. ii; and René Maury, *L'intégration européenne* (Paris: Sirey, 1958), p. 40.

25 H. G. Johnson, "The European Common Market—Risk or Opportunity?" *Weltwirtschaftliches Archiv*, Vol. LXXIX, No. 2 (1957), p. 269. Also S. Dell, "Economic Integration and the American Example," *Economic Journal*, March, 1959, pp. 39–42.

26 Cambridge: At the University Press, 1948.

27 *Ibid.*, pp. 27, 33–36.

these differences, Rostas did not reach definite conclusions. He noted that the ratio of horsepower per worker in American and British manufacturing bears the same relation as the ratio of output per worker in the two countries, but he warned that such a correlation does not exist in individual industries.[28] Rostas also used the hypothesis of relating market size and productivity. The results of the estimates led him to believe that some correlation between market size and productivity actually existed, since the United States enjoyed the greatest relative advantage mostly in those industries where the American market was relatively large,[29] and, in the one case where the American market was smaller (fish curing), absolute productivity was also smaller. On the other hand, Rostas pointed out that large differences in market size were often associated with less than average productivity differences and vice-versa.[30]

With respect to the first hypothesis relating capital-labor ratios and productivity, it should be noted that an industry-by-industry comparison shows little systematic relationship between, on the one hand, horsepower per worker or fuel input per worker and, on the other hand, labor productivity.[31] Furthermore, even if in each industry the ratio of the capital-labor coefficients between the two countries were equal to the ratio of labor productivities, the existence of such a relationship would not establish the proposition that intercountry productivity differences could be ascribed—wholly or in most part—to differences in capital-labor ratios, since the results would depend on the choice of the production function. If, for example, a Cobb-Douglas function of the form $O = 1.01 L^{0.75} C^{0.25}$ is used, a capital stock 170 per cent larger (this figure corresponds to the relationship of American

28 *Ibid.*, pp. 52–54.

29 Packing materials (glass containers, tin cans), durable mass-produced goods (automobiles, radios), and standardized industrial products (rubber tires, electric lamps, rubber). Cf. *ibid.*, pp. 33–34.

30 *Ibid.*, pp. 33–34, 59. Marvin Frankel prepared similar estimates for the years 1947–48 and found that, if the data were adjusted by eliminating industries with regional and local markets, a positive relationship between market size and productivity could be established. The coefficient of correlation of 0.70 between the two variables indicates that about 50 per cent of the variance in American-British productivity ratios could be accounted for by the variance in market size between the two countries. See his *British and American Manufacturing Productivity* (Urbana: University of Illinois Bulletin, Bureau of Economic and Business Research, 1957), p. 66. Frankel discounts the significance of this result, however, asserting that the cause-and-effect relationship between market size and productivity is not clear (*ibid.*, p. 72). On this point, cf. p. 113 below.

31 Horsepower and fuel consumption ratios are regarded as representative of the capital stock (Rostas, *op. cit.*, pp. 52–53; also Frankel, *op. cit.*, pp. 43–45).

and British capital-labor ratios for manufacturing as a whole) would result in a less than 30 per cent productivity differential.[32] The remaining discrepancy must be explained by differences in the production functions of the two economies, which, in turn, reflect differences in market size and technology, when the use of advanced technological methods is also influenced by the size of the market.[33]

Recent findings of an OEEC study, encompassing over half the entire manufacturing sector and making use of more refined methods than those employed in previous estimates, indicate a high degree of correlation between the volume of output and output per worker in an industry-by-industry comparison of American and British manufacturing. The rank correlation coefficient between output indices and output per worker indices is 0.789 for 44 manufacturing industries, and the degree of correlation would increase further if correction was made for industries with regional markets. Differences in market size appear to be responsible for the relative productivity advantage of the United States in the manufacturing of metal cans, automobiles, agricultural machinery, paper and card containers, etc., and for the British relative advantage in shipbuilding, sugar refining, tanneries, grain milling, woolen and worsted products, and cutlery.[34] The OEEC study also shows that unit cost ratios follow differences in labor productivity, although discrepancies are slightly smaller here.[35] This result indicates that differences in labor productivity give a good approximation to unit cost differences; hence the positive correlation between market size and productivity also implies the existence of a similar relationship between the size of the market and real costs.

[32] This production function was derived from American data for the period 1899–1922 by Paul H. Douglas. See his *The Theory of Wages* (New York: Macmillan Co., 1934), pp. 133–34.

[33] Differences in resource endowments would be another explanatory variable, but this cannot account for the all-pervading differences in American and British productivity that can be found especially in industries producing for a mass market, where the natural resource content of output is often negligible (cf. Frankel, *op. cit.*, pp. 30–40).

[34] "Output" refers to net output (value added), and the relevant indices express American data in percentages of British data. See D. Paige and G. Bombach, *A Comparison of National Output and Productivity of the United Kingdom and the United States* (Paris: Organisation for European Economic Co-operation, 1959), pp. 69–71, 75–76. For manufacturing as a whole, output per worker in the United States is 292 measured in British prices and 256 at American price weights when British productivity is taken as 100 (*ibid.*, p. 55). All data refer to 1950.

[35] *Ibid.*, pp. 60–61. Similar results have been reached by Frankel (*op. cit.*, p. 45). Unit cost data refer to net costs, excluding the cost of material, fuels, and other purchased inputs.

Evidence supplied by J. H. Young in a comparative study of the American and Canadian economies gives further support to the market-size hypothesis.[36] Young compared output and productivity in 22 American and Canadian industries and—after the exclusion of the cement industry, which has many regionally located small plants in the United States—found a rank correlation coefficient of 0.76.[37] On the basis of available evidence Young concludes: "It could be argued with some validity that [the size of the market] appears to be the most important single factor" in explaining differences in productivity in Canadian and American manufacturing.[38]

It should be added that in examining the correlation between the size of the market and productivity, industry by industry, we consider the impact of market size on economies internal to the firm or industry but exclude the effects of interindustry relationships. Yet, as will be argued at a later point, a larger market also affects productivity through the transmission of technological change between industries, as well as through its effect on specialization. An additional qualification is that uncertainty associated with the introduction of new products and processes is also likely to be less significant in a wider market. These considerations indicate that the numerical results that were cited may understate the correlation between market size and productivity.

The Market-Size Hypothesis: Criticism and Further Evidence

Arguing against the proposition that the advantages of a large market result in a higher level of productivity in the United States as compared with the United Kingdom, Rothbarth and, in his wake, Frankel asserted that the United States had already possessed a productivity advantage over Britain in 1870, although at that time the

[36] "Some Aspects of Canadian Economic Development" (unpublished dissertation submitted to Cambridge University, England, 1955). Also "Comparative Economic Development: Canada and the United States," *American Economic Review, Papers and Proceedings*, May, 1955, pp. 80–93.

[37] If the cement industry is included, the coefficient is 0.70 ("Some Aspects of Canadian Economic Development," p. 78). The correlation is measured between indices of output and productivity when American data are expressed as a percentage of Canadian data.

[38] *Ibid.*, p. 86. Some other observers go even further and assert that three quarters (or more) of the productivity differential between Canadian and American secondary manufacturing can be attributed to differences in market size. See D. H. Fullerton and H. A. Hampton, *Canadian Secondary Manufacturing Industry* (Ottawa: Queen's Printer, 1957), p. 159, also chap. 4.

American market was probably smaller than the British.[39] The legitimacy of this conclusion is open to doubt, however. It is well known that large-scale production methods had been used in the United States as far back as 1850 in the production of small arms, clocks, locks and other hardware, window frames, doors, carts, etc., and that the application of mass-production methods resulted in higher productivity in these fields. Mass production, in turn, was made possible by the existence of a large market for these products. D. L. Burn points out that all contemporary explanations "lay considerable stress on the peculiarities of the market, particularly its size."[40] Consequently, there may be more truth in the reverse of the Rothbarth-Frankel proposition: the United States had early productivity advantages in those industries where a wider market was available. This conclusion is supported by the findings of a German study which imply that, around 1870, American manufacturing productivity, on the average, might not have been greater than British productivity.[41] The latter result would suggest that the American advantage in industries with a larger market was counterbalanced by disadvantages of industries possessing a relatively smaller market.

At this point, we also have to deal with an often raised objection against the market-size hypothesis, according to which the line of causation between market size and productivity (or real costs) is indeterminate.[42] It is not alleged here that the relationship of market size and productivity would be unidirectional. Rather, an increase in productivity will enlarge the market by raising national income and by augmenting demand for a particular product via a reduction in costs. But the introduction of modern technology is also conditioned

[39] E. Rothbarth, "Causes of Superior Efficiency of U.S.A. Industry as Compared with British Industry," *Economic Journal*, September, 1946, p. 384, and M. Frankel, "Anglo-American Productivity Differences: Their Magnitude and Some Causes," *American Economic Review, Papers and Proceedings*, May, 1955, pp. 104–5.
[40] "The Genesis of American Engineering Competition, 1850–70," *Economic History*, January, 1931, p. 305.
[41] B. Buxbaum, "Der amerikanische Werkzeugmaschinen- und Werkzeugbau im 18. und 19. Jahrhundert," *Beiträge zur Geschichte der Technik und Industrie* (1920), Vol. X, pp. 121–54. On the other hand, Frankel believes that "American productivity began to forge ahead of British productivity somewhere between 1830 and 1860" (*British and American Manufacturing Productivity*, p. 27). He adds that "it is unlikely that the United States could have lagged behind Britain for long after 1830–60, and it is unlikely that she could have surpassed the latter much before that period" (*ibid.*, p. 28).
[42] Cf., e.g., Frankel, *British and American Manufacturing Productivity*, p. 72; Solomon Fabricant, "Study of the Size and Efficiency of the American Economy," *Economic Consequences of the Size of Nations*, pp. 47–50.

by the size of the market, and the existence of a bidirectional relationship does not reduce the importance of the market-size hypothesis, since the two variables reinforce each other.

For individual industries, an increase in output contributes to higher productivity in various ways: adoption of large-scale production methods is easier; producers are more willing to undertake new investments; machines of better quality are used, since the average age of capital is lower; institutional resistance to change is weaker; etc. Autonomous technological improvements, on the other hand, widen the market for the industry's products, and the interaction of the two variables augments the effect of each, contributing thereby to further gains in output and productivity. On the national economy level, an increase in the size of the market raises productivity via the workings of internal and external economies, intensified competition, lessening uncertainty, etc. An improvement in productivity, in turn, enlarges the market through its effect on higher incomes. We find a multiplier-type relationship here when the mutual interdependence of incomes and productivity reinforces the effect of any of them and gives a leverage to the impact of third factors increasing productivity.[43]

The latter conclusion can provide an explanation for the observed interrelationship between the growth of output and the rate of increase of productivity over time. P. J. Verdoorn has found in a study encompassing the periods 1870–1914 and 1914–30 that, in various industries of a number of advanced economies, productivity has been increasing approximately as the square-root function of the volume of output.[44] If so, a 100 per cent rise in output would be accompanied by over a 41 per cent increase in productivity.[45] The relationship between the increase of output and productivity growth is emphasized also by Paige and Bombach, who found that the gap in productivity levels between most American and British industries had been widen-

[43] This argument draws on Scitovsky's analysis in *Economic Theory and Western European Integration*, pp. 119–20.

[44] "Fattori che regolano lo sviluppo della produttività del lavoro," *L'Industria*, No. 1 (1949), pp. 45–53, and "On an Empirical Law Governing the Productivity of Labor," *Econometrica*, April, 1951, pp. 209–10. For an application of these findings to integration in Europe, see *Overdrukken*, No. 22, of the Dutch Planning Bureau.

[45] Verdoorn actually calculates with 45 per cent, when the limits are given as between 41 and 57 per cent. Cf. *L'Industria*, No. 1 (1949), pp. 45–46. For a discussion of further estimates leading to results similar to those of Verdoorn, see Colin Clark, *The Conditions of Economic Progress* (London: Macmillan & Co., Ltd., 1957), pp. 350–74; also F. W. Kendrick, "Productivity Trends: Capital and Labor," *Review of Economics and Statistics*, August, 1956, pp. 248–57.

ing and that in each country productivity gains were the greatest in the rapidly growing industries.[46]

Another way of establishing the proposition that a widening of the market will raise the level of productivity in manufacturing is to abstract from the interrelationship between per capita incomes and productivity. Then, for a given per capita income level, population can be taken as an indicator of market size. A larger population will make possible the exploitation of large-scale economies in various branches of manufacturing, both directly through its effect on final demand and indirectly via demand for intermediate products. The consequent lowering of costs permits the expansion of these sectors, partly at the expense of sectors that do not experience increasing returns, partly at the expense of imports.

H. B. Chenery, in an ingenious analysis of cross-section data of fifty-one countries, has explored the impact of the growth of per capita incomes and population on industrialization. He found that if the income level is held constant at $300 per year, an increase in population from 2 to 50 million causes per capita output to nearly double in manufacturing as a whole and to increase by more than 250 per cent in industries where large-scale economies are most significant.[47] In Latin America, for example, differences in the size of population alone would be expected to cause Brazil to have twice as much per capita manufacturing production as Guatemala.

Aside from the limitations of this procedure that arise from the unreliability of data, differences in economic policies, etc., it should be emphasized that, by reason of the assumed constancy of per capita incomes, Chenery understates the total effect of market size on productivity. Actually, not only will an increase in population raise productivity, but the ensuing increase in incomes will in turn enable producers to use large-scale production methods, and the interrelationship between market size and productivity will give a leverage to the effects of third factors.

These findings indicate that the size of the market is an important variable in determining the level of productivity. This does not mean, however, that the impact of factors other than market size could not outweigh the advantages of a larger market. High levels of produc-

[46] Op. cit., pp. 71–72.
[47] The industries in question are textiles, paper, printing, rubber, chemicals, petroleum products, metals, machinery, and transport equipment. See Chenery, op. cit., pp. 645–46.

tivity in small countries, such as Belgium, Switzerland, or Sweden, require the introduction of further explanatory variables. A stronger sense of community, a higher standard of education, and a greater capacity to adjust are often cited to explain the high per capita incomes in these countries.[48] It can be added that the small rich countries were already far advanced in industrialization before the First World War, when barriers to international economic intercourse were less formidable. Some of these nations did not undergo the ordeals of the two world wars; others had colonies to rely upon. Political stability attracted foreign capital to these countries, and their advantageous location also contributed to the rise in real incomes.

Sociological and psychological factors play an important role not only in small nations but in larger countries as well. It is often noted, for example, that the high degree of social integration, as well as the enterprising character of the American people and good labor discipline, have been conducive to high levels of productivity in the United States. Through its effect on the homogeneity of tastes, on factor movements, etc., social integration has an important bearing on the exploitation of large-scale economies in a common market, too.

In the presence of these noneconomic factors, we have to give a cautious formulation to the market-size hypothesis: under *ceteris paribus* assumptions, a wider market will make possible the attainment of higher levels of manufacturing productivity. As for the case of economic integration, this proposition implies that a fusion of national markets would improve the growth prospects of the participating countries. Belgium and Holland, for example, may be thriving individually, yet the integration of their economies enables them to reach higher productivity levels.

Large-Scale Economies in Present-Day Integration Projects

The foregoing discussion of the interrelationship between market size and productivity suggests that large-scale economies would accompany economic integration. The question arises as to what extent these findings can be applied to present-day integration projects. With regard to Europe, Gottfried Haberler raised doubts about this possibility. Haberler pointed out that economic integration in the

48 See Simon Kuznets, "The Economic Growth of Small Nations," *Economic Consequences of the Size of Nations*, pp. 14–32; W. A. Jöhr and F. Kneschaurek, "Study of the Efficiency of a Small Nation—Switzerland," and L. Duquesne de la Vinelle, "Study of the Efficiency of a Small Nation—Belgium," *ibid.*, pp. 54–77 and 78–92.

United States came about in an early period of economic development under conditions of comparative economic liberalism, and, if its various areas had had "a hundred years to harden into independent states with well-protected economies," it is "more than doubtful that there would be today a United States of America."[49] Phrasing the problem in this way, the center of attention is shifted from the economic to the political sphere. Recent developments in the European Common Market indicate that Haberler might have been unduly pessimistic in this regard and overestimated the power of vested interests. This is not to deny the difficulties in the way of exploiting the potential advantages of a large market in Europe. Differences in language, in customs, and in tastes are likely to hinder the creation of a unified market and the standardization of a number of commodities.[50]

TABLE 2

CHANGES IN PRODUCTION AND INTRA-AREA TRADE IN EUROPE, 1913–51*

	APPROXIMATE PERCENTAGE CHANGE IN	
	Volume of Commodity Production	Volume of Intra-Area Trade
1913–28.....................	+15	± 0
1928–38.....................	+15	−10
1938–51.....................	+30	+12
	+70	+ 2

*SOURCE: UN Economic Commission for Europe, *Economic Survey of Europe since the War* (Geneva, 1953), p. 214. The figures do not include the U.S.S.R.

Another way of establishing the proposition that a widening of the market will raise the level of productivity in Europe is to argue in reverse and to examine the effects of the decrease in the effective size of the market during the interwar period. The figures of Table 2 demonstrate that trade-and-payments restrictions and more intensive use of the weapons of monetary, fiscal, and other policies by the individual states considerably reduced economic intercourse within the European economy. In view of available evidence, one is bound to agree with Ingvar Svennilson that "the arbitrary combinations of resources within smaller or larger national areas had a decisive influence on long-term growth in Europe as a whole. It is likely that the ex-

49 "Economic Aspects of a European Union," *World Politics*, July, 1949, p. 440.
50 On this point, see pp. 137–38 below.

istence of this national structure slowed down, not only the growth of some less favoured countries, but also the general development of Europe's joint resources."[51] *Ceteris paribus,* it can be argued that integration in Europe will accelerate the growth of productivity.

The comparison of the American and British economies indicates that a fusion of national markets will make possible the exploitation of large-scale economies not only for the smaller European countries but also for countries of the size of France and Germany. The dynamic effects of integration are likely to be even greater in Latin America, considering that the limited size of national markets is one of the main obstacles to the development of manufacturing industries in this area, and a widening of the market through integration can provide a powerful inducement for growth. By reason of the lower stage of economic development they occupy, the integration of the Latin-American countries offers greater opportunities for economies internal to the firm, economies internal to the industry, and external economies in interindustry relations than a union of highly developed European economies. These advantages are reduced, however, by reason of higher transportation costs on the more spread-out Latin-American continent.

After this general discussion of the interrelationship between market size and productivity, in the following chapters we shall examine various factors that contribute to large-scale economies in an integrated area. Separate treatment will be allotted to the effects of integration on (a) economies of scale, (b) external economies, (c) market structures, (d) technological change, (e) risk and uncertainty, and (f) investment.

The hypothesis is advanced here that economic integration will permit the exploitation of economies internal to the firm that had previously not been forthcoming because of the limited size of the market. Such gains could not be obtained if the integrated national economies had been large enough to exploit all sources of internal economies prior to integration. It will be argued, however, that, in present-day integration projects, economies of scale can be appropriated, at least in some branches of production, in a wider market.

The concept of external economies used here comprises all forms of intra-industry and interindustry relationships that contribute to cost reductions. A distinction will be made between external econo-

51 *Growth and Stagnation in the European Economy* (Geneva, 1954), p. 41.

mies operating outside the market mechanism (spreading of technological and organizational know-how and development of a managerial class and a skilled labor force in a large market) and those operating via the market (cost reductions through interindustry repercussions and interdependence via income changes). Finally, both technological and pecuniary elements are present in changes of the industrial structure through specialization.

The effects of integration on market structures will be analyzed in their relationship to the degree of competition. Following Scitovsky, the argument will be presented that economic integration is likely to intensify competition after the removal of discrimination between producers. The disappearance of monopoly and quasi-monopoly positions, in turn, contributes to a more efficient use of resources and provides incentive for improvements in production methods. At the same time, an increase in the average size of the firm may raise the amount of research expenditures, and large-scale economies of research are likely to be forthcoming on the firm level and on the national economy level as well.

Furthermore, integration will reduce risk and uncertainty in the economic intercourse of the union members. In the present-day world, various factors contribute to the riskiness of foreign transactions. Uncertainties are associated with the complexity of trade regulations and with the possibility of unilateral changes in tariffs and other forms of trade restrictions, foreign-exchange regulations, and economic policies in general. Finally, integration is bound to bear influence on investment activity, since new investments will be necessary to exploit the potential economies of large-scale production and changes will occur in the allocation of investment funds, too.

Chapter 6

ECONOMIES OF SCALE

The chief advantages of production on a large scale are economy of skill, economy of machinery and economy of materials.

—Marshall

Concepts of Internal Economies[1]

Marshallian internal economies are customarily interpreted in a static sense: decreasing costs are said to prevail if the firm's cost curve is downward-sloping and reversible. An increase in the quantity produced will then lead to lower costs, and a subsequent reduction in output would re-establish the previous cost relationships. Adjustments are assumed to take place in the long run, which leaves sufficient time for the depreciation of old equipment. Marshall does not give separate consideration to intraplant and interplant economies and attributes economies of scale to the specialization of workers, the application of machinery, and the more economical use of materials.[2]

The static concept of internal economies drew objections from Schumpeter, who argued that the firm's cost curve is ordinarily U-shaped also in the long run, and reductions in costs take the form of a downward shift of the curve. According to Schumpeter, cost reductions result from innovating activity, which he defined as the application of new combinations of productive factors or, alternatively, as the setting-up of a new production function.[3] The concept of the production function, as used by Schumpeter, is different from the "abstract" production function. The latter formulation assumes perfect knowl-

1 In this chapter the expressions "internal economies" and "economies of scale" will be used interchangeably to denote economies internal to the firm.

2 Alfred Marshall, *Principles of Economics* (8th ed.; London: Macmillan & Co., Ltd., 1956), p. 232. Here and elsewhere in the text, references are made to the average cost curve of the firm (or plant).

3 "The Instability of Capitalism," *Economic Journal*, September, 1928, pp. 361–86, and *Business Cycles* (New York: McGraw-Hill Book Co., Inc., 1939), Vol. I, pp. 87–102.

edge of all possible alternatives on the part of the decision maker;[4] thus the entrepreneur would have only routinizable managerial functions, the best alternative being automatically chosen at any point of time. In a more realistic model, only a limited number of alternative processes are considered simultaneously,[5] and an increase in the size of the market will offer new alternatives to the firm. The use of production methods which had not been in the entrepreneur's horizon before can now be viewed as the setting-up of a new production function. Changes will come about in time, and some of the cost-reducing elements will prove to be irreversible. The irreversibility of some forms of internal economies was also admitted by Marshall, who, in an appendix to the *Principles,* called attention to the "limitations of the use of statical assumptions in regard to increasing returns."[6]

Actually, internal economies of both a static and a dynamic character contribute to the so-called economies of scale. Their discussion is included in Part II of this study, however, by reason of our emphasis on dynamic elements in the case of economic integration. Scale economies will be considered under two headings: economies internal to the plant and economies internal to the firm and external to the plant. Only the "real" economies of scale, i.e., those which entail a reduction of input needs per unit of output, will be examined. Cost reductions for the plant (firm) that are not associated with any real saving for the economy as a whole (e.g., lower prices paid to suppliers by reason of the increased bargaining power of the large firm) fall outside our topic.

Intraplant Economies

The following are the main forms of economies internal to the plant:[7]

a) For various types of equipment, such as containers, pipelines,

---

[4] On this point, see T. C. Koopmans, *Three Essays on the State of Economic Science* (New York: McGraw-Hill Book Co., Inc., 1957), pp. 68–71.

[5] See H. A. Simon, "A Behavioral Model of Rational Choice," *Quarterly Journal of Economics,* February, 1955, pp. 99–118.

[6] *Op. cit.,* pp. 664 ff.

[7] For references, see P. Sargant Florence, *The Logic of British and American Industry* (London: Routledge & Kegan Paul, 1953), pp. 49–60; E. A. G. Robinson, *The Structure of Competitive Industry* (Chicago: University of Chicago Press, 1958), chap. ii; T. M. Whitin and M. H. Peston, "Random Variations, Risks, and Returns to Scale," *Quarterly Journal of Economics,* November, 1954, pp. 601–12; Harvey Leibenstein, "The Proportionality Controversy and the Theory of Production," *ibid.,* November, 1955, pp. 619–25; and Schumpeter, *Business Cycles,* Vol. I, pp. 87 ff.

compressors, etc., cost is a function of the surface area, whereas capacity is directly related to volume. From this principle, engineers derived the .6 rule, according to which the increase in the cost of equipment of this sort is given by the increase in capacity raised to the .6 power.

b) Cost increases are less than proportional to the growth of volume in the case of bulk transactions. Savings derived from large-scale handling, shipping, etc., come under this heading.

c) The principle of massed reserves indicates a cost saving as output increases in the case of inventory holdings of finished products and materials, since optimum safety allowances which provide protection against random variations vary proportionately with the square root of output. The same principle applies to the holding of cash balances for liquidity purposes, to auditing, sampling, and to repair facilities.

d) Large-scale production will be necessary for the optimum use of various kinds of indivisible equipment. According to "the principle of multiples," first noted by Babbage in his *Economy of Manufactures*, maximum efficiency in the use of combined units of equipment requires the entire plant's capacity to be equal to some common multiple of the capacities of individual units of efficient size.

e) At higher rates of output, economizing is possible in a number of nonproportional activities, such as design, production planning, research, channeling and collecting of information, etc. Either these activities require a high level of output for optimal operation, or their cost rises less than proportionately with an increase in output.

f) Production in larger quantities warrants the application of advanced technological methods that call for the use of specialized equipment, higher capital intensity, or assembly-line production.

g) Besides the use of specialized equipment, larger size makes possible the specialization of workers and will enable the firm to buy the best management.

The importance of these cost-reducing factors will vary among industries and according to plant sizes. In the present context, emphasis is laid on the so-called "structural economies"[8] (*a, d, e, f, g*), since these are likely to be of greater consequence in the case of economic

---

[8] Whereas structural economies cannot be reaped with existing equipment and organization of production, marginal economies do not require changes in plant and organization and are operative also in the case of a small increase in output. See J. E. Meade, *Trade and Welfare. The Theory of International Economic Policy*, Vol. II (London: Oxford University Press, 1955), pp. 36–37.

integration where the size of the market increases significantly. Among the factors that check the exploitation of economies of scale in a union, transportation costs and product differentiation deserve mention.

The literature on economic integration abounds in unsubstantiated claims as to the possibilities of internal economies, while authors critical of integration have voiced rather pessimistic views.[9] No a priori answer can be given to this question, since economies of scale depend on the size of the area, on differences in tastes, on transportation costs, and so forth. An appraisal of available evidence on various industries, however, will help us in exploring the possibility of reaping economies of scale in present-day integration projects. We shall make use of various approaches to test the hypothesis that integration may lead to the exploitation of internal economies. Most of the evidence collected concerns problems of European economic integration, where comparisons with the United States will prove to be helpful. Separate consideration will be given to the Latin-American integration projects. The analysis of internal economies will also prepare the ground for the discussion of problems of specialization, competition, and technological change in an integrated area.

The arguments used in denying the possibility of obtaining economies of scale in an integrated Europe are usually based on one of two propositions: (a) the size of the plant is approximately the same in the United States and in relatively smaller countries, such as Great Britain and Canada; (b) statistical estimates do not indicate any relationship between plant size and productivity. It is then argued that an extension of the market over, for example, its present size in the United Kingdom, France, or Germany would not lead to economies of scale.

As to the first proposition, American and British plant sizes have been recently compared by Frankel and Florence. It has been shown that the average size of plants measured by the number of workers employed is approximately the same in the two countries or, at most, is only slightly larger in the United States. Similar results have been reached in the comparison of American and Canadian plant sizes by Rosenbluth.[10] The absence of a positive correlation between plant size and productivity was first advanced by Rostas, and the same propo-

9 For references, see nn. 15–20 in Chap. 5.

10 Marvin Frankel, *British and American Manufacturing Productivity* (Urbana: University of Illinois Bulletin, Bureau of Economics and Business Research, 1957), p. 60; Florence, *op. cit.*, p. 36, and Gideon Rosenbluth, *Concentration in Canadian Manufacturing Industries* (Princeton: Princeton University Press, 1957), p. 85.

sition was made by Frankel.[11] Both Rostas and Frankel used American and British data to test the hypothesis, comparing relative differences in average plant sizes and productivity in selected industries.

A Comparison of Plant Sizes

A critical examination of the above propositions requires, in the first place, the choice of an appropriate yardstick for measuring the size of the plant. One is bound to agree with Joel Dean, that "a measure which corresponds most closely to economic capacity is the best."[12] Various indicators, such as employment, output, fuel consumption, and capital equipment, have been suggested for this purpose. Difficulties in the valuation of capital and possibilities of saving in fuels at higher output levels can be mentioned as the main objections against the latter two methods. It is sometimes argued that the employment index gives the best results, since the cause-and-effect relationship between output and productivity is not always clear. But the same qualification applies, to some extent, also to the use of employment as an indicator. In addition, two further objections of considerable importance can be levied against the employment measure. First, the number of workers is only one of the determinants of capacity, and, second, capital-intensive methods of higher efficiency can actually reduce employment *pari passu* with an increase in capacity. Therefore, the use of the employment measure is likely to give a downward bias to the estimated relationship between plant size and productivity.

Theoretically, output appears as the best measure of capacity if the assumption is made that all firms produce at the lowest point of their average cost curves. Although this is not likely to be true, "it may be hoped that in industries with a continuous range in possible size of plant . . . a statistical averaging of observations will give a curve of about the same shape as the theoretical function."[13] If output figures are used for measuring capacity, the results obtained by comparing the average number of workers per plant will change significantly. While the employment measure showed little difference in the average

11 L. Rostas, *Comparative Productivity in British and American Manufacturing Industry* (Cambridge: At the University Press, 1948), p. 60, and Frankel, *op. cit.*, p. 63.

12 *Managerial Economics* (New York: Prentice-Hall, 1951), p. 306.

13 *Ibid.*, p. 306. Output is used as an indicator also in J. Steindl, *Small Business and Big Business* (Oxford: Basil Blackwell, 1945), pp. 18–24. For an extensive discussion of the difficulties encountered in the measurement of plant sizes, cf. C. A. Smith, "Survey of the Empirical Evidence on Economies of Scale," *Business Concentration and Price Policy* (Princeton: Princeton University Press, 1955), pp. 213–30.

size of manufacturing plants between the United States and the United Kingdom, the previously observed disparities in labor productivity indicate that, in terms of output, American plants are 2.5–3 times larger than British plants. The differences in the average size of plants would appear even greater if comparison were made with France, Italy, or Belgium.[14]

Note, however, that international comparisons of plant sizes can provide only approximate magnitudes without any claim for precision. Dissimilarities in statistical methods and in the groupings of industries reduce the value of the estimates.[15] In addition, the coverage of small industry differs not only internationally but also—at least in the case of the United States—from one census to another. Solomon Fabricant notes that differences in "cutoff points" may lead to the underestimation of plant sizes in the United States as compared with those in other countries.[16]

The Relationship between Plant Size and Productivity: Industry Studies

If output is used as a measure of plant size, manufacturing plants appear to be considerably larger in the United States than in other industrialized countries. It is a different problem whether a positive correlation between plant size and productivity also exists. In Frankel's opinion this relationship cannot be established, no matter whether the size of the plant is measured by output or by employment.[17] Closer inspection reveals, however, that the method employed by Frankel (and Rostas) in arriving at the alleged absence of interdependence between plant size and productivity has certain deficiencies that do not permit one to reach meaningful conclusions. By comparing ratios of

---

[14] Some information on the size of manufacturing plants in the countries participating in the European Common Market is provided in P. L. Mandy and G. de Ghellinck, "La structure de la dimension des entreprises dans les pays du marché commun," *Revue Economique*, May, 1960, pp. 395–413.

[15] On the difficulties that beset statistical comparisons of plant sizes within the Common Market, see L. Cohen, "Un exemple de l'impossibilité de certaines comparaisons statistiques: la taille des établissements industriels dans les pays du marché commun," *Etudes et Conjoncture*, February, 1959, pp. 197–208.

[16] "Study of the Size and Efficiency of the American Economy," *Economic Consequences of the Size of Nations*, ed. E. A. G. Robinson (London: Macmillan & Co., Ltd., 1959), p. 45. Actually, in 1947 and 1948 respectively, the "cutoff point" was establishments employing 10 persons in the United States and 11 persons in the United Kingdom. (The reader should note that the statistical concept of establishment roughly corresponds to that of the plant.)

[17] *Op. cit.*, pp. 57–58.

average plant sizes and labor productivity between the United States and Great Britain, *industry by industry,* and calculating a correlation coefficient between these variables, a *ceteris paribus* assumption is made as between industries. If the optimum plant size, the shape of the cost curves, and the dispersion of plant sizes differ considerably for individual industries, a positive correlation between the ratios of average plant sizes and labor productivity may not be found, even if the plant cost curves show internal economies in *every* industry. Furthermore, the aggregation of data referring to a heterogeneous group of commodities, such as tin containers, paper sacks, cured fish, and manufactured ice, conceals the possibility that economies of scale can be found in *some* of these industries. To reach more reliable results, we then have to consider individual industries rather than an aggregate of industries.

Industry studies have been carried out with respect to American, German, and New Zealand manufacturing. In these cases all or most manufacturing industries have been examined. In the United States, if establishments are classified according to the value of output, the data of the 1939 Census of Manufacturing give a strong indication of productivity increasing with size of establishment in each of the twenty industry groups, with 142 increases and 17 decreases recorded in detailed calculations.[18] The German data indicate that productivity increases with size in most of the 41 industries that are divided into three or more size groups, while a negative correlation between size and productivity was found in the meat-processing industry only.[19] Finally, in New Zealand manufacturing, where plant size is measured by the number of workers employed, 31 industries show increasing productivity, 26 constant, and 7 decreasing productivity with size, whereas 15 industries exhibit, first, an increase and later a decrease in productivity.[20]

[18] See J. Johnston, "Labour Productivity and the Size of Establishment," *Bulletin of Oxford University Institute of Statistics,* November–December, 1954, p. 351. Were we to accept the method advocated by Johnston and use an indicator that combines output *and* employment in measuring the size of the plant, nine industry groups would show increasing, three industries constant, and none decreasing productivity, while eight industries display no relationship or do not fit Johnston's classification (*ibid.,* p. 352).

[19] Statistisches Bundesamt, Wiesbaden, "Die Kostenstruktur in der gewerblichen Wirtschaft," *Statistik der Bundesrepublik Deutschland,* Vol. XLIX. Cited in Karl Borch, "Productivity and Size of the Firm," *Productivity Measurement Review,* February, 1958, pp. 47–51. The basis of the classification is the value of output. Data refer to 1950.

[20] J. W. Rowe, "Productivity and Size of Establishment in New Zealand Manufacturing," *Productivity Measurement Review,* May, 1958, pp. 36–39. The industries with increasing productivity to size produce 40 per cent of value added in manufacturing. Data refer to 1956.

These results lend support to the view that productivity increases with size in many industries. The interpretation of the estimates derived from industry studies raises various problems, however, especially in connection with the heterogeneity of products within an industry, as statistically defined. J. M. Clark first noted that standardization in a large market leads to the specialization of various plants in different products.[21] Further studies have shown that, in a number of industries, specialization often leads to smaller, rather than larger, plant sizes.[22] Taking into account the possibility of horizontal and vertical specialization, two opposite tendencies will affect the size of the plant. Whereas economies of scale tend to enlarge the plant's size, specialization leads to its reduction. This process can be visualized by imagining a growing plant producing various intermediate and final products, when a further extension of the operations would result in the continuous splitting-up of the plant in vertical and horizontal directions. While all the newly created plants (which may operate in the framework of the same firm or as independent firms) may enjoy economies of scale, their size might be smaller than that of a non-specialized plant.

The existence of economies of scale, then, does not imply that gigantic plants are necessarily more efficient than others of relatively smaller size, if the latter are specializing in a narrower range of products. Economies of scale may continue without a "disintegration" of the production process, however, in certain localized industries, such as waterworks, electricity plants, gasworks, brewing, etc.; in industries requiring large indivisible equipment, as steel making and shipbuilding; and in those where the product is highly complex and is built of a great number of small parts, e.g., typewriters, watches, and cash registers.[23] In addition, various factors, such as the objective of spreading risks, the availability of particular productive services, and the application of research conducted in the framework of the firm, may tend to increase the size of the plant through diversification.

The above considerations qualify the results of the industry

21 *Studies in the Economics of Overhead Costs* (Chicago: University of Chicago Press, 1923), p. 96.

22 P. Sargant Florence, *Investment, Location, and Size of Plant* (Cambridge: At the University Press, 1950), pp. 50–51, 88. Similar conclusions have been reached in G. J. Stigler, "The Division of Labor Is Limited by the Extent of the Market," *Journal of Political Economy*, June, 1951, pp. 185–93, on the basis of data published in *Industrial Location and National Resources* (Washington: National Resources Planning Board, 1943).

23 Cf. Robinson, *op. cit.*, p. 32.

studies. A further qualification is introduced if the regional character of some products with relatively high transportation costs is taken into account. The error possibilities due to these factors and to others to be mentioned below can be reduced if plant sizes and efficiency are compared with regard to homogeneous products, with attention paid also to the regional nature of the market, if any.

Plant Size and Efficiency for Homogeneous Products

In attempting to establish the validity of the hypothesis of economies of scale, we are actually inquiring into the relationship between plant size and efficiency. An adequate measure of this relationship would be the comparison of unit costs for different plant sizes. In industries comprising heterogeneous products, however, costs are difficult to compare. Consequently, we have used labor productivity as an approximation. This procedure may have a considerable margin of error in industries where the proportion of labor cost in total cost varies as between products. In addition, the higher capital intensity of larger firms can lead to an overestimation of the degree of correlation between plant size and efficiency if data on labor productivity are used as a "proxy" for efficiency.[24] For industries producing homogeneous goods, this error possibility can be avoided by correlating plant size with the unit cost of the product.

Empirical data collected by the U.S. Tariff Commission were presented by J. M. Blair in an article on "The Relation between Size and Efficiency of Business."[25] The figures show efficiency markedly increasing as a function of size over the whole range of output for cement, Bessemer pig iron, basic pig iron, Bessemer and open-hearth ingots, crude petroleum, and sugar. Also for the United States, a National Bureau publication cites empirical studies for the paper industry, creameries, and electricity generation, all of which show increasing returns to scale. In the case of electricity generation, for example, variable cost falls from 2.0 to 0.8 cents per kilowatt-hour as capacity increases from 1,000 to 100,000 kw.[26] On the other hand, lit-

[24] This is not necessarily so, however, since the application of more advanced technological methods associated with higher capital intensity may reduce rather than increase the cost of capital per unit of output in modern plants.

[25] *Review of Economics and Statistics*, August, 1942, pp. 125–35. Estimates refer to various dates between 1910 and 1939. Plants are classified in 4–15 groups according to size; size is measured in physical output units, cost as average cost per unit of output.

[26] "Cost and the Size of Plants and Firms," *Cost Behavior and Price Policy* (New York: National Bureau of Economic Research, 1943), pp. 243–47, 259–60.

tle or no economies of scale are shown with regard to fertilizers, baker-ies, and rubber tires.[27]

Rostas collected empirical information on various British indus-tries and found efficiency increasing with size in the production of margarine, cement, tinplate, creamery butter, forged and foundry pig iron, tobacco, copper and brass, in spirit-distilling and in ship-build-ing. Rostas' data showed medium plants to be the most efficient in butter blending and fertilizers, whereas efficiency appeared to decrease with size in acid pig iron and sugar refining.[28] For the years 1946–48, reports of official committees reached inconclusive results for the wool industry, furniture, footwear, rubber tires, calico printing, electric lamps, and matches, while small-scale production was shown to work with lower unit costs in lace manufacturing and in the production of rubber footwear.[29]

Empirical investigations on efficiency in plants of different size may give rise to errors in connection with the valuation of certain cost items (e.g., depreciation), differences in the utilization of capacity, or overtime work. These deficiencies are eliminated if the probable unit costs of plants of different size are estimated on the basis of tech-nological information. Managerial or engineering estimates have de-ficiencies of their own, however, primarily because subjective ele-ments often influence the results. This method was used with regard to petroleum refineries in the United States, in which case comparable cost items showed constant or decreasing costs in the function of size.[30] Subsequently, J. S. Bain attempted to determine, with the help of managerial and engineering estimates, the minimum scale of the plant required for lowest unit costs in twenty American manufactur-ing industries.[31] Taking into consideration submarkets due to re-gional pattern[32] and product differentiation,[33] in six or eleven of the

[27] J. M. Blair, "Technology and Size," *American Economic Review, Papers and Proceedings*, May, 1948, pp. 148–50.

[28] L. Rostas, *Productivity, Prices, and Distribution in Selected British Industries* (Cambridge: At the University Press, 1948).

[29] Cf. John Jewkes, "Are the Economies of Scale Unlimited?" *Economic Conse-quences of the Size of Nations*, pp. 105–8.

[30] *Cost Behavior and Price Policy*, p. 246.

[31] *Barriers to New Competition* (Cambridge, Mass.: Harvard University Press, 1956), chap. 3. The data refer to 1951.

[32] Flour, cement, petroleum refining, steel, metal containers, meat packing, gypsum products.

[33] Shoes, canned fruits and vegetables, farm machinery except tractors, automobiles, fountain pens.

twenty cases—depending on whether the largest or the smallest sub-market is used as a basis—the proportion of the relevant market capacity needed for a plant producing on an efficient scale exceeds 10 per cent.[34]

On the basis of estimated optimal scales and the rise of production costs on suboptimal scales, Bain concludes that very important scale economies exist in the manufacturing of automobiles and typewriters and moderately important economies in the production of cement, farm machinery, rayon, steel, and tractors. Minimum optimal scales are large, but no information is available on cost increases at lower output levels for copper, gypsum products, fountain pens, and metal containers, whereas in the other industries under consideration economies of scale appear to be relatively unimportant.[35]

Managerial estimates are used in J. H. Young's cited "Some Aspects of Canadian Economic Development." The evidence supplied by American manufacturers operating plants in both the United States and Canada reveals that in a number of industries the smaller size of the Canadian market restricts the size of the plant and inhibits the use of more efficient equipment, which would result in lower production costs. Examples are various types of electrical equipment, heating and air-conditioning units, radios, automobile parts, medicinal and pharmaceutical preparations, fountain pens, breakfast cereals, etc.[36] Similar conclusions have been reached by Rosenbluth with regard to the iron and steel industry. Noting the impact of the smaller market on efficiency, Rosenbluth adds that Canada is in a much better position to adopt American techniques than other economies of comparable size located farther from the United States, the reason being that specialized machinery can be imported from the United States if the size of the market does not allow its manufacture, and repair services, parts, and training facilities are more easily accessible.[37] Thus the disadvantages of the small market for other economies of similar size are likely to be greater than those observed in the Canadian economy.

[34] Bain, op. cit., pp. 72–77. The market is not segmented in the manufacturing of distilled liquors, rubber tires and tubes, rayon, soap, cigarettes, copper, tractors, and typewriters.

[35] Ibid., pp. 81–82.

[36] Pp. 64–67, 80–82. See also "Comparative Economic Development: Canada and the United States," American Economic Review, Papers and Proceedings, May, 1955, p. 91.

[37] Rosenbluth, op. cit., pp. 72, 85.

We have presented findings for various countries based on empirical evidence and technological and managerial information. The estimates include data on heterogeneous and homogeneous industries. Available information suggests that, as a general proposition, we can establish the existence of economies internal to the plant in a number of industries. No attempt is made to generalize this rule to all industries, but this is not even necessary to show that gains from production on a large scale can be reaped in an integrated area. Economic integration would give rise to economies of scale even if internal economies were operating in some industries only. It is a different question at what size the market is large enough to reap *all* possible economies of scale and how substantial these economies are in various integration projects.

European Economic Integration and Economies of Scale

The possibilities of economies of scale in an integrated Europe have been analyzed in general terms by Tibor Scitovsky. Scitovsky endorses the proposition that "as a general rule, the more efficient the method the higher the rate of output to reach minimum per unit costs, or, to put it differently, the larger the optimum size of the plant,"[38] and he maintains that, for various reasons, optimal production methods are not employed in many European industries. Small national markets, lack of standardization in consumer goods, parts, and components, the absence of the "spirit" of competition, and the low rate of accretion of demand are said to contribute to this result.[39]

An increase in the size of the market would then shift the demand curves for the products of the imperfectly competitive firms, and the expansion of production would make possible the use of more efficient production methods. The opportunities for standardization in a wider market offer further potential gains. Finally, the larger yearly increase in the demand for various commodities will facilitate the introduction of large-scale production in newly established plants. In regard to the potential economies of scale within the framework of the European Common Market, we shall examine, first, the probable effects of integration on the employment of large-scale production meth-

---

[38] *Economic Theory and Western European Integration* (Stanford: Stanford University Press, 1958), p. 112. The reader is reminded here that this proposition—although it applies to a number of industries—does not hold for all branches of manufacturing.
[39] *Ibid.*, pp. 24–25, 119–30.

ods in different industries and, second, the possibilities of standardization within individual plants.[40]

To begin with, economies of scale can be obtained in some new branches of manufacturing. Potential gains derived from the development and use of atomic energy are a prime example. Atomic power stations are still in an experimental stage, and a substantial improvement in technological methods will be necessary to make atomic energy competitive with oil. In the framework of the European Atomic Energy Community the cost and risk associated with this activity can be spread over the six participating countries. Furthermore, none of the member countries could ensure the efficient operation of fuel fabrication and chemical processing plants that serve a number of reactors.[41]

With respect to the steel industry, the United Nations Economic Commission for Europe estimated optimum capacity levels for a continuous strip mill at 1,300,000 tons of crude steel equivalent per annum for a plant producing flat products; 600,000 tons for a plant producing heavy sections; and 500,000 tons for light sections.[42] These estimates compare with Bain's data, according to which 1–2.5 million of ingot tons are the yearly output of an optimal integrated steel plant; costs are 5 per cent higher at a capacity of 0.5 million tons and increase significantly at lower output levels.[43] Nevertheless, in the years prior to the creation of the European Coal and Steel Community, nine new plants to produce flat products had been built in Europe, but only two of them were modern continuous strip mills of optimum size. Similar observations were made with regard to plants producing heavy sec-

[40] It should be recalled here that we proposed the use of gross national product and per capita income figures to indicate the size of the market for manufacturing products. In 1955, gross national products calculated as the geometrical average of GNP figures measured at European and at United States relative price weights for the Common Market countries were the following: Germany, 57.6; France, 48.6; Italy, 31.5; the Netherlands, 11.4; and Belgium, 10.8 billion U.S. dollars. The same method gives a gross national product of $377.2 billion for the United States. Per capita income figures are: Germany, $1,140; France, $1,120; Italy, $630; Netherlands, $1,040; Belgium, $1,240; average for the Common Market, $990; United States, $2,310. See Milton Gilbert and Associates, *Comparative National Products and Price Levels* (Paris: OEEC, 1958), pp. 23, 87.

[41] Cf. *A Target for Euratom: A Report* (May, 1957), p. 32, and Georges Vedel, "Euratom," *Revue Economique*, March, 1958, pp. 213–32.

[42] United Nations Economic Commission for Europe, *European Steel Trends in the Setting of the World Market* (Geneva, 1949), p. 62.

[43] Bain, *op. cit.*, p. 236. It is added that a range of products outside the flat-rolled category, produced, e.g., from electric furnaces, can be made fairly efficiently with semi-integrated operations depending on scrap iron or purchased pig iron or with integrated operations at capacity levels of 100,000–500,000 annual ingot tons.

tions.[44] More efficient plants have been built since the inauguration of the European Coal and Steel Community, however.[45]

In the framework of the Common Market, there are further possibilities for the exploitation of economies of scale in the smelting and refining of copper, zinc, tin, and lead, where, at present, no single European firm produces as much as the leading firms in the United States. Large-scale production can contribute to more efficient operation in the manufacturing of die casters and brass founders, too.[46]

Especially the smaller member countries—for example, Belgium and Italy—are at a disadvantage in metal manufacturing by reason of their limited domestic market. In some branches of this industry, the growth of the market will open opportunities for more efficient production on a larger scale in the other member countries, too. Hollow-ware, metal windows, cutlery, and simpler tools are examples.[47] In general engineering, the use of large-scale production methods is rather exceptional in most countries participating in the Common Market.[48] In this industry, large firms are to gain particularly in machine-tool manufacturing, where the present tendency is toward the production of more efficient, self-contained machinery with high operating speeds. Increased automation in American machine-tool production is bound to be followed in the framework of the European Common Market, and the possibilities of automation give promise for economies of scale in all participating countries.

It is often pointed out that economies of scale can be reaped in a larger European market in the field of electrical engineering, where domestic appliances, household meters, fractional horsepower motors, and smaller industrial motors are typical mass-production items. The production of refrigerators, for example, exceeds 700,000 units a year in some American factories, while in Europe the largest output of a single factory is 65,000 units annually. It is estimated that, for some domestic appliances and certain standard lines of light equipment where the manufacturing process can be made nearly auto-

[44] Cf. K. K. F. Zawadzki, "The Economics of the Schuman Plan," *Oxford Economic Papers*, June, 1953, pp. 185–86.

[45] Cf. Louis Lister, *Europe's Coal and Steel Community* (New York: Twentieth Century Fund, 1960), pp. 82–84.

[46] Economist Intelligence Unit, *Britain and Europe* (London, 1957), pp. 81–82.

[47] L. Duquesne de la Vinelle, "Study of the Efficiency of a Small Nation—Belgium," *Economic Consequences of the Size of Nations*, p. 85; V. A. Marsan, "The Experience of Italy," *ibid.*, p. 154, and *Britain and Europe*, pp. 92–93.

[48] Marsan, *op. cit.*, pp. 159–60; *Britain and Europe*, p. 99.

matic, costs may continue to fall even when the output of a plant reaches one million units a year. For items with a greater degree of product differentiation, such as washing machines or refrigerators, the optimum scale is about 500,000 a year in the United States and somewhat less in Europe. Nevertheless, the diversity in standards, voltages, and ranges of power will hinder the full development of mass production.[49]

In automobile production, 600,000 units is said to be the optimum scale in the United States. Costs are moderately higher at 150,000 units and substantially higher at 60,000 units. The use of indivisible equipment appears to be the determining factor. The Big Three in the United States operate ten to seventeen assembly plants, one engine plant per model, and—with the exception of Chrysler—one body plant each. General Motors and Ford manufacture more automobiles each than the nineteen European producers put together. In 1955 most European automobile models were produced in series of less than 100,000.[50]

It is questionable, however, whether integration in Europe will actually lead to the production of much larger series of individual automobiles. It is possible that—at least until the impact of increased incomes is felt—the freeing of trade will result in more interchange of automobiles between countries, without a reduction in variety or a significant rise in the production of various makes. This will certainly increase consumer satisfaction but not necessarily efficiency in production. Nonetheless, economies of specialization will be forthcoming in the production of automobile parts. This problem will be taken up in the next chapter.

The limited size of the domestic market is said to be the reason for the use of inefficient small-scale methods in heavy engineering in Belgium and Italy. Railway rolling stock and heavy electric machinery are singled out in this connection.[51] These considerations do not apply to the larger countries of the Common Market, however, inasmuch as the present size of their plants appears sufficient for the exploitation of economies of scale. On the other hand, none of these countries

[49] 6th Report of the OEEC, *From Recovery towards Economic Strength*, Vol. I (Paris: Organisation for European Economic Co-operation, 1955), p. 187, and *Britain and Europe*, pp. 117–27.

[50] Bain, *op. cit.*, pp. 245–47, and *From Recovery towards Economic Strength*, Vol. I, pp. 187–88.

[51] Duquesne de la Vinelle, *op. cit.*, p. 85, and Marsan, *op. cit.*, pp. 154–55.

manufactures transport airplanes, the production of which could be undertaken in a larger market.

Many European, especially German, chemical firms already enjoy the advantages of large size. But there exist a number of small firms which will succumb to the competition of large-scale enterprises that can take advantage of internal economies resulting from indivisibilities in plant and equipment.[52]

The Canadian experience can be cited in regard to cotton textiles. According to managerial information, higher productivity in the United States as compared with Canada is due to the fact that, while approximately the same assortment of products is manufactured in both countries, in the large American market a number of mills can specialize in one single type of fabric and the Canadian mills produce 5 to 100 types. The short production runs and numerous changes in quality and construction represent cost disadvantages, especially in dyeing and printing. Similar conclusions have been reached with regard to the British textile industry.[53] We shall return to the possibilities of standardization in the European Common Market at a later point.

Synthetic fabrics also offer opportunities for economies of scale. In the manufacturing of rayon yarn, for example, optimal operation requires 20,000–25,000 tons annual output per plant, costs increase by about 8 per cent for a plant of half of this size and by 25 per cent for a plant with one quarter of the optimal output. At the same time, the entire yearly production is around 10,000 tons in Belgium and 30,000 tons in the Netherlands.[54]

Further examples of potential economies of scale in the Common Market are paper and allied products, chinaware, glass, furniture, leather, and footwear, although gains from large-scale production will be smaller and are more difficult to establish in these fields. On the other hand, no economies of scale are likely to be forthcoming in the production of some metal manufactures, instruments and electronic controls, heavy generators, dyestuffs, antibiotics, clothing, etc. The reasons are labor intensity, quality requirements, differences in speci-

[52] Cf. *Britain and Europe*, pp. 164–88.
[53] Cf. Young, "Some Aspects of Canadian Economic Development," pp. 179–80, and the findings of the *Report of the Cotton Textile Mission to the United States of America* (London: Her Majesty's Stationery Office, 1944).
[54] Bain, *op. cit.*, p. 241; *Statistical Yearbook, 1959* (New York: United Nations, 1959), pp. 208–9.

fications, and, with regard to clothing, differences in tastes.[55] In some industries—for example, in screw machine products, lumber and timber products, meat packing, manufactured ice, and condensed and evaporated milk—technological change may even point in the direction of smaller optimum plant size.[56]

These considerations suggest that integration will make the exploitation of economies of scale possible for a number of industries in the European Common Market. The potential gains are especially pronounced in the small and medium-sized member countries: in Belgium-Luxemburg, the Netherlands, and Italy. Gains from scale economies will be forthcoming, although to a lesser extent, in several French and German industries, too. In this connection, the possibility of standardization on a large market should also be noted.

Two meanings of the concept of standardization can be distinguished. Standardization may refer either to the establishment of standards, in order to make possible the interchangeability of parts and components produced by *different* manufacturers, or to the reduction of product variety by *individual* producers. The former is not a necessary consequence of an enlargement of the market; thus we shall be concerned primarily with the latter here.

If, within a given product group, the same assortment of commodities is manufactured in countries of different size, two consequences may follow. First, plants in a small country may specialize in a few varieties of a product manufactured on a small scale, thereby forgoing economies internal to the plant; second, each plant may produce many varieties of a given commodity and thus restrict the advantages of manufacturing large series. An enlargement of the market, with the variety of products maintained, will then have a double effect: plants producing on a small scale can extend their operations, and plants that have hitherto manufactured a large variety of commodities can now specialize in a few lines of production. The first alternative has been discussed above, the second will be examined in the following.

We have already noted that production runs are generally longer in American textile manufacturing plants than elsewhere. Conditions are similar in several branches of engineering and metal manufacture—not only in the production of consumer goods but also in tool-

55 *Britain and Europe*, Part II.
56 Cf. Blair, "Technology and Size," p. 140

making and in the manufacturing of various intermediate products. P. J. Verdoorn suggests that, in explaining productivity differentials between the United States and Europe, differences in the length of the production run may be more important than differences in plant sizes.[57] Even if the same assortment of commodities was produced in European countries as in the United States (some believe that a greater degree of product differentiation exists in the former), production would take place in more diversified establishments in Europe.[58] Diversification, in turn, requires frequent change-over in production, and the short production runs impose additional costs on the firm and on the economy.

First, the change-over involves some direct costs, such as the cost of resetting machines, labor-hours spent in shifting from one production process to another, and the expenses accompanying the reorganization of work. Second, if frequent changes are made in the pattern of production, the use of specialized equipment will be forgone, and the fixed costs associated with a particular production process (the cost of design, that of preparing molds, etc.) will be spread over a smaller quantity of output. Finally, short production runs entail the loss of future improvements in manufacturing efficiency along the "learning curve," which shows labor productivity increasing as a function of accumulated output. In several industries, empirical studies indicated an 18–20 per cent gain in productivity as accumulated output doubled.[59]

Economic integration in Europe will then contribute to an increase in productivity also through a reduction in the variety of products manufactured by individual producers. The proposition has often been advanced, however, that standardization cannot be achieved in the heterogeneous European market. In criticism of this view, we have already pointed out that the consumption of the same social strata in the member countries offers possibilities for standardization after

---

[57] *Economic Consequences of the Size of Nations*, p. 346.

[58] C. D. Edwards notes that the size of the country probably has a significant effect on the structure of large enterprise, since, in a small economy, a domestic concern can become big only by diversification. Cf. his, "Size of Markets, Scale of Firms, and the Character of Competition," *Economic Consequences of the Size of Nations*, p. 124.

[59] Such results have been reached, for example, in the study of manufacturing efficiency in a large American machine-tool building firm, in shipbuilding, and in the production of air-frames (W. Z. Hirsch, "Manufacturing Progress Functions," *Review of Economics and Statistics*, May, 1952, pp. 143–55). Cf. also the results cited by Verdoorn in *Economic Consequences of the Size of Nations*, p. 346.

trade barriers have been removed. Changes in the social structure and rising incomes in the union will reinforce this tendency, and the greater purchasing power of the working classes will lead to mass consumption in consumer durables. Also, differences in consumption habits do not hinder the standardization of intermediate products. Finally, less frequent changes in the style of consumer durables may bestow a differential advantage upon European producers as compared with those in the United States.

It should be added that, even in industries where economies of scale can be exploited to the full in each member country, an enlargement of the market will affect productivity growth through its influence on the degree of competition. The probable effects of integration on the competitiveness of market structures will be examined in Chapter 8.

Internal Economies in Latin-American Union Projects

Available information on possible economies of scale in the Latin-American integration projects is much scantier than for Europe.[60] The proposition has often been advanced that economic integration will permit Latin-American countries to obtain important scale economies, but little has been done as yet to substantiate this assertion. We shall present here the available information on individual industries, followed by a brief discussion of certain characteristics of the Latin-American market as compared with the situation in Europe. The existing market for industrial products, the size of industrial plants, product differentiation, transportation costs, and the potentialities for the future growth of markets and plant sizes will be the variables considered.

A comparison of Bain's data on the estimated optimum capacity of certain industries and the yearly output of these industries in various countries (Table 3) illustrates the possibility of obtaining economies of scale in the Latin-American integration projects under consideration. The reader is warned, however, that Bain's estimates reflect economic conditions in the United States and that different factor-price ratios in the less developed countries of Latin America

---

[60] In the foregoing discussion we concentrated on problems of the Common Market and paid little attention to the Free Trade Association of the "Outer Seven." The reader will find valuable information on the latter in *Britain and Europe*.

TABLE 3

OPTIMAL PLANT SIZES AND ANNUAL OUTPUT IN SELECTED INDUSTRIES*

	Shoes (Thousand Pairs)	Cement (Thousand Tons)	Crude Steel (Thousand Tons)	Rayon Yarn (Thousand Tons)	Cigarettes (Millions)	Copper (Refined) (Thousand Tons)
Approximate optimal size................	600–2,500	400	1,000	20–30	20,000	85
Increase of unit cost at 50% of optimal capacity..........	Insignificant	10%	18%	8%	1%	No estimate
At 25% of optimal capacity.........	Moderate	30%	33%	25%	2%	No estimate
Argentina...........	9,706	2,471	244	14	24,423	.....
Brazil..............	.....	3,755	1,299	25	46,632	.....
Chile..............	7,100	727	348	2	5,250	440
Mexico............	1,962	2,539	988	13	32,948	61
Paraguay...........	.....	7	.....	.....	461	.....
Peru...............	3,748†	544	.....	1	2,034	38
Uruguay...........	.....	.....	.....	1	.....	.....
El Salvador.........	273†	87	.....	.....	817	.....
Guatemala.........	.....	122	.....	.....	1,724	.....
Honduras..........	.....	.....	.....	.....	953	.....
Nicaragua..........	526†	40	.....	.....	777	.....

*SOURCE: For information on optimal scale, see Bain, *Barriers to New Competition*, pp. 228–48, and, with respect to the steel industry, *A Study of the Iron and Steel Industry in Latin America*, pp. 112–16. With the exception of the production of shoes and cigarettes, costs increase sharply at outputs lower than 25 per cent of optimal capacity. Data on output are from *Statistical Yearbook, 1959* and refer to 1958 or to the last preceding year for which information is available. Symbol . . . means that output figures are not available.
†Figures include the production of shoes with non-leather uppers.

may warrant smaller optimum size. Nevertheless, these figures give at least some indication of potential gains from operation on a larger scale, and in some of these branches optimal capacity is not very sensitive to factor-price differentials.

It has further been suggested that the establishment of the Latin American Free Trade Association will permit the exploitation of economies of scale in the manufacturing of excavation and construction equipment, automobiles, heavy vehicles and railway equipment, chemicals, etc.[61] With regard to the countries participating in the Central American Common Market, it is noted that in most industries

[61] Cf., e.g., Octaviano Campos Salas, "La zona de libre comercio de América Latina," *Comercio Exterior*, March, 1960, pp. 140–43, and Plácido García Reynoso, "Probables efectos del Tratado de Montevideo en la industrialización de América Latina," *El Trimestre Económico*, April–June, 1960, pp. 193–202.

plants either are too small or cannot fully utilize their capacity because of the limited size of national markets. The textile, footwear, and cement industries are frequently mentioned in this connection. In further branches of manufacturing, one or two plants of economical size will be sufficient to supply the entire area. These so-called integration industries will be created under the auspices of the integration program.[62]

Information on potential economies of scale in particular industries within the framework of the Latin-American integration projects is rather limited. Some general conclusions can, however, be reached if we compare certain characteristics of the Latin-American market with those of the Common Market in Europe.

To begin with, considerable differences exist with regard to the size of the market for industrial products. We have seen in Chapter 2 that the combined gross national product of the countries participating in the Latin American Free Trade Association amounts to about one fourth of the GNP of the Common Market countries, while gross national product in the Central American Common Market does not even reach 1 per cent of the latter. The differences in market size for manufactured goods are even larger than differences in national incomes, considering that higher per capita incomes in Europe imply that a larger share of income is spent on industrial products.[63] Among individual countries, only the Brazilian market might exceed, and that of Mexico and Argentina approximate, the size of the market for industrial products in Belgium or in the Netherlands.

As a general observation, it can be stated that plants are of smaller size in Latin America than in Europe. However, an unpublished study of the UN Economic Commission for Latin America indicates that, in certain branches of the mechanical and electrical industries, Brazilian and Argentine plants are larger than those of small European countries. This is said to follow from the fact that the attitude prevailing in several countries in Europe to aid small-scale industry finds little scope in Latin America. Nevertheless, these cases cannot

[62] See United Nations Department of Economic and Social Affairs, *La integración económica de Centro-América* (1956), chaps. v–vi, and "Central American Economic Integration Programme: Evaluation and Prospects," *Economic Bulletin for Latin America*, October, 1959, pp. 38–39.

[63] Calculating with the appropriate population figures, national incomes per capita in the Latin American Free Trade Association appear to be one third, in the Central American Common Market one fifth, of per capita incomes in the European Economic Community.

be regarded as more than exceptions to the general rule stated above.

The advantageous position of the Latin-American countries with regard to product differentiation should also be noted. In contradistinction to the situation in Europe, more uniformity in tastes can be observed, and the variety of manufactured commodities (e.g., consumer goods) is rather limited. Although this is bound to change as a higher stage of economic development is reached, the largely standardized American market is likely to serve as a model rather than the heterogeneity of tastes presently existing in Europe.

Our observations on the extent of national markets, the size of average plants, and the possibilities of standardization indicate that the scope for the exploitation of economies of scale is considerably greater in the Latin-American integration projects than in Europe. As an important qualification, the cost of transportation should be mentioned. For a number of industries the distance factor limits the effective size of the market to a greater or less degree (e.g., steel, cement, etc.). The distance factor becomes relevant, for example, in trade between Mexico and the other participants of the Latin American Free Trade Association and also within Brazil as compared to, for example, Belgium. We can speak of a "trade-off" between economies of scale and transportation costs, and it is clear that, in some branches of manufacturing, the distance factor will limit the possible exploitation of scale economies in a Latin-American union.

Notwithstanding the restraining effects of the cost of transportation, the Latin American Free Trade Association, as well as the Central American Common Market, offers substantial opportunities for internal economies. This proposition is greatly strengthened if we consider the possibilities of economic development within the integrated area, with the concomitant creation of new industries. To give some indication of prospective developments, the projections of the UN Economic Commission for Latin America can be cited. According to these, in order to satisfy expected demand in an integrated Latin America, steel production would have to increase from 2.6 to 32.3 million tons, the manufacturing of passenger automobiles from nil to 1,300,000 vehicles, the production of machinery and equipment from $200 million to $5,400 million, and chemical production from $1,700 to $7,200 million in the period 1955–75.[64] The reader is

[64] *The Latin American Common Market*, pp. 71–78. In Brazil, however, 16,500 cars were produced in 1958 (*Statistical Yearbook, 1959*, p. 253).

warned, however, that these figures have been derived by deducting the amounts that are likely to be imported, given the availability of foreign exchange, from estimated demand, and in most cases actual production possibilities have not been considered. Nevertheless, although the projections cannot be regarded as realistic figures, they may be useful in indicating general trends.

Interplant Economies

In the present chapter we have given an extensive discussion of economies internal to the plant. Some remarks are also due on the possible extent of interplant economies that can be attained in the framework of the firm.[65] A firm may operate plants which produce commodities on the same stage of manufacturing (horizontal integration), or different stages of the production process may be divided between the plants (vertical integration).

Aside from historical accident, horizontally integrated firms operate more than one plant if the product is differentiated (shoes, cigarettes, automobiles); if different products are related through some activity common to them, such as research; or if savings in transportation cost can be achieved in the event of regionally located plants (steel, cement, gypsum products). Multiplant economies are said to arise from integrated management and staff functions, bulk buying of material, and marketing of products. The extent of these economies, as estimated by J. S. Bain for the United States, appears to be rather small. For products for which numerical estimates have been made (steel, shoes, cement, soap, gypsum products, cigarettes), savings due to multiplant operations in no case exceed 5 per cent of cost per unit.[66] Benefits can be derived from the diversification of firms, however, if the firm's experience or the results of its research activity can be profitably used in the manufacturing of related commodities.

The integration of different stages of production is often regarded as a device to ensure markets and/or materials for certain products. Such a procedure does not guarantee any cost savings for the economy as a whole and will therefore not be considered here. Savings in fuel and transportation cost can be attained in the case of integrated steel-works (coke ovens, blast furnaces, steel furnaces, and

---

[65] It should be recalled that, for the purposes of the present study, those economies are relevant that represent a saving for the economy as a whole arising from the multiplant operation of the firm.

[66] Bain, *op. cit.*, pp. 89–90. Also Blair, "Technology and Size," pp. 150–51.

rolling mills), however. Interplant economies due to verticality in steel production may result from an enlargement of the market in Europe and also in Latin America. We have already considered this form of savings in our discussion of integrated steel plants.

Available information indicates that some degree of interplant economies can be obtained in firms operating several plants. Nevertheless, the smallness of the estimates for the United States and the absence of information on other countries do not permit any definite judgment on the possible extent of multiplant economies. Also, in a number of industries, interplant diseconomies (e.g., the increasing cost of administration and management) may outweigh the cost advantages of multiplant operation. Therefore, the further discussion of this problem would be of little use and will not be pursued here.

Chapter 7   EXTERNAL ECONOMIES

> Those internal economies which each establishment has to arrange for itself are frequently very small as compared with those external economies which result from the general progress of the industrial environment.
>
> —Marshall

Concept and Classification of External Economies

It is often claimed that the introduction of the concept of external economies by Marshall was meant to rescue long-run competitive equilibrium in the presence of increasing returns.[1] A rereading of the *Principles* suggests, however, that Marshall did not share the excessive preoccupation of his followers with competitive equilibrium. Marshall was aware of the fact that "economic problems are imperfectly presented when they are treated as problems of statical equilibrium, and not of . . . growth,"[2] and—although he was far from presenting a complete theory of growth—his valuable insights into problems relating external economies and economic progress foreshadowed later, modern treatment.

Marshallian external economies are not the bucolic ones of the bee-orchard-honey type[3] but are all closely connected with the development of the economy. They are said to depend on "the general development of industry," on "the growth of correlated branches of industry," on "the general progress of industrial environment," and on the increase of the size of the market in general.[4] External econo-

---

[1] Cf. F. M. Bator, "The Anatomy of Market Failure," *Quarterly Journal of Economics*, August, 1958, p. 356.

[2] Alfred Marshall, *Principles of Economics* (8th ed.; London: Macmillan & Co., Ltd., 1956), p. 382. See also p. 104 above.

[3] J. E. Meade's famous example of direct interaction between producers, when the beekeeper's bees enjoy the free foods provided by the apple grower's orchard blossoms.

[4] *Op. cit.*, pp. 221, 264, 365, 267–68.

mies include "the many various economies of specialized skill and specialized machinery, of localized industries and production on a large scale," the "increased facilities of communication of all kinds," trade knowledge, skilled labor force, etc.[5] The pervading theme in the discussion of external economies is their interaction with the growth of the economy. Marshall also points out that many of these economies are irreversible, so that the gains derived from increased production are not lost if output returns to its former level.[6]

Since Marshall's time the concept of external economies has received varied treatment. Some authors, like Frank H. Knight, tend to dismiss external economies altogether;[7] others have attempted to classify and reclassify them in a static framework.[8] The dynamic interpretation of external economies is of recent origin.[9] In the present study, external economies will be defined as a divergence between social and private product, when social and private products are interpreted as the present value of future (direct and indirect) benefits. This definition includes both static and dynamic external economies in production but excludes external effects in consumption.

In regard to external economies as defined here, we shall first distinguish between economies operating outside the market mechanism and those working through the market.[10] As a further subdivision within the first group, we also differentiate between static economies and those operating through time. This threefold classification

5 *Ibid.*, pp. 267, 237, 365–66.

6 *Ibid.*, Appendix H.

7 "Some Fallacies in the Interpretation of Social Cost," *Readings in Price Theory* (Homewood, Ill.: Richard D. Irwin, Inc., 1952), pp. 160–79.

8 Jacob Viner, "Cost Curves and Supply Curves," in *Readings in Price Theory*, pp. 198–232; J. E. Meade, "External Economies and Diseconomies in a Competitive Situation," *Economic Journal*, March, 1952, pp. 54–67; M. C. Kemp, "The Efficiency of Competition as an Allocator of Resources. I. External Economies in Production," *Canadian Journal of Economics and Political Science*, February, 1955, pp. 30–42; Bator, *op. cit.*, pp. 351–79.

9 Cf., e.g., Paul Rosenstein-Rodan, "Problems of Industrialisation of Eastern and South-Eastern Europe," *Economic Journal*, June–September, 1943, pp. 202–11; Tibor Scitovsky, "Two Concepts of External Economies," *Journal of Political Economy*, April, 1954, pp. 143–51; Marcus Fleming, "External Economies and the Doctrine of Balanced Growth," *Economic Journal*, June, 1955, pp. 241–56; Ragnar Nurkse, *Problems of Capital Formation in Underdeveloped Countries* (Oxford: Basil Blackwell, 1953); Arthur Lewis, *The Theory of Economic Growth* (Homewood, Ill.: Richard D. Irwin, Inc., 1955); Albert Hirschman, *The Strategy of Economic Development* (New Haven: Yale University Press, 1958).

10 Our unit of reference is the firm, so we will discuss economies that are external to the firm, no matter whether they are internal or external to the industry.

will prove to be useful in examining the interrelationship of external economies and growth.[11]

The time element is absent from the static external economies, which are the only kind compatible with static equilibrium. Direct interaction between producers, the use of a common pool of resources, and Meade's concept of the creation of "atmosphere"[12] belong to this category. The first form of static external economies can be represented by the bee-orchard example; the second prevails if fishermen or oil-drillers use a common pool of fish or oil; the third is typified by increased rainfall due to afforestation. In the first two instances the quantity of the unpaid resource decreases by its use, while it remains unchanged in the third case. Nevertheless, the use of "atmosphere" is also limited by the number of producers who have access to it. In the celebrated example of afforestation, for instance, only the farmers of a certain region benefit. Static external economies are favored examples of textbooks but have little importance in the real world. They are even less relevant for economic integration and will not be discussed here.

The second category of external economies operates through time and outside the market mechanism. It comprises the spreading of technological and organizational know-how and the development of a managerial class and a skilled labor force. One could argue that, at any given point of time, the acquisition of techniques and the hiring of labor takes place from a "pool" of knowledge and skilled personnel (the former is analogous to Meade's atmosphere, the latter to the pool of oil and fish), so that the existence of this type of external economies is consistent with static general equilibrium, *if* technological knowledge and skills are considered as given. However, firms not only enjoy existing technical knowledge and skills but also constantly create and develop them. The nonmarket interaction of firms in this field consists not only in the sharing and using of existing technical know-how, but technology also "begets" new technology and contributes to further progress. Putting it in a different way, technology and skills are developed through use. We face a dynamic process in the growth and

11 A fourth kind of external economy—the impact of market size on specialization —will be considered separately, since this refers to changes in the *structure* of industries rather than to the interrelationship of *existing* industries.

12 "Atmosphere" is defined by Meade as a fixed condition of production which is unchanged in quantity irrespective of use. See J. E. Meade, *Trade and Welfare. The Theory of International Economic Policy*, Vol. II (London: Oxford University Press, 1955), p. 41.

acquisition of skills and the development of technological and organizational knowledge; hence—for the discussion of problems of economic growth—the static interpretation of this category of external economies would be of little use.[13]

The third category of external economies is, too, a phenomenon of dynamic change, but, unlike the second, it operates through the market. These pecuniary economies include market interactions between industries that entail a divergence between private profitability and social productivity. Pecuniary external economies have no relevance for static equilibrium: in static theory, prices (and output) are considered as resulting from a given market situation, and we do not inquire into the historical process of how these prices have come about. They are of importance, however, under conditions of dynamic change, since they affect the growth of the economy. This warrants a more detailed discussion of external economies operating through the market.

Pecuniary External Economies

Pecuniary economies may take the form of direct market interactions or may operate through income changes. In the first case, industries are interconnected as buyers and suppliers of raw materials and intermediate products; in the second, as suppliers of consumer goods. We will first examine the direct market interactions of producers and discuss interdependence via changes in incomes at a later point.

The direct interdependence of industries on the market can be analyzed under varying assumptions. We may assume that (*a*) there are no internal economies and factor supplies are inelastic but a fixed amount of net investment takes place; or (*b*) internal economies are absent but factor supplies are elastic; or (*c*) there are economies internal to the firm or to the industry, while factor supplies may be elastic or inelastic.

In all these cases, two types of market interactions will be distinguished: the impact of an expansion in industry A on output-using

[13] The creation of social overhead capital comprising educational and hygienic facilities necessary for developing a labor force that will possess the required qualities also belongs to this category. This relationship is not unidirectional, however. As H. W. Singer rightly points out, industrial development also reacts "on the general level of education, skill, way of life, inventiveness, habits, store of technology, creation of new demand, etc." ("The Distribution of Gains between Investing and Borrowing Countries," *American Economic Review, Papers and Proceedings,* May, 1950, p. 476).

industry B and on input-producing industry C.[14] The expansion of industry A, in turn, might have been prompted by an increase in the demand for its product or by the introduction of an innovation. An increase in demand for the commodity manufactured by industry A will raise the demand for the product of input-producing industry C, while an innovation in A will reduce the price of its product that is used as an input in industry B. At the same time, if the innovation is output-increasing and input-using,[15] demand for C's products will also increase. The effects of an innovation of the latter type will be examined below.

In case (a),[16] if an innovation takes place in industry A, the price of the products manufactured in industries A and B will fall, and their production, as well as output in input-producing industry C, will expand. Nevertheless—since factor supplies are assumed to be inelastic —prices of other commodities will rise. The real effect of the innovation on the national product will be equivalent to the output produced with the inputs saved in industry A at its original production level—to which its possible impact on the allocation of investment funds should be added.

Under the assumption of perfect foresight, investment decisions in all industries will be guided by correct anticipations of future demands and relative prices, and private profitability and social productivity considerations will coincide. Removing the assumption of perfect foresight, these decisions will be based on present prices, which only imperfectly reflect future scarcities. In the absence of information on the expansion of industry A, less than the efficient amount will be invested in industries B and C, and—without the corresponding developments in the buyer and supplier industries— investment in A will also be less than desired. Thus, from a given amount of investment funds available in the economy, more will be

14 Further types of market interactions between industries are mentioned by Scitovsky (op. cit., p. 149): industry A's products may be complementary to those of industry D, and the factors used by industry A may find substitutes in industry E's products. In addition, external diseconomies are generated in industry F, the products of which are substitutes for those of industry A, and in industry C, whose products are complementary (in other uses) to the factors used by industry A. These secondary repercussions will not be discussed here, although this does not amount to the denial of their importance.

15 See the classification of innovations given in Oscar Lange, "A Note on Innovations," Readings in the Theory of Income Distribution (Philadelphia: Blakiston Co., 1946), pp. 181–96.

16 This case is discussed in Scitovsky's article.

spent in other fields than would be considered desirable. This is equivalent to saying that the private profitability of an investment in industry A understates its social productivity.

Our results will be modified under case (*b*), where it is assumed that at least some of the factors of production are available in elastic supply. This is the case discussed by Rosenstein-Rodan, Lewis, and Nurkse. The first two of these authors assume an elastic labor supply; Nurkse, on the other hand, assumes an elastic supply of capital. If the high elasticity of the labor supply is interpreted as involuntary unemployment and if the elastic supply of capital means that, in the absence of a minimum rate of earnings, capital will be used for unproductive purposes, the expansion in industries B and C represents a real gain for the economy. In other words, if the supplier and buyer industries can utilize hitherto unused resources,[17] the innovation raises national product through (*a*) its input-saving effect in industry A and (*b*) its impact on the expansion in interdependent industries. Now the private profitability of an investment in industry A will not only understate its social productivity, but it is also possible that the government will have to undertake an unprofitable investment in A in order to ensure the desired expansion in the interrelated industries.[18]

Under more general assumptions, in case (*c*), an innovation in industry A gives the possibility of obtaining economies of scale in some of the industries involved. Supply industries will be able to use large-scale production methods as their output increases, while at succeeding stages of production the lowering of input prices can have a similar effect. In other words, a successful innovation in an industry producing intermediate goods will induce suppliers and buyers to reconsider their production methods and to employ hitherto not applied advanced technology. The newly applied technology might have been known to the entrepreneur before, it may represent new application of existing scientific knowledge, or it may be associated with new developments through research.

The transmission of technological change may also take the form

[17] Besides labor and capital, these considerations apply also to unutilized waterpower and mineral supplies.

[18] This kind of pecuniary external economy assumes an eminent place in most writings on economic development. It is often pointed out that in underdeveloped countries the creation of economic overhead capital (transportation facilities, electricity, water, gas, sewage, etc.) will make the expansion of manufacturing industries possible.

of a circular process. In England around 1800, for example, a circular flow ran from iron making to steam engines to coal mining and to iron making again. Under such a configuration, technological improvements have a magnified impact, since increased productivity in one industry reverts to it in the form of cheaper inputs. All these repercussions—vertical or triangular—form part of a response mechanism that contributes to the advancement of technology as the economy grows. At a given stage of expansion, further gains are forthcoming if elastic factor supplies restrain increases in the prices of productive factors.

The foregoing considerations focus attention on the interdependence of industries. All industries are sources and recipients of external economies; thus the concept should not be limited to the impact of the provision of economic overhead on other industries but should include the effects and intereffects of an expansion in any industry. As Rosenstein-Rodan expressed it, "complementarity makes to some extent all industries basic."[19] But Rosenstein-Rodan neglected to add that industries, in addition to being complementary, are also competitive in their demand for resources.

Emphasis on complementary relationships at the expense of competitive interrelations between industries led Rosenstein-Rodan and Nurkse to concentrate their attention on external economies operating via income changes. Under this conception, the installation of efficient large-scale plants in the production of certain consumer goods would generate demand for other items of consumption by raising real income, but the introduction of large-scale technology is checked by the limited size of the market in underdeveloped countries. According to these authors, the economies of scale referred to here could be captured if an increase in incomes was achieved as a result of the joint installation of plants of efficient size in a number of industries. This argument, in turn, was criticized by Marcus Fleming who expressed the opinion that "so long as factors of production are in fixed supply, the introduction of large-scale production units is likely to give rise not to economies but to diseconomies in other industries unless the former industries are already big enough for the introduction of the new plant to make possible a net reduction in the resources employed there."[20]

[19] *Op. cit.*, p. 208.
[20] *Op. cit.*, p. 247.

Fleming's discussion indicates the possibility of external diseconomies as parallel advances are made in a number of fields. Beneficial effects through income changes will nevertheless occur if the supply of resources is elastic or if internal or external economies have raised national income and the resulting increase in demand for consumer goods has made possible the introduction of efficient large-scale production methods in some industries. Reinterpreting the argument, we can state that, besides the direct market interaction of industries, an innovation in any industry will bring additional gains, inasmuch as the concomitant increase in income allows for the use of large-scale technology in industries for whose products demand has risen. Finally, in a negative sense, the thesis presented by Rosenstein-Rodan and Nurkse deserves attention by reason of the emphasis given to the restrictive effects of limited markets on industrial expansion. The latter problem will be our concern in the section that follows.

Market Size and External Economies

Various authors commented on the role of interindustry relationships in the process of economic growth. The importance of "linkages" between various industries was first noted by Schumpeter, who directed attention to the impact of the emergence of new industries on the growth of a national economy.[21] Recently, François Perroux examined the role of an *industrie motrice* in economic development. Perroux expounds the thesis that a growing industry creates external economies for supplier and user industries and that these industries, together with the *industrie motrice,* form a "pole of development," which, in turn, contributes to the growth of the economy.[22] Arguing along similar lines, Hirschman advises underdeveloped countries to establish industries producing intermediate products, where the combined amount of the backward and forward linkage effects is the largest.[23]

These explanations lay great stress on how a key industry affects the development of the linked industries but fail to specify the *conditions* which need to be fulfilled for the key industry to expand. Con-

21 "The Instability of Capitalism," *Economic Journal,* September, 1928, pp. 361–86.
22 "Note sur la notion de 'pôle de croissance,'" *Economie Appliquée,* January–June, 1955, pp. 309–20. For a similar formulation, cf. Singer, *op. cit.,* pp. 473–85.
23 *Op. cit.,* chap. 6. The concept of backward and forward linkages refers to quantitative relationships between interdependent industries that are derived from an input-output table. Note that the assumption of constant technological coefficients excludes the consideration of changes in costs.

cerning these conditions, economic historians have paid ample attention to the side of supply, but only recently has there been some consideration given to demand factors.[24] This long-time neglect of demand factors is far from justified, however. The availability of materials is not sufficient to warrant the development of an industry, as long as satisfactory outlets are not found for its product. The market for industrial expansion might become available at home as a result of an increase in per capita incomes and population, the introduction of new wants, military demand, or demand for the purposes of further transformation, or abroad in the form of possibilities for exportation.

Historical experience gives evidence of the restrictive effects of limited markets on the expansion of various industries and of manufacturing industry in general. It is noted, for example, that, notwithstanding the early cost-reducing innovations in weaving and spinning, the development of the British textile industry did not accelerate until the domestic market expanded sufficiently and large-scale sales in foreign markets became profitable.[25] The breakthrough in the textile industry, in turn, provided a stimulus for the iron industry via demand for steam engines and textile machinery. The availability of export markets was instrumental also in the expansion of other British manufacturing industries as witnessed by the large share of exports in British industrial production during the nineteenth century.

Export possibilities were of prime importance in the industrial development of Continental countries, too. The expansion of the German metallurgical and engineering industries, for example, would not have been possible without foreign markets. Military expenditures and—in its initial stage—railroad building, too, influenced industrialization through demand for the products of heavy industry. This line of thought can be conveniently summed up by referring to Goran Ohlin's conclusion, according to which "the first step towards . . . an understanding of the growth process is simply to pay as much

[24] This charge cannot be levied against German historians. See, for example, Werner Sombart's *Luxus und Kapitalismus* and *Krieg und Kapitalismus*. However, in the English-language literature a plea made three decades ago for more concern with demand factors has met with little response. See E. W. Gilboy, "Demand as a Factor in the Industrial Revolution, *Facts and Factors in Economic History* (Cambridge, Mass.: Harvard University Press, 1932), pp. 620–39.

[25] W. W. Rostow notes that from the beginning of its development a very high proportion of the British cotton-textile output, reaching 60 per cent by the 1820's, was exported. See his *The Stages of Economic Growth* (Cambridge: At the University Press, 1960), p. 54.

attention to the growth of an industry's market as is usually lavished on the growth of its capacity."[26]

The evidence cited above indicates that exports provided an important market outlet for the advanced economies of today during their period of industrialization.[27] On the other hand, for present-day underdeveloped countries—besides the disadvantages of facing countries with a developed industrial structure—tariffs and other forms of trade barriers, payments restrictions, divergences in economic policies, and political uncertainty constitute serious obstacles in the way of basing the expansion of manufacturing industries on export possibilities. At the same time, the domestic market seldom provides sufficient outlet either.

A comparison of recent experience in Puerto Rico and in Chile can serve to illustrate this point. Although the Chilean economy possesses considerable natural advantages over Puerto Rico, the record of the latter has been far more favorable. This result could not have been obtained, had Puerto Rican producers not possessed free access to the United States market. The availability and—in the absence of political uncertainty and exchange-rate variations—the stability of the American market make it possible for Puerto Rico to concentrate on those industries in which she possesses cost advantages.[28] On the other hand, tariffs and other artificial obstacles to trade restrict Chile's possibilities of developing export-oriented industries, and the expansion of manufacturing industries is further limited by the smallness of the domestic market.

More generally, under present-day conditions, underdeveloped countries face the choice between the parallel development of a number of industries and the concentrated growth of a few branches of manufacturing. Both these methods have certain advantages and disadvantages. To begin with, the first method would provide external economies for the industries in question through their interrelationships in production and their interdependence via increased incomes. By reason of the observed interdependence in production, the manu-

[26] "Balanced Economic Growth in History," *American Economic Review, Papers and Proceedings*, May, 1959, p. 353.

[27] With respect to the United States, our conclusions apply to the development of particular regions which benefited from unobstructed trade with other regions in the framework of a large national market.

[28] See Werner Baer, "Puerto Rico: An Evaluation of a Successful Development Program," *Quarterly Journal of Economics*, November, 1959, pp. 645–71.

facturing of any commodity becomes more profitable, the greater the availability of the necessary inputs, complementary goods, and outlets for further transformation. In the expression of Tibor Scitovsky, "it is generally desirable and profitable to expand simultaneously, and in the proportions determined by technological production coefficients, the production and productive capacity of all goods whose relation to each other is that of factor to product or common factor to the same product."[29] Similarly, consumer demand for the products of any industry depends on incomes generated through the expansion of other industries.

Potential external economies that find their origin in the interdependence of industries in production and consumption would speak for the simultaneous expansion of all interrelated industries. In most underdeveloped countries, however, various limitations interfere with the parallel development of a number of industries. Simultaneous advances on all fronts are restricted by the quantities of productive factors available and the feasible amount of new investment, as well as by the size of the national markets. Given these limitations, production units of optimum size will often not be profitable, and thus potential economies of scale will be forgone.

Supply limitations would permit the exploitation of economies of scale if the available resources were used for developing a limited number of industries. Concentrated growth may also be more conducive to technological progress, since a fast rate of expansion gives scope to the introduction of new technological methods. This proposition finds support in the evidence supplied on the interrelationship of the rate of increase of output and the growth of productivity. Concentrated growth will meet with important barriers on the demand side, however. Since domestic demand is unlikely to follow the lopsided production pattern, discrepancies will be created between the structure of demand and supply. The time-honored method of removing these discrepancies is foreign trade. Yet, under present-day conditions, the expansion of exports in new lines of production faces difficulties by reason of the obstacles and uncertainties in foreign trade. In addition, the newly developed industries are unlikely to attain cost advantages, since they will not enjoy external economies that

29 "Growth—Balanced or Unbalanced?" in *The Allocation of Economic Resources: Essays in Honor of B. F. Haley* (Stanford: Stanford University Press, 1959), p. 211.

would result from the development of related industries. In other words, the comparative advantage of any given industry will depend on interindustry interrelationships. As a result, nations that concentrate their development in a limited number of industries often face the unhappy choice between installing plants of less than optimum capacity and building ahead of demand. The second alternative has been chosen in several Latin-American countries, where a large number of firms operate with excess capacity, especially in Argentina and Mexico and also in Brazil.[30]

The arguments presented here should suffice to demonstrate the difficulties that underdeveloped countries face in balanced and in unbalanced growth.[31] Many of these obstacles can be removed if the market is enlarged through integration. In the latter case, external economies associated with the simultaneous development of interrelated industries can be appropriated, and the advantages of concentrated growth can also be exploited. The possibility of reaping external economies through the interdependence of industries in production and in consumption appears, then, as a powerful argument for economic integration.[32] Integration is not a panacea for curing all economic ills, however, and its beneficial effects can follow only if sociological, psychological, and political obstacles to development have been surmounted. Finally, the position taken in this study should not be interpreted as a plea for less trade. Besides increased trade relations within the integrated area, increasing productivity is expected to contribute to the competitiveness of export industries, as well as to a rising demand for imports from third countries as a consequence of increased incomes.

The external economies argument for integration has especial force in underdeveloped countries. This should not mean, however, that it would find no scope in advanced industrial economies. Kuznets

30 See p. 55 above.

31 We have concentrated our attention here on those aspects of the balanced-unbalanced growth controversy that are relevant to our topic. The reader can find valuable material on the broader issues of this problem in previously cited writings of Nurkse, Lewis, and Hirschman, as well as in Paul Streeten, "Unbalanced Growth," *Oxford Economic Papers*, June, 1959, pp. 167–90, and Scitovsky, "Growth—Balanced or Unbalanced?" pp. 207–17, to which this exposition owes much.

32 For similar conclusions, see Baer, *op. cit.*, pp. 666–67, 670; Scitovsky, "Growth—Balanced or Unbalanced?" pp. 216–17, and John Sheahan, "International Specialization and the Concept of Balanced Growth," *Quarterly Journal of Economics*, May, 1958, p. 197.

maintains that all small countries face certain disadvantages by reason of the limited domestic market, the uncertainty of foreign trade, and the absence of a diversified industrial structure.[33] Integration, on the other hand, would give rise to external economies through the interdependence of industries. An increase in the size of the market is likely to create "growing points" that will permit the introduction of advanced technology in the supplier and buyer industries. These changes may take the form of chain reactions when innovations in one industry generate external economies through the transmission of technological change to vertically interdependent industries.[34] An expansion in industries producing final commodities will have a similar effect on preceding stages of manufacturing. Further gains will be obtained as the growth of productivity in particular industries allows the application of large-scale production methods in other sectors through the demand-increasing effects of rising incomes.

Specialization in a Large Market[35]

So far we have discussed nonmarket interactions between industries and external economies operating through the market under the assumption that the structure of existing industries remains unchanged. However, an increase in the extent of the market also changes the structure of individual industries. Allyn Young first analyzed in his justly celebrated article the impact of an enlargement of the market on specialization. Young emphasized that a wider market makes it possible to segregate various functions of an industry into specialized undertakings that will then constitute new industries. This diversification process allows for the use of specialized machinery and leads to specialization in labor and management. Young also pointed out that the scale of operations of the newly created industries "merely reflects the size of the market for final products of the industry or in-

---

33 Cf. Simon Kuznets, *Six Lectures on Economic Growth* (Glencoe, Ill.: Free Press, 1959), pp. 92–98.

34 See pp. 149–50 above. Cf. also the interesting discussion of the relationship between the vertical interdependence of industries and technological change in W. P. Strassmann, "Interrelated Industries and the Rate of Technological Development," *Review of Economic Studies*, October, 1959, pp. 16–22.

35 The concept of specialization will be interpreted here to mean vertical specialization: changes in the structure of existing industries. Horizontal specialization, the standardization of products manufactured in individual plants, has already been discussed in the previous chapter.

dustries to whose operations their own are ancillary. And the principal advantage of large-scale operation at this stage is that it again makes methods economical which would be uneconomical if their benefits could not be diffused over a large final product."[36]

Subsequently, Young's ideas were further developed by G. J. Stigler. Stigler expressed the opinion that certain processes carried out by the firm were subject to increasing, and others to decreasing, returns. At a given time, these functions may be too small to support a specialized firm or firms. With an increase in output, processes subject to increasing returns will be taken up in the framework of a new firm (or firms) constituting a new industry (or industries). Stigler adds that firms specializing in these activities cannot wield monopoly power since the demand for their products is elastic: the old firms will refuse to pay a price higher than the average cost of the process to them. With a further expansion of the market, the newly created industry becomes competitive, and the splitting of processes continues.[37]

More generally, the wider the market, the larger will be the economies of specialization. A small market may permit the maintenance of one or even a few optimal plants producing certain machines or durable consumer goods, but a small country will not be able to produce various parts, components, accessories, and capital goods on an optimum scale and will not sustain the optimum operation of certain subsidiary and ancillary activities. The importation of components, accessories, etc., is not a remedy, partly because in most cases the end-products are not homogeneous, partly because repair services and training facilities may not be available.

The interrelationship between the size of the market and specialization has been studied in respect to various industries. A favored example of the process of disintegration concomitant with increased output is that of the metal industry in the Birmingham area in Brit-

---

[36] "Increasing Returns and Economic Progress," *Economic Journal*, December, 1928, p. 539. Young illustrates his theory with the case of the printing trade, where the printers were originally producers of wood-pulp, paper, type metal, specialized tools and machines, etc., which functions later became separate industries.

[37] "The Division of Labor Is Limited by the Extent of the Market," *Journal of Political Economy*, June, 1951, pp. 185–93. It can be added that there is no need for assuming that some processes exhibit intrinsically increasing, and others decreasing, returns. The economies of specialization are connected rather with changes in technology, when the cost curves of different activities will shift downward as the expansion of the market makes the application of hitherto not employed technological methods possible.

ain. There plants have come to specialize vertically in certain processes and services, such as founding, casting, forging, tool-making, and repairs, and horizontally in the manufacture of needles and pins, safes and locks, domestic hollow ware, electric heat and cooking apparatus, batteries, electrical machinery, etc. It was also indicated that the subdivision of processes conferred advantages on the British textile industry over, for example, German textile manufacturing, where specialization was less developed.[38]

The automobile industry is another frequently used example. Bain notes that interchangeability of automobile parts among United States producers makes possible the exploitation of large-scale economies in their production. This applies to the manufacture of such components as electrical and ignition systems, heaters, steering wheels, hydraulic brakes, bearings, oil pumps, transmissions, batteries, spark plugs, gauges, radiators, springs, etc.[39] These parts and accessories had originally been manufactured by the car producers, and have come to be produced by separate undertakings as car output has expanded. The period after the Second World War has seen an increased degree of subcontracting, and many small enterprises were formed to supply a certain producer with one or more components.

The economies of specialization will be exhausted on a relatively low level of economic development in some industries (e.g., tanneries) but require a highly developed industrial structure in others (automobiles, machine tools, etc.). Recent developments in the United States and other industrialized countries bear witness to the continuing process of specialization in these economies. This conclusion appears to be supported by numerical estimates referring to the United States. S. Wickham proposed to measure the degree of vertical integration as the percentage share of value added in the value of output, and he noted that this quotient was smaller for the fifty largest American firms than for American manufacturing industry in general.[40] Stigler also shows that in 1939, in the United States, vertically integrated, rather than vertically disintegrated, establishments were found in

---

[38] Cf. P. Sargant Florence, *Investment, Location, and Size of Plant* (Cambridge: At the University Press, 1948), pp. 54–57, and S. J. Chapman, *Work and Wages* (London: Longmans, Green, and Co., 1904), Vol. I, p. 166.

[39] J. S. Bain, *Barriers to New Competition* (Cambridge, Mass.: Harvard University Press, 1958), p. 247.

[40] "Observations sur l'intégration et diversification des entreprises," *Revue Economique*, July, 1953, pp. 490–94.

smaller industries.[41] A further subdivision of activities is expected from the spreading of automation, and there seems to be no reason for a slackening in the process of specialization even in an economy of the size of the United States. A fortiori, gains from specialization can be expected in a union of economies which possess a market smaller than that of the United States.

External Economies in Present-Day Integration Projects

We have discussed here various forms of external economies and their way of action. At this point we shall briefly examine the applicability of our findings to present-day integration projects. Separate consideration will be given to nonmarket interactions, pecuniary economies, and the economies of specialization.

Among nonmarket interactions, external economies in technical and organizational knowledge are likely to be more important than in labor skills. The latter will be operative, however, if countries participating in a union have surpluses and deficits in various skills, since, through migration, new skills can be acquired by the inhabitants of any country who formerly lacked them. As regards technological (and organizational) know-how, the effects of economic integration will be felt in four ways. First, discoveries in basic research may be made better use of in a larger and more diversified market;[42] second, integration will contribute to the spreading of existing knowledge among particular industries of different countries; third, closer contact between competing national industries is likely to increase the rate of technological change; fourth, the trend toward larger business units can also be conducive to technical progress. We shall return to the last proposition in Chapter 8.

These nonmarket interactions can be of importance in all integration projects. The generally low standards of technological knowledge will make considerable improvements possible in Latin America, but gains are likely to be forthcoming in Europe also. Bertil Ohlin is of the opinion, for example, that the diffusion of knowledge will con-

41 *Op. cit.*, p. 190. For information on European industries, see J. Houssiaux, "Quasi-intégration, croissance des firmes et structures industrielles," *Revue Economique*, May, 1957, pp. 385–411.

42 On the external economies of basic research, see R. R. Nelson, "The Simple Economics of Basic Scientific Research," *Journal of Political Economy*, June, 1959, pp. 297–306.

stitute one of the most important sources of gain in a European union.[43]

Interindustry relationships, too, will contribute to economic development in the Latin-American integration projects. The fusion of national markets will make possible simultaneous advances in a number of fields, as well as the application of large-scale technological methods in individual industries. A widening of the market will also permit the development of new branches of manufacturing, especially in the field of metallurgy, metal manufacturing, and engineering. Both the emergence of new industries and the expansion of old ones can contribute to the utilization of hitherto unused or underutilized resources, particularly labor and mineral supplies, and can lead to induced technological improvements.[44]

The interindustry transmission of technological change will be operative also in European integration projects. An increase in the demand for one industry's product or an innovation in any given industry will contribute to economic growth through interindustry repercussions that take the form of induced technological change. External economies of this type will benefit particularly the smaller member countries. The interdependence of industries through changes in incomes will have similar effects.

Further gains will be forthcoming as a result of increased specialization in a wider market. The importance of the economies of specialization for European integration projects has frequently been noted.[45] In this connection an evaluation of the problems of specialization in Great Britain deserves full quotation: "There are a number of cases in which the size of the British home market is apparently too small to encourage rapid progress. . . . In certain industries the British market has not been big enough to encourage the growth of specialist producers of equipment—who themselves might have created new possibilities of progress."[46] The industries in question are paper,

[43] "Problèmes d'harmonisation et de coordination des politiques économiques et sociales," *Revue d'Economie Politique*, January–February, 1958, p. 283.
[44] For an attempt to measure numerically the extent of external economies in the steel industry and metal manufacturing in Latin America under varying assumptions, see H. B. Chenery, "The Interdependence of Investment Decisions," in *The Allocation of Economic Resources*, pp. 82–120.
[45] Cf., e.g., International Labour Office, *Social Aspects of European Economic Cooperation* (Geneva, 1956), pp. 11–12, and *Economic Consequences of the Size of Nations*, ed. E. A. G. Robinson (London: Macmillan & Co., Ltd., 1960), pp. 356, 436.
[46] C. F. Carter and B. R. Williams, *Industry and Technical Progress* (London: Oxford University Press, 1957), p. 155.

bread, rubber, plastics, fine chemicals, aircraft, and scientific instruments.

Carter and Williams' findings show that, at the present stage of industrial development, even a market as large as the British does not permit sufficient specialization in a number of industries. These conclusions can then be applied to France and Germany, where the size of the market is about the same as in Britain. The existing limitations of specialization are even more significant in the smaller countries of the European Common Market, such as Belgium and the Netherlands, and in the countries participating in the Free Trade Association of the "Outer Seven."

Among industries in which a widening of the market leads to increased specialization, we have already mentioned the production of automobile parts and components as an example. In Italy and to a lesser degree Germany, parts and components are produced by the car manufacturer; hence the scope for potential specialization and standardization in a unified market is quite considerable.[47] Similar conclusions have been reached with regard to semimanufactures using nonferrous metals, and increased specialization may contribute to the reduction of unit costs also in machine building and in some other industries manufacturing intermediate products.

Great emphasis is laid on gains from specialization in Latin America. The United Nations Economic Commission for Latin America conducted studies on the possibilities of specialization in the pulp and paper industry and in cotton textiles. Similar conclusions have been reached with regard to several branches of heavy industry. Intra-industry specialization will be a likely consequence of integration in railroad-equipment manufacture, for example.[48] Possibilities for specialization in further manufacturing industries can be illustrated by the example of Brazil, which possesses the largest national market in Latin America. In the latter country an increased degree of specialization has been observed in recent years in metal manufactur-

47 *Britain and Europe*, pp. 136–37.
48 Cf. United Nations Department of Economic and Social Affairs, *The Latin American Common Market* (1959), p. 33; United Nations, *Pulp and Paper Industry in Latin America* (New York, 1955); United Nations, *Labor Productivity of the Cotton Textile Industry in Five Latin American Countries* (1951); Plácido García Reynoso, "Probables efectos del Tratado de Montevideo en la industrialización de América Latina," *El Trimestre Económico*, April–June, 1960, pp. 193–202; and S. S. Dell, *Problemas de un mercado común en América Latina* (Mexico, D.F.: Centro de Estudios Monetarios Latinoamericanos, 1959), p. 33.

ing and engineering. In the production of electric motors, electric and gas ranges, sewing machines, and metal furniture, for example, there has been a tendency to subcontract the foundry part of the production process and, to a lesser extent, also various operations, such as stamping, forging, thermal treatments, etc., to specialized firms. The Brazilian automobile industry provides another example. Prior to the introduction of automobile production in Brazil, a large number of automobile parts and components were manufactured for replacement in individual plants. Since then, only one or two parts or components have been produced in each plant, and these specialized plants are of smaller size than the establishments that had a more diversified production pattern before.[49]

It should be noted, however, that gains from specialization can be partly offset by transportation costs. This consideration has relevance for the Latin American Free Trade Association, where economic distances between Mexico and Argentina, or between the eastern parts of Brazil and Chile, will interfere with intra-industry specialization among these countries. Specialization, then, can contribute to agglomerative tendencies; the latter will be discussed in Chapter 9.

[49] For information concerning the Brazilian experience, I am indebted to Nuno Fidelino de Figueiredo of the UN Economic Commission for Latin America.

Chapter
8 FURTHER DYNAMIC FACTORS

Europe would develop tremendously if she had a customs union. In the end, the United States and other outsiders may benefit rather than be hurt.
—Gottfried Haberler, in *Hearings on Foreign Economic Policy* (84th Cong., 1st sess.), p. 530

Economic Integration and Market Structures

In François Perroux's opinion, the effect of a union on the degree of monopoly is *the* decisive factor in determining the economic consequences of integration.[1] Although this proposition may overstate the significance of changes in market structures in a union, one may certainly rank the problems of competition among those of primary importance. As to the possibilities of competition in an integrated area, opinions differ widely. Some authors believe that integration *will* increase the power of monopolies and/or cartels; others maintain that cartel agreements *should* be reached in an economic union; finally, some contend that economic integration leads to more competition.

Kurt Rothschild first presented the view that powerful monopolies would arise in an integrated area and that the increased degree of monopoly would create inefficiencies in resource allocation.[2] Kindleberger also declares that cartel agreements are likely to be reached in a customs union and adds that, if competition actually did increase, potential large-scale economies would be forgone.[3] Finally, Perroux maintains that the common market is "the fruit of the capitalism of monopolies," and that the abolition of customs barriers will inevitably

1 *L'Europe sans rivages* (Paris: Presses Universitaires de France, 1954), p. 482.
2 "The Small Nation and World Trade," *Economic Journal*, April, 1944, pp. 26–40.
3 "European Economic Integration," in *Money, Trade and Economic Growth: Essays in Honor of J. H. Williams* (New York: Macmillan Co., 1951), p. 66.

result in a strengthening of monopoly positions, accompanied by the formation of international cartels.[4]

While these authors contend that economic integration is bound to increase the power of monopolies and cartels, others maintain that there is need for cartelization in an economic union. Maurice Byé asserts, for example, that cartel agreements within the union are beneficial, since mutual gain would result "from the disappearance of certain competitive struggles, from a pooling of market research and advertising and from mutual adaptation of [the] conditions of production."[5] Byé adds that "for advantages of this kind to be maximized, it is necessary that the degree of monopolistic pressure in the Union be no smaller than it previously was in the most monopolistic of the member nations."[6] The same line of thought is followed by Jan Tinbergen, according to whom, "in the field of specialization and interplant cooperation . . . direct steps seem to promise more than the indirect forces of competition might, in the end, perform."[7]

The propositions advanced by Byé and Tinbergen are based on a disregard of the possible beneficial effects of competition. This will become apparent if the meaning of the term "competition" is clarified. As Tibor Scitovsky noted, competition should not be understood to mean merely large numbers of firms coexisting in a market but should rather refer to the ability and willingness of producers to encroach upon each others' markets.[8] Competitive pressures can take the form of price and nonprice competition as well, when the latter includes research, development of new products, and styling. Under this definition, competition is desirable because it contributes to the elimination of inefficient producers and provides inducement for technological improvements. On the other hand, the proposed cooperation of producers may lead to restrictive practices which can hinder the exploitation of the advantages of a wider market.

Besides the problem of the desirability of competition, we also

4 "Les formes de la concurrence dans le marché commun," *Revue d'Economie Politique*, January–February, 1958, p. 377; also *La coexistence pacifique*, Vol. II: *Pôles de développement ou nations?* (Paris: Presses Universitaires de France, 1958), pp. 200, 338.

5 "Customs Unions and National Interests," *International Economic Papers*, No. 3 (London: Macmillan & Co., Ltd., 1953), p. 222.

6 *Ibid.*

7 "On the Theory of Economic Integration," in *Selected Papers* (Amsterdam: North Holland Publishing Co., 1959), p. 150. Similar arguments are presented in André Marchal, *Les ententes et les concentrations dans le marché commun* (Brussels: Services d'Information des Communautés Européennes, 1959).

8 *Economic Theory and Western European Integration* (Stanford: Stanford University Press, 1958), p. 124.

have to deal with the question whether competition would be intensified in an integrated area. In contradistinction to the previously cited pessimistic views, a number of authors have expressed the opinion that economic integration will stimulate competition. J. E. Meade argues, for example, that "a large free-trade area will itself help to improve the efficiency of the domestic economic system by working as an effective antimonopoly device."[9] Some authors go even further and assert that the greatest potential gain in a union will originate in the beneficial effects of increased competition.[10]

Various factors can contribute to the increase in competition in an integrated area. To begin with, a wider market sustains a greater number of efficient production units. Even if a small country were able to support firms of optimum size in various branches of manufacturing, it would rarely be possible to have a number of efficient firms competing in a small market. There is no contradiction, then, between the possibility of reaping economies of scale and enjoying the advantages of intensified competition in an integrated area. Although the number of producers in the union decreases as inefficient firms disappear, still a greater number of producers will be competing in the enlarged market than in the narrow national markets. More specifically, in industries where only one or a few firms operate within the boundaries of a national economy, the removal of tariffs increases the number of potential competitors and will thereby loosen monopolistic and oligopolistic market structures. In sectors characterized by national monopolies, oligopoly will become the dominant market structure, while in oligopolistic industries the size of the group will increase. As a result, the market power of national monopolies is bound to decline, and the broadening of oligopolistic structures is likely to reduce the possibilities of oligopolistic coordination and collusion. In a larger group, both overt and tacit collusion have less chance to continue; thus nonprice competition and also price competition can become more effective.

Competition is often thwarted for reasons other than the market

9 *Problems of Economic Union* (Chicago: University of Chicago Press, 1953), p. 14. Cf. also J. Dobretsberger, "Théorie des territoires économiques," *Economie Appliquée*, January–March, 1950, p. 80.

10 Cf. A. Frumento, "Le regole di concorrenza fra imprese industriali nella Comunità Economica Europea," *Rivista Internazionale di Scienze Economiche e Commerciali*, January, 1958, pp. 1–56, and Maurice Allais, *L'Europe unie—route de la prospérité* (Paris: Calmann-Lévy, 1960), pp. 53–54. A somewhat more guarded position is taken, but the gains from intensified competition are also emphasized, in Scitovsky, *op. cit.*, especially, chap. iii.

power of monopolies and collusive oligopolies. Scitovsky argues that in many European countries a number of factors, such as close personal relations between individual businesses, the quest for a quiet life and stable income, and the underestimation of demand elasticities, contribute to the policy of low turnover and high profit and inhibit effective competition.[11] Economic integration would extend the market open to each producer and increase the number of firms that he considers his competitors. This is likely to make competition less personal and more effective by lessening the fear of retaliation and the individual producer's misgivings about encroaching upon other producers' markets. In addition, new products imported from member countries will compete with home-produced goods, and a high degree of substitution between products belonging to the same commodity group is expected to intensify competition. The effectiveness of competition will also be fostered by an increased flow of information on market outlets within the union.

Changes in government policies concerning small business, too, may stimulate competition in the framework of an economic union. In some European countries—of which France is a prime example—government subsidies to small, inefficient firms are widespread. If we take into account the greater fiscal burden of the large firm, it can rightly be said that the inefficient production units are subsidized at the expense of more efficient producers. At the same time, the small firm takes away markets from its larger counterparts and hinders their expansion. It is conceivable that the pressure of foreign competition will induce national governments to revise this policy after the freeing of tariff barriers. The governments will no doubt realize that the assistance given to inefficient producers hampers future progress, thereby weakening the chances for effectively competing with the enterprises of other member countries. In addition, in industries where the freeing of tariff barriers will exert a downward pressure on prices, the cost of protecting the small firm will increase. Finally, the coordination of economic policies is bound to reduce the possibility of providing such protection along with the power of small-scale producers to bring pressure on the governments in order to obtain preferential treatment.

These considerations imply that, other things being equal, integration will contribute to more effective competition within a

11 *Op. cit.*, pp. 26–28, 116 ff.

union. It is a different question that producers may seek cartelization in the form of strengthening national, or establishing international, cartels as a "remedy" against intensified competition. No a priori answer can be given to this question since economic, sociological, and political conditions differ among countries, and these will greatly influence the outcome. Nevertheless, it can be argued that, inasmuch as national cartels were designed to protect the interest of inefficient small-scale producers, the diminution of the power of these groups would reduce the danger of cartelization. An attenuation of close personal relations between businesses in a larger area can have a similar effect. Efficient producers may no longer be willing to abide by the rules of cartels or gentlemen's agreements if they must thereby forgo the possibilities of expansion in a wider market. Furthermore, also in cases when cartel agreements are maintained, the power of large enterprises is likely to increase within these arrangements, thereby contributing to an increased degree of nonprice competition. Last but not least, as long as international cartels are not established, the effectiveness of existing national cartels will diminish.

The last-mentioned factors indicate that the restrictive effect of the cartels can be expected to decrease in a union. Yet there may be a tendency to establish supra-national cartels in some industries in order to divide up the market. Against these and other practices, the use of governmental anticartel policy cannot be forgone. In other words, integration will be conducive to competition, but the benefits of increased competition can be safeguarded only by instituting appropriate measures against restrictive practices.

Market Size and Concentration: Some Empirical Evidence

The above arguments lead to the conclusion that, under *ceteris paribus* assumptions, competition is expected to become more intensive in a larger market. Although "other things" are never equal in the real world, a comparison of economies of different size may shed some light on the validity of this proposition.

No statistical measures have been devised to give numerical expression to the competitiveness of national economies, even though degrees of concentration have been compared between the United States and some other industrialized economies. A high level of concentration does not necessarily indicate a low degree of competitiveness in terms of our definition, however, since a cartel of a great many small firms may greatly restrict competition, whereas a few large firms may engage in vigorous nonprice competition. Nevertheless, it is likely that a higher degree of concentration will offer greater opportunities for restrictive agreements, and thus data on concentration may still be of some use in evaluating the competitiveness of different economies.

In a study on *Concentration in Canadian Manufacturing Industries,* Gideon Rosenbluth notes that "the difference in the size of the United States and Canadian economies is strikingly reflected in the levels of concentration in the two countries. With very few exceptions, comparable industries are more highly concentrated in Canada. . . . The difference in concentration must . . . be the result of a difference in the number of firms, which is in nearly all cases much smaller in Canada."[12] Similar results have been obtained in a comparison of American and British manufacturing. Whereas, on the average, the four largest firms produce 19 per cent of the industry's output in the United States, the corresponding figure is 33 per cent in the United Kingdom.[13] The smaller British market affects the degree of competition especially in industries manufacturing highly specialized products. It is noted that in certain branches of manufacturing the market cannot support more than one or a few producers. The lack of sufficient competition, on the other hand, is said to hinder technological progress.[14]

The Italian market is smaller than the British; hence the possibilities of effective competition are less, too. This problem has been explored by V. A. Marsan, whose conclusions deserve full quotation:

[12] (Princeton: Princeton University Press, 1957), pp. 19–20.

[13] Gideon Rosenbluth, "Measures of Concentration," in *Business Concentration and Price Policy* (Princeton: Princeton University Press, 1955), pp. 57–95. No comparable estimates have been prepared with regard to the countries participating in the European Common Market. Data are available only on the percentage of workers employed by the upper fifth of all firms ranked by size in particular industries. These figures show considerable similarities between the Common Market countries, but they are of little use in arriving at any conclusions concerning levels of concentration by reason of the deficiencies of the employment measure used, the intercountry differences in classification procedures, and the grouping-together of 20 per cent of the firms in each industry. Objections can also be raised against the use of the Gini coefficient, which is a measure of dispersion rather than concentration. For the relevant data, see Communauté Economique Européenne, Commission, *Rapport sur la situation économique dans les pays de la Communauté* (Brussels, 1958), pp. 75–76.

[14] C. F. Carter and B. R. Williams, *Industry and Technical Progress* (London: Oxford University Press, 1957), p. 155.

There are numerous sectors where, owing to the limited size of the home market, an economic scale of production entails a position very close to monopoly. If one considers the percentage share of national output accounted for by one or very few firms (often grouped together), it appears that concentration of industry is now very high in Italy in far more sectors than in the case of larger-sized economies. The basic reason, even if not the only one and not in every case, is that in many sectors the capacity of efficient plant is very close to, or sometimes larger than, the domestic outlet.[15]

Another comparison refers to the percentage share of output produced by the largest firms in Belgium and the United States. It has been shown that, whereas the largest enterprise in Belgium produces 23 per cent of output in the cotton industry, 67 per cent in oil refining, 26 per cent in paper and allied products, and 41 per cent in canned food, the production of the four largest firms in the United States amounts only to 13, 37, 16, and 27 per cent of industry output in the above branches of manufacturing.[16] Although this list is highly selective and differences in the coverage of industries give occasion for errors, the figures are suggestive in indicating relative differences.

These findings can be interpreted to indicate the existence of some degree of correlation between market size and competitiveness. This is not to deny the importance of other factors, such as the prevailing attitude toward competition, government regulation of restrictive practices, etc. In the United States, for example, antitrust legislation contributed to the maintenance of effective competition in various industries. At the same time, our hypothesis receives support from the consideration of recent trends in concentration in the Canadian economy, while, with regard to the United States, M. A. Adelman concluded that "the extent of concentration shows no tendency to grow, and it may possibly be declining."[17]

Problems of Competition in Present-Day Integration Projects

We have presented some theoretical arguments concerning the

[15] "The Experience of Italy," *Economic Consequences of the Size of Nations,* ed. E. A. G. Robinson (London: Macmillan & Co., Ltd., 1959), p. 160.
[16] Jacques Paridant de Cauwere, "Le problème des investissements dans le marché commun," *Les Annales du Marché Commun,* No. 6 (1958), p. 13.
[17] "The Measurement of Industrial Concentration," *Review of Economics and Statistics,* November, 1951, p. 295; also Comments by C. D. Edwards, G. W. Stocking, E. B. George, and A. A. Berle, with a Rejoinder by Adelman in *Review of Economics and Statistics,* May, 1952, pp. 156–78. On Canada, see Rosenbluth, *op. cit.,* p. 20.

impact of economic integration on market structures, which seem to point in the direction of greater competitiveness. Empirical evidence on levels of concentration in national economies of different size appears to strengthen this conclusion and implies a possible loosening of monopolistic and oligopolistic market positions after integration. In actual integration projects, however, various factors may counteract these tendencies; hence it is of interest to look at the prospects of competition in the European Common Market and in the Latin-American unions.

With regard to the European Common Market, the experience of the Coal and Steel Community can be instructive. It appears that the ECSC has contributed to increased competition through the abolition of tariffs, through the equalization of transportation rates, and through its action against subsidies, price discrimination, and other forms of restrictive practices. Although there seems to have been international collusion among steel firms (but not among coal mines) in setting prices after the abolition of price controls in 1953, there is little indication of continued international collusion.[18] The publication of prices required by the Treaty and some degree of success in the implementation of anticartel measures have also had a beneficial effect on competition. On the other hand, the steel producers of the ECSC appear to be acting as a cartel toward third countries, and intra-union competition is restricted by the payment of interfirm compensations to inefficient producers.[19]

The Coal and Steel Community has taken a firm stand against cartels but raised less objections against concentration within individual member countries. The High Authority is of the opinion that concentration is likely to increase productivity and that, at the same time, it is not dangerous to competition by reason of the increased market size. The biggest steel producer in the Community, for example, controls less than 10 per cent of output, whereas in the United States, U.S. Steel leads with 30 per cent and the three largest producers taken together are above the 50 per cent mark.[20] The differences in the degree of concentration are even greater if comparison is made

18 William Diebold, *The Schuman Plan* (New York: Frederick A. Praeger, 1959), pp. 257 ff.

19 On these and related issues, see Louis Lister, *Europe's Coal and Steel Community* (New York: Twentieth Century Fund, 1960), chaps. 6–8.

20 Diebold, *op. cit.*, pp. 376–77.

with the situation existing in the member countries' markets taken individually. Nevertheless, the establishment of vertical combinations, especially in the Ruhr, can be regarded as a warning sign for the future.[21]

As for the Common Market itself, the Treaty does not contain a provision for prohibiting concentration and forbids only the abuse of dominant market position. The signing of the Treaty actually brought about a movement toward concentration within various industries in Germany and elsewhere, as well as some degree of interpenetration among the enterprises of the participating countries. Banks and other financial institutions play an eminent role in this process, and American capital also participates in it.[22] However, by and large, these changes indicate a greater degree of concentration within a member country only, with a decline in the market power of individual firms on the enlarged market. Exceptions are industries in which the existence of international corporations may limit the decrease in the level of concentration. In rubber manufacturing, for example, Dunlop, Goodyear, and Michelin operate plants in two or three member countries of the Common Market. It is also possible that, in some branches of manufacturing, monopolistic groups will increase their power after the abolition of the inner tariff walls and will be able to raise profits by widening price differentials between the union's market and foreign markets. This may be the outcome in some branches of the chemical industry, whose past history suggests the possibility of internationalization of present national restrictions.

National legislations of countries participating in the Common Market differ greatly with regard to cartels. Whereas French, Italian, and Belgian laws are generally permissive toward cartels, the abuse principle is prevalent in the Netherlands, and, with certain important exceptions, cartels are prohibited in Germany. The Common Market Treaty builds on the principle of the prohibition of cartels, but the interpretation and the application of the relevant paragraphs are a

---

21 See Maurice Byé, "Les problèmes posés par la Communauté européenne du charbon et de l'acier," *Revue Economique*, November, 1960, pp. 842–44.

22 For detailed information, see Jacques Trempont, "Reflexions sur les concentrations industrielles en Allemagne Fédérale," *Revue du Marché Commun*, March, 1960, pp. 108–13; Henri Claude, "Les banques françaises dans l'Europe des trusts," *Economie et Politique*, March–April, 1959, pp. 48–57; and Jacques Austruy, "La règlementation des ententes et les pouvoirs compensateurs dans le Marché Commun," *Revue Economique*, September, 1960, pp. 782–85.

matter of considerable controversy.[23] A further problem is whether these regulations would be circumvented through so-called gentlemen's agreements, tacit collusion, etc. Such *ententes* are certainly a possibility; yet—as we pointed out before—the profit motive is likely to give incentive to more competition in a larger area, since personal connections, the fear of retaliation, etc., will have less restrictive effect on producers in encroaching upon each other's market. The prospects of competition can also be improved if information is made available on products, services, prices, and market possibilities.[24] Finally, producers' restrictive agreements will certainly be less widespread if cartels are prohibited, as compared with the case when cartel agreements did not face legal obstacles or were even legally enforceable, as in the Germany of the 1920's.

The chances of competition in Latin America appear to be gloomier than in Europe. There has been little discussion on prohibiting restrictive agreements between producers, and if mention is made of the need for more competition, the arguments offered are overly general. The Report of the first session of the Working Group on the Latin American Regional Market (Santiago, Chile, February, 1958) stated, for example, that "the essence of a regional market lies in its competitive character."[25] In later pronouncements, however, it was proposed to postpone the reduction of tariff barriers for commodities that would face intra-area competition. To support this proposal, the difficulties of readjustment and the possibility of bankruptcy for inefficient enterprises have been cited.[26] However, it is questionable how competition can become effective in the future if the life of inefficient production units is perpetuated. In the absence of competition, the sheltered high-cost producers may well go on expanding and will have little incentive to improve their production methods.

Some observers believe that greater competition will result in the

23 On the controversy, see e.g., Saverio Ilardi, "Competition Rules in the EEC Treaty," *Review of the Economic Conditions of Italy*, May, 1959, pp. 316–32 and Theodor Faist, "Die Wettbewerbsbestimmungen für Unternehmen in der europäischen Wirtschaftsgemeinschaft und in einer europäischen Freihandelszone," *Aussenwirtschaft*, December, 1955, pp. 297–311.

24 For a good discussion of some of these points, cf. Jacques Houssiaux, *Concurrence et marché commun* (Paris: Editions M. Th. Genin, 1960), pp. 1–10.

25 United Nations Department of Economic and Social Affairs, *The Latin American Common Market* (1959), p. 34.

26 Cf. *ibid.*, pp. 18–20, 86.

integration projects now under implementation.[27] The Montevideo Treaty supplies little evidence in support of this proposition, however, considering that the early reduction of duties on manufactured goods is not provided for in the Treaty. At the same time, in the absence of regulations on producers' restrictive agreements, the formation of cartels faces few obstacles in this area. Finally, in Central America, there is evidence of pressure coming from the side of the industrialists to institute measures against what is termed "ruinous competition."[28]

In the discussion of competition in Latin-American unions, we have to consider the so-called complementarity agreements, too. These are preferential arrangements between countries closely linked by geographical proximity or common interests that provide for the apportionment of the manufacturing of various parts and components used in the same production process. Although the Report of the first session of the Working Group emphasized that "the specialization in industries . . . must be the outcome of the free interplay of economic forces" and added that "it is inconsistent with this principle to accord specific countries the exclusive right to install certain industries or activities,"[29] the second session of the Working Group (1959) advocated the adoption of complementarity agreements.[30] A provision for complementarity agreements is also contained in the Montevideo Treaty, although the Treaty requires the concurrence of two thirds of the participating countries and also the setting of a time limit for each complementarity agreement.

These arrangements obviously involve the danger of establishing monopoly positions by giving preferential treatment to selected industries. It is conceivable, however, that in some situations complementarity agreements will be advantageous for economic development to the extent that they contribute to the establishment of hitherto nonexistent branches of manufacture. It is hoped that the safeguards contained in the Montevideo Treaty will ensure that the complementarity agreements adopted will not amount to the exclusion of potential competition.

27 Cf. e.g., Z. L. Savoia, "El area de libre comercio entre Argentina, Brazil, Chile y Uruguay," *Economia y Finanzas,* November, 1959, p. 9.

28 Cf. Centro de Estudios Monetarios Latinoamericanos, *Boletin Quincenal,* November, 1959, pp. 389–90.

29 *The Latin American Common Market,* p. 31.

30 *Ibid.,* pp. 48–49.

A similar problem is that of the so-called integration industries in Central America. These industries are established by agreement of all countries participating in the union. This arrangement has the advantage of contributing to the creation of new industries that would not be established otherwise because of uncertainties associated with foreign markets. However, the very same rules might become a source of protectionism, since it may be necessary to raise tariffs permanently, in order to shelter the "integration industries" from foreign competition.

Autonomous Technological Change

In Chapter 5 we distinguished between autonomous and induced technological change: whereas induced technological change follows an increase in the size of the market, autonomous technological improvements bear no direct relationship to market size. Nevertheless, some degree of indirect causation can be established between the latter two variables via expenditures on research. The relationship between market size and research activity can be demonstrated in two ways: (a) by postulating large-scale economies in research and (b) by arguing that an enlargement of the market brings about a more than proportional increase in research expenditures. In the following we shall discuss these propositions both on the firm level and on the national economy level.

We have seen above that, after the freeing of tariff barriers, economies of scale will be realized in a number of industries, and thus the share of large firms in the market will rise. The increase in the average size of the firm may contribute to technological progress through large-scale economies in research and through a more than proportional expansion of the firm's research activity. To begin with, research and development conducted in the framework of the firm often involves a fixed cost greater than what can be borne by small enterprises.[31] In addition, the large firm possesses an advantage in the case of diversified production, where discoveries made in basic research carried out within the enterprise or new knowledge acquired in the development of individual products can be utilized in a wider field.

31 On this point cf. Marshall's dictum, according to which small firms are at a disadvantage because they cannot afford much research and are often unable to develop their inventions for lack of capital (*Principles of Economics* [8th ed.; London: Macmillan & Co., Ltd., 1956], p. 234).

Large-scale economies in research have come to command increasingly greater attention in recent years, in some cases also at the expense of economies of scale in production. Actually, the dividing line between these two phenomena is by no means clear-cut. An increase in the size of the firm requires research activity to devise new, or to apply previously known, technological methods for large-scale production, and the development of new products in a large, diversified firm also makes research activity necessary.

Large-scale economies in research can provide a reason for a more than proportional increase in research activity as the firm grows. Large firms have the further advantage of possessing a greater amount of resources for research expenditures, they have better access to the capital market, and they are likely to have the longer time horizon necessary to form long-term development plans, to undertake basic research, etc.[32] All these factors can contribute to an increased share of expenditures on research and development in larger firms. This proposition has received some support from empirical evidence referring to the United States. H. H. Villard shows that in six American industries under review, with one exception, spending on research as a percentage of output increases with the size of the firm.[33]

If large enterprises spend more on research and also enjoy large-scale economies in research, they are likely to be technologically more progressive than their smaller counterparts. The testing of this hypothesis encounters difficulties in the choice of the variables considered and by reason of the influence of third factors on the data. Nevertheless, observations made with regard to American and British industries can be of some use. Almarin Phillips studied 28 American industries and found that industries with larger production units tended to have a higher rate of technological progress than industries in which small firms were dominant.[34] Results for the United Kingdom are inconclusive although case studies indicate, that "while progressiveness

[32] For a summary and references on the controversy about the relationship between bigness and progress, see my "Success Criteria for Economic Systems," *Yale Economic Essays*, Spring, 1961, pp. 14–16.

[33] See "Reply" to a Comment by J. Schmookler on Villard's "Competition, Oligopoly, and Research," in *Journal of Political Economy*, December, 1959, pp. 633–35. The industries examined are food and kindred products, chemicals and allied products, fabricated metal products, machinery, electrical equipment, and professional and scientific instruments.

[34] "Concentration, Scale and Technological Change in Selected Industries, 1899–1939," *Journal of Industrial Economics*, June, 1956, pp. 179–93.

is possible (and does occur) at all sizes of organization, there are special disabilities attaching to certain types of small firms which make financial success (and presumably in consequence, outstanding technical progress) more difficult to achieve."[35]

An increased share of research expenditures in national income would accompany integration as the average size of the firms increased and larger firms spent more on research. Further gains could be expected from large-scale economies of research that would materialize on the national economy level. Even if two countries of different size spend the same proportion of their national income on research and development, the lower aggregate amount of research expenditure puts the smaller country at a disadvantage. In the first place, the small country will not be able to cover many important fields of scientific advancement, although more diversified research activity has a greater chance for success.[36] In addition, similar to the case of individual firms, in some fields a large amount of research expenditures of the nature of a fixed cost is required to carry out the necessary experiments, without which little progress can be made.[37] Finally, a larger and more diversified economy can make better use of the results of its basic research and of discoveries made in individual industries.

It can be concluded that integration will be conducive to autonomous technological improvement, since large-scale economies in research can be reaped on both the national and the firm level, and it is also likely that more will be spent on research and development after the freeing of trade barriers. The latter conclusion is reinforced by the prospects of accelerated growth in an integrated area. These beneficial effects of integration on autonomous technological change are expected to follow in the European Common Market as well as in Latin-American integration projects.[38]

[35] Carter and Williams, op. cit., p. 186. Also pp. 121, 126.

[36] This has been noted, for example, in the comparison of the United States and the United Kingdom. See ibid., p. 156; also Economic Consequences of the Size of Nations, pp. 136, 374–76.

[37] This factor is held responsible for the relative backwardness of the Italian chemical industry, which is said to suffer from its inability to conduct research on an adequate scale (cf. Marsan, op. cit., p. 154). The development of atomic energy provides another example.

[38] With regard to the European Common Market, similar conclusions have been reached in E. Tuchtfeld, "Intégration économique et progrès technique," in Demain l'Europe sans frontières (Paris: Plon, 1958), pp. 91–113, and A. Maddison, "Industrial Productivity Growth in Europe and in the U.S.," Economica, November, 1954, p. 315.

Risk and Uncertainty in Foreign Transactions

The risk element in foreign trade can be attributed to two main causes: uncertainty with regard to restrictions existing at any point of time and uncertainty with respect to the possibility of future changes in restrictions or in economic policies. Both types of uncertainty have an adverse effect on foreign transactions, since producers include an additional risk premium in their calculations and prospective transactions are thereby discouraged.

The first type of uncertainty is associated with the complexity of administrative regulations on foreign trade. The risk of incurring unforeseen costs or penalties and the possibility of the invalidation of transactions can be mentioned in this regard.[39] In the United States, for instance, there are a hundred acts that affect importation, and the interpretation of these acts leaves room for potential surprises for the trader. Costly litigation must sometimes be resorted to for the protection of the traders' rights. The expenses of litigation are augmented by the costs that arise from delays in the settling of cases. To give an example, the number of classification cases in the U.S. Customs Courts averaged 80,000 a year during the period 1949–53, and only about 7 per cent of the cases were disposed of during any given year. Classification difficulties assume the greatest proportions for new commodities, thereby hindering the expansion of foreign trade.[40] Similar is the effect of foreign-exchange restrictions and import quotas when the trader often does not know whether the quota will be filled or the exchange allotment for a particular commodity will be exhausted before the foreign transaction reaches completion.

A further source of uncertainty is the possibility of changes in restrictions and policies. As long as the trader can never be sure when a foreign country will change tariff levels, subsidies, quotas, and exchange restrictions, the normal flow of goods will be disrupted. Uncertainty associated with variations in exchange rates can also be mentioned here, since, for an individual producer, devaluation in a foreign country is equivalent to the imposition of a tariff. Finally, the possibility of changes in monetary, fiscal, and social policies, as well as political uncertainty, increases the risk of the trader.

[39] Cf. G. A. Elliott, *Tariff Procedures and Trade Barriers* (Toronto: University of Toronto Press, 1955), p. 6.

[40] *Ibid.*, pp. 88–89.

The described causes of risk and uncertainty in foreign transactions may also interfere with the application of large-scale technology, which calls for large and stable markets. In view of the precariousness of foreign outlets, producers will often not be willing to invest in equipment designed for mass production. The high fixed cost of machinery and equipment increase the risk of possible losses suffered by the entrepreneur, and the inclusion of a risk premium in the cost calculations will reduce the profitability of large-scale production methods. In such cases, the private profitability of these processes will understate their social productivity, and less efficient technology will be adopted.

The cost of entering the foreign market is another consideration. This cost includes the expenses incurred in changing production design to suit foreign customers and the expense of establishing repair facilities, and selling outlets. In the face of the uncertainty associated with foreign sales, firms will often be hesitant to undertake the expenses involved in entering a foreign market. It has been noted, for example, that European steel producers are reluctant to effect the retooling and reconversion of equipment necessary to comply with American specifications, since they have no assurance that the American tariff policy will not change in the future.

For the economy as a whole, the precariousness of foreign markets means that the government is often compelled to encourage the manufacturing of some products of strategic importance in order to avoid embarrassment in case the supply of these commodities is cut off. In Simon Kuznets' opinion, "so long as international anarchy prevails, and so long as political independence is desired, there will be justification for keeping within a country's boundaries activities whose products are indispensable and whose supply might be cut off; for devoting a substantial proportion of resources to economically unproductive uses . . . and for limiting the economically profitable use of resources if it makes the country too dependent in the long run."[41] It should not be forgotten, however, that these considerations often lead to the use of spurious arguments designed to establish the need for protection.

The importance of these factors is difficult to evaluate, since the degree of uncertainty varies greatly between countries and also over

[41] "Economic Growth of Small Nations," *Economic Consequences of the Size of Nations*, p. 26.

time. In Robert Triffin's opinion, in Europe "uncertainty and instability over policy was far more disturbing than any degree of restriction."[42] It is not easy to pass judgment on this assertion. Compared to the pre–First World War period, uncertainty in foreign transactions has increased considerably as a result of intensified state intervention in economic life; in Europe it was especially significant in the years following the Second World War but has declined in importance since. In the present situation, uncertainty is a greater obstacle to trade in Latin America than it is in Europe. The successive exchange reforms, multiple exchange rates, quotas, and bilateral agreements have inhibited trade primarily among the Latin-American countries themselves.[43]

The establishment of a customs union means the permanence of commitments as far as the abolition of tariffs and other forms of trade restrictions are concerned and thus removes the uncertainty associated with these restrictions and with changes in restrictions as well. On the other hand, uncertainty due to possible changes in monetary, fiscal, and other policies will continue to exist in a union as long as coordination of economic policies has not been achieved.

Some degree of uncertainty in trade relations will also be maintained if liberal escape clauses provide the possibility of reinstatement of trade restrictions. This danger is rather small in the European Common Market, where the consultation of member countries should precede the use of the escape clause. On the other hand, the possibility of invoking this provision unilaterally in the Latin American Free Trade Association may have detrimental effects on trade. Finally, possible changes in commercial policies on trade with third countries undertaken by individual members of a free-trade area provide an element of uncertainty.

Investment Activity in a Union

Besides its effect on commodity trade, the lessening of uncertainty associated with national frontiers will influence investment activity through its impact on investments in export industries and on foreign investments. Further effects of integration on investment are related to the reallocation of production and changes in production

---

[42] *Economic Consequences of the Size of Nations*, p. 411.
[43] Cf. *Inter Latin American Trade: Current Problems*, p. 52, and p. 55 above.

methods that follow the removal of tariff barriers within an integrated area. Finally, in a common market, the flow of funds between member countries is facilitated by the establishment of an integrated capital market. As a result, both the volume of investment and the allocation of investment funds can be affected.

The impact of integration on the volume of investment was first examined by C. P. Kindleberger, who argued that the integration of industrial economies may have an inflationary effect in periods of excessive aggregate demand and a deflationary effect in periods of deflation.[44] In the former case, plants operate under full capacity, so that any reallocation of resources will require new investment, while the depreciation of the old equipment takes time. On the other hand, excess capacity during deflation is said to permit the expansion of production by efficient firms without new investment, while depreciation allowances of less efficient establishments would not be reinvested. It is difficult to conceive of a situation where integration had a deflationary effect, however. Under the conditions postulated by Kindleberger, there would be disinvestment in *all* firms prior to integration. After the freeing of tariff barriers, disinvestment would go on in the less efficient firms—and disinvestment cannot accelerate because it is limited by the amount of depreciation—while the more efficient enterprises may stop disinvesting, as their share in the market rises. Consequently, under more realistic assumptions, economic integration will have an expansionary or, at least, a neutral effect in a period of deflation.

Under full utilization of capacity—and this is the relevant case in industrialized countries under present-day conditions—the reallocation of production from high-cost to low-cost sources of supply will place additional demands on efficient firms. Some of this demand might be satisfied by an increase in the number of shifts worked, but social factors and the shortage of skilled labor limit multishift operation. Consequently, new investments will be required to accommodate this demand. New plants will also be built in industries where hitherto unexploited economies of scale can be appropriated. In addition, new equipment will be needed in order to achieve specialization, although the experience of the postwar years suggests that the conversion of existing equipment for new uses can relieve some of the pressure.

The increased demand for investment funds cannot be regarded

44 *Op. cit.,* pp. 65–66.

solely as a transitional problem, since the construction of large-scale plants and specialized equipment will take a long time and the expansion of production in any one industry will provide inducement for further investments in supplier and user industries through interindustry repercussions. The need for increased investments is especially pronounced in a union of underdeveloped countries, where integration takes place *pari passu* with economic development. In these countries, self-sustained growth will require an enduring increase in the rate of investment. The question arises how the increased volume of investments will be financed. Domestic savings or foreign investments are possible sources of financing. With regard to the former, different considerations are relevant in the case of underdeveloped countries and for industrialized economies.

Low per capita incomes and the riskiness of investment can be mentioned among the factors that are responsible for low saving ratios in underdeveloped countries. In the presence of appropriate government policies, integration can lead to an increase in the proportion of incomes saved in these countries through its effect on economic growth. Higher rates of return and reduced risk and uncertainty on new investment are expected to further contribute to this outcome.

While a sustained increase in the share of savings in national income is a likely consequence of the integration of underdeveloped countries, such a result does not necessarily follow in a union of advanced economies. At higher levels of development, there is no evidence that large markets would be associated with higher saving ratios or that the proportion of national income saved would increase as per capita incomes rose. Nevertheless, also in industrialized economies, greater stability and less uncertainty in a union might raise the saving ratio. Corporate saving, too, may increase as large firms capture a greater share of the market. Furthermore, higher returns due to increased productivity could elicit a larger amount of savings, while income redistribution favoring the lower-income classes would act in the opposite direction. Finally, in an inflationary situation, forced savings would be extracted from fixed-income recipients through price rises.

In addition to increased domestic savings (voluntary or forced), the inflow of foreign funds, too, might become an important source of financing in an integrated area. New foreign investments could take the form of equity or portfolio investments. The possibility of selling on a large market and the endeavor to get behind the tariff wall would provide inducement for the establishment of plants by foreign concerns. Also, the expectation of earning a higher return would induce foreigners to lend more to governments or to individual enterprises operating in the countries participating in a customs or economic union.

It is well known that the flow of American capital into the countries participating in the European Common Market shows signs of acceleration. Several American enterprises are setting up subsidiaries in these countries, and there has been increased interest among American investment companies in European stocks and bonds. The need for foreign investments is especially acute in the Latin-American integration projects, where domestic savings are far from adequate to satisfy the demand for investment funds. It is likely that these projects will also attract foreign, especially American, capital, as soon as they approach realization. Integration in Central America, for example, gave impetus to the inflow of United States capital, and American investors also expressed interest in the Latin American Free Trade Association.

Notwithstanding possible increases in the amount invested, changes in the allocation of investment funds can be more important than the increase in the volume of investment—at least in a union of developed economies. Integration can affect the pattern of investment through a reallocation of production, the use of advanced technological methods, lessened uncertainty, and—in a common market—the creation of an integrated capital market.

The reallocation of production from higher-cost to lower-cost sources will have a parallel effect on the pattern of investment. The introduction of mass-production methods, as well as horizontal and vertical specialization in a wider market, will also lead to a more efficient use of investment funds by increasing the relative importance of large-scale and specialized equipment at the expense of inefficient, small-scale machinery. Furthermore, as we noted before, the increased market share of large firms is bound to give rise to an expansion of financing from retained earnings. This can contribute to the growth of efficient firms but may also impair the interindustry mobility of investment funds.

We have already referred to the impact of uncertainty in international trade on investments. In independent national economies some potential investments in export industries are not carried out because of the risk associated with foreign transactions. The inclusion of a risk premium in the profitability calculation of industries producing for export markets creates a divergence between private profitability and social productivity and results in less investment in these fields than desirable, allocating more funds to sectors that cater to domestic demand. Integration is expected to remedy the ensuing misallocation of investment funds by lessening uncertainty in intra-area trade. At the same time, lessened uncertainty will lead to an increased amount of long-term investment which was not considered profitable before.

In regard to the intra-union movements of investment funds, uncertainty associated with prospective changes in regulations on factor movements, in exchange rates, taxes, and national economic policies in general, acted as deterrents before the establishment of the union. The risk of nationalization, uncertainty about the transfer of earnings and the repatriation of capital, and the possibility of government price and wage fixing all had similar consequences. The creation of an integrated capital market removes at least some of the sources of uncertainty and contributes to a better use of investment possibilities within the union.

In the foregoing discussion we implicitly assumed that market forces would effect the reallocation of investment. Some economists argue, however, that market criteria are unsatisfactory guides in allocating investment funds, and hence investment plans should be prepared by the participating nations and a central agency should coordinate these plans.[45] At the same time, others contend that, in the absence of an "unequivocal, objective, and quantitatively definable" criterion, the central planning of investments would give a solution greatly inferior to that attainable on the free market.[46]

In postwar Europe, the efforts of the Organisation for European Economic Co-operation to establish coordinated national investment plans have failed, and such a proposition is not likely to be adopted in the framework of European integration projects, since it is deemed to impair the workings of the market mechanism. However, govern-

[45] Cf. e.g., Maurice Byé, "Localisation de l'investissement et communauté économique européenne," *Revue Economique*, March, 1958, pp. 188–212; and André Philip, "Social Aspects of European Economic Co-operation," *International Labour Review*, September, 1957, pp. 244–56.

[46] Wilhelm Röpke, "Europäische Investitionsplannung: Das Beispiel der Montanunion," *Ordo*, Vol. VII (1955), p. 86; also Walter Eucken, "La pénurie de capitaux et les investissements en Europe," *Synthèses*, February, 1950, pp. 301–8.

ment participation will be required in investments where private capital cannot perform the task satisfactorily (e.g., the construction of atomic installations), and—as will be shown in the following chapter —there is need for the coordination of regional development plans. The central authorities can also contribute to the efficient allocation of investment funds by supplying information on investments undertaken in different industries of the participating countries, thereby making the capital market more "transparent" and easing the task of the entrepreneurs in comparing investment alternatives. The latter purpose is served, for example, in the European Coal and Steel Community by the High Authority's reports on investment activity in the coal and steel industries of the member countries.

The role of central agencies in financing the creation of social and economic overhead capital (especially in the construction of transportation facilities and electricity-generating equipment) will be much more important in the underdeveloped countries of Latin America than in Europe. In addition, some degree of coordination in the lending and borrowing operations of the national governments is likely to become necessary in the Latin-American integration projects in order to avoid discriminatory treatment of national industries. Finally, the lack of a developed capital market will augment the task of common financial institutions in facilitating long-term investment through lending and borrowing operations and investment guarantees.

The Impact of a Union on Nonparticipating Economies

In Part I of this study we reached the conclusion that under static assumptions the integration of national economies reduces the welfare of third countries through trade diversion and through the deterioration of their terms of trade. Third countries would benefit in the long run, however, if the dynamic factors discussed in Part II were strong enough to counteract these adverse consequences. The dynamic effects of integration will be beneficial for nonparticipating economies, inasmuch as rising income levels in the union will lead to increased imports.

Actually, even though dynamic factors may need a long time for their full operation, the "short-run" and the "long-run" changes may overlap to a significant degree, so that fluctuations in trade between member and nonmember countries will be damped. To give an example, at the time when the European Payments Union was established, the opponents of this move often argued that the payments agreement among the Western European countries would reduce the volume of trade between overseas countries and Western Europe. The facts have disproved this assertion, and the complex of effects which previously might have been regarded as being of a short-run or long-run character have brought about a considerable increase in intra-European trade and in trade between Europe and the outside world as well.

The question arises: How can we ascertain the long-run effects of integration on nonmember countries? M. E. Kreinin advanced the argument that a union is trade-diverting if intra-area trade increases faster than trade with third countries.[47] This definition is based on unrealistic assumptions, however; it implicitly assumes that the marginal propensities to import from member and from nonmember countries are identical and that the establishment of the union has had no effect whatsoever on economic growth. Actually, the increase in trade with third countries can be partly attributed to rising incomes resulting from integration, so that Kreinin's concept will not indicate trade diversion. Trade diversion could be estimated only if we ascertained how much trade with third countries would have taken place in the absence of integration.

An interesting attempt was made to assess the possible trade-diverting effects of the European Common Market by Erdman and Rogge.[48] These authors distinguish between a *Präferenzeffekt* and a *Wachstumseffekt* of the union on third countries. The former refers to the static trade-diverting effect, the latter to the boost given to imports as a result of the accelerated growth of incomes in the Common Market. It is rather uncertain, however, to what degree integration will contribute to growth. To get around this problem, Erdman and Rogge accepted GATT's estimate, according to which, between 1953–55 and 1973–75, the gross national product of the Common Market countries would increase by about 90 per cent in the absence of integration; and they also made use of figures provided by GATT for illustrative purposes which assumed a 120 per cent, or, alternatively, a 150 per cent increase in national income during the same period *after* integration.[49]

[47] "On the 'Trade-Diversion' Effect of Trade Preference Areas," *Journal of Political Economy*, August, 1959, pp. 398–401.

[48] Paul Erdman and Peter Rogge, *Die europäische Wirtschaftsgemeinschaft und die Drittländer* (Basel: Kyklos Verlag, 1960).

[49] Cf. GATT, *The Possible Impact of the European Economic Community, in Particular the Common Market, upon World Trade*, Trade Intelligence Paper No. 6 (Geneva, 1957).

The conclusion is reached that, over the period under consideration, trade-diverting effects will predominate with regard to about
50 per cent of agricultural imports from the temperate zone (bread
grains, fish, meat, dairy products, some fruits, vegetables—amounting
to about 16 per cent of Common Market imports from third countries), although this outcome would be partly due to the expected
artificial stimulation of domestic production that would have occurred
also without the Common Market's establishment. No adverse effects
are likely to occur, and foreign suppliers may even benefit from the
creation of the Common Market in the case of the remaining categories of nontropical agricultural imports (forest products, tobacco,
textile materials, etc.). With respect to tropical products (18 per cent
of Common Market imports), third countries stand to gain, considering the high income elasticity of demand for these products and the
limited capabilities of the associated territories for future expansion.
This conclusion is further strengthened if we consider the possibility
that some of the former colonies of the member countries might not
participate in the Common Market. For nonagricultural raw materials (11 per cent of imports), it is expected that the income effects
will predominate and the relative share of domestic production will
decline, while the future of energy imports (16 per cent of imports)
will depend on the substitution of oil for coal and the development of
atomic energy. Taking into account that the latter will not reach the
originally expected magnitudes, the net effect on foreign imports is
likely to be positive. Less can be said about trade in industrial products (23 per cent of imports), where technological change, economic
policy measures, etc., will greatly influence the outcome. Beneficial
effects are said to predominate in capital-goods imports, while third
countries are likely to lose in the case of chemicals and some metal and
paper products. Nevertheless, given the high income elasticity of demand for industrial products, nonparticipating countries, on balance,
are likely to benefit rather than lose.

Taken together, available information suggests that, in the European Common Market, the growth effect may outweigh the preference
effect in the course of a twenty-year period if the national income of
the Common Market countries increases at least by 120 per cent. This
result can be attributed primarily to increased imports of raw materials, fuels, and various categories of industrial products at higher
income levels.[50] The beneficial effects are further strengthened if we

50 See Erdman and Rogge, *op. cit.*, chap. v.

consider a longer time span. Less optimistic conclusions can be reached with regard to the long-run effects of the Free Trade Association of the "Outer Seven," however, by reason of the complementarity of these economies and their geographical location.

The problem of trade diversion is of a different character in Latin America than in Europe. Whereas, in Europe, integration is expected to contribute to the further growth of industrialized economies, economic development in Latin America represents a structural change from an economy based on primary activities to an expansion of manufacturing industries. Given the restricted possibilities of most Latin-American countries for expanding traditional exports[51] and the observed correlation between per capita incomes and the share of manufacturing in national income,[52] industrialization appears to be desirable in these countries.[53] Industrialization, however, has been shown to be associated with import substitution, in the sense that the share of domestic production in expenditure on industrial goods increases. Third countries will then be adversely affected by reason of the static trade-diverting effects and the substitution of domestic production for imports accompanying industrial development. On the other hand, nonparticipating countries will benefit because an industrially developed country becomes a good market for the products of economies whose development has taken place earlier. Chenery's data indicate that although the growth in industrial production far outstrips the increase in imports of manufactured goods as the income level rises, the share of industrial imports in national income shows only a slight decline.[54] On balance, then, other industrialized countries are likely to gain inasmuch as their exports to formerly less developed countries will reach a higher level *after* the process of industrialization has advanced.

These considerations imply that integration of underdeveloped economies will benefit third countries inasmuch as it contributes to economic development. Such a result would not be obtained in the Latin-American area, however, if the projections of the UN Economic Commission for Latin America were realized, since, according to

[51] Cf. *The Latin American Common Market*, pp. 57–60.

[52] Cf. H. B. Chenery, "Patterns of Industrial Growth," *American Economic Review*, September, 1960, pp. 635–38, and Bela Balassa, "Comment," *ibid.*, June, 1961, pp. 394–97. Estimates are based on the cross-section data of fifty-one countries.

[53] Note that industrialization in Latin America should not be construed to mean an absolute decline in primary production but rather a relative decrease in these activities as compared to manufacturing.

[54] Cf. Chenery, *op. cit.*, pp. 640–42.

these, in 1975 the value of imports from the outside world would be only slightly higher than in 1955.[55] It can be argued that, in the absence of integration, imports would reach a higher level. Nevertheless, it should not be forgotten that the projected import substitution in Latin America cannot be ascribed solely to integration but also to economic policies which will supposedly be followed. And it can safely be said that, in most of Latin America, substitution of domestic production for imports would take place even in the absence of integration as a result of conscious efforts toward industrialization behind high tariff walls. Thus one should compare the effects of a policy of industrialization in an integrated area with those of the same policy followed within national boundaries. Our previous discussion has shown that development coupled with integration will be more advantageous than industrialization in the framework of independent national economies. Since in the small national markets economies of scale can often not be appropriated and the external economies of balanced expansion cannot be obtained, the cost of setting up new industries in terms of alternatives forgone will be high and rising so that export activities may at the end be endangered; on the other hand, in the wider market of an integrated area, individual countries can avoid expanding industries for which they are not suited and can enjoy internal and external economies. The resulting growth in incomes, then, would put third countries in a more advantageous position than if the policy of industrialization was followed by the Latin-American countries individually.

55 *The Latin American Common Market*, pp. 64–68.

PART III

Integration and Economic Policy

Chapter 9 — REGIONAL PROBLEMS IN A COMMON MARKET

The following may be deemed to be compatible with the Common Market: aids intended to promote the economic development of regions where the standard of living is abnormally low or where there exists serious underemployment.

—Article 92/3 of the Treaty establishing the European Economic Community

Location Theory and Regional Analysis

Until recently, regional problems within the framework of a national economy received but scant attention in the economic literature and in public discussions. Various factors contributed to this apparent neglect. First, traditional economic theory ignored the locational aspects and concentrated on the domestic-international dichotomy. Second, under the classical assumptions of price and wage flexibility and factor mobility within a country, there seemed to be little need for the discussion of regional issues, since differences in income levels could not have endured. Finally, after the depression of the 1930's had shattered the general belief in laissez-faire as an all-out cure for economic problems, increased government intervention was first confined to national issues and was extended to regional problems with a time lag.

After a long period of comparative neglect, the past twenty years have seen important developments in regional analysis. These developments came from two sources: intensified theoretical analysis of the economic problems of regions and increased attention given to regional issues by the policy-makers. The two lines of approach appeared intertwined in some earlier contributions, such as the British *Report on the Location of Industry*[1] and the American *Industrial Lo-*

[1] London: Political and Economic Planning, 1939.

191

cation and Natural Resources,[2] and this interaction has been maintained since, as witnessed, for example, by a recent study on Puerto Rican refinery-petrochemical-synthetic-fiber complexes[3] or by the discussion of regional problems in the European Common Market.

Among the antecedents of regional analysis in economics, the Weber-Lösch location theory, Florence's work on industrial agglomeration, and Perroux's discussion of the poles of development deserve attention.[4] Both Weber and Lösch examined the emergence of economic regions in the framework of their respective location theories, while Florence started out with an empirical investigation of the organization and location of industries and inquired into the causes of industrial agglomeration, making use of the Marshallian analysis of external economies. Although of recent origin, Perroux's discussion of the poles of development and their effect on regional economic growth is also mentioned here, partly because of its independence from developments elsewhere, partly because of its profound effect on regional analysis in Continental Europe. Finally, credit for the latest developments in the theoretical analysis of regional problems should be given to E. M. Hoover, Walter Isard, and other American economists.[5]

Regional problems have an important part in the discussion of economic integration plans, too. Herbert Giersch was the first to present the view that economic integration would weaken the tendency toward agglomeration along national lines but would, at the same time, intensify regional agglomeration tendencies.[6] François Perroux lays great stress on the proposition that economic integration will in-

2 Washington: National Resources Planning Board, 1943.

3 W. Isard, E. W. Schooler, and T. Vietorisz, *Industrial-Complex Analysis and Regional Development* (New York: M.I.T.–John Wiley & Sons, 1959).

4 Cf. Alfred Weber, *Theory of Location of Industries* (Chicago: University of Chicago Press, 1929); August Lösch, *The Economics of Location* (New Haven: Yale University Press, 1954); P. Sargant Florence, *Investment, Location, and Size of Plant* (Cambridge: At the University Press, 1948), and *The Logic of British and American Industry* (Chapel Hill: University of North Carolina Press, 1953); François Perroux, "Economic Space: Theory and Applications," *Quarterly Journal of Economics*, February, 1950, pp. 89–104, and "Note sur la notion de 'pôle de croissance,'" *Economie Appliquée*, January–June, 1955, pp. 307–20, and other writings, cited below.

5 Cf., e.g., E. M. Hoover, *The Location of Economic Activity* (New York: McGraw-Hill Book Co., Inc., 1948); Walter Isard, *Location and Space Economy* (New York: M.I.T.–John Wiley & Sons, 1956), and the literature cited therein. Walter Isard's *Methods of Regional Analysis* (New York: M.I.T.–John Wiley & Sons, 1960) reached me too late to be considered in the writing of this chapter.

6 "Economic Union between Nations and the Location of Industries," *Review of Economic Studies*, No. 2 (1949–50), pp. 87–97.

crease regional disparities.[7] These authors and others who do not project an enhancement of regional disparities in a union emphasize the need for the coordination of regional policies in an integrated area with a view to developing regions with low per capita incomes.[8]

For an evaluation of these views, we have first to define the concept of a region. In view of the many conflicting definitions used, one may well agree with Walter Isard, who maintains that "the choice of a particular set of regions . . . depends on the particular problem to be examined."[9] In the present context we are interested in differences in per capita incomes and in the development possibilities of regions. The purpose of such an investigation is best served if the interdependence among individual incomes in the process of development is employed as a criterion.[10]

The use of this definition is justified by the hypothesis that a region grows and decays as an entity, rather than having its income change as the outcome of a sum of independent variations in particular activities located in the region. Nevertheless, changes in the demarcation of regions due to the changing pattern of economic relationships should not be left out of account. Such a qualification is especially important in the case of large population movements, as experienced in the United States, but is of less significance, for example, in the European area, given present political boundaries. It will assume importance, however, in the event of economic integration in Europe and also in Latin America, since new regions may develop over the old frontiers.

Agglomerative Tendencies in Regional Development

Many of the basic ideas in regional analysis date back to Alfred Weber's work on location theory. In discussing the development of

[7] See, for example, *L'Europe sans rivages* (Paris: Presses Universitaires de France, 1954), pp. 274 ff., and *La coexistence pacifique*, Vol. II: *Pôles de développement ou Nations?* (Paris: Presses Universitaires de France, 1958), pp. 201, 261, 346.

[8] Cf., e.g., Paul Romus, *Expansion économique régionale et Communauté Européenne* (Leiden: A. W. Sythoff, 1958), p. 334; see also United Nations Department of Economic and Social Affairs, *The Latin American Common Market* (1959), pp. 88–89.

[9] "Regional Science, the Concept of a Region, and Regional Structure," Regional Science Association, *Papers and Proceedings*, Vol. II (1956), pp. 1–14.

[10] For definitions along similar lines, cf. J. L. Fisher, "Concepts in Regional Economic Development," Regional Science Association, *Papers and Proceedings*, Vol. I (1955), W1–W20, and E. M. Hoover and J. L. Fisher, *Regional Aspects of Economic Growth and Decay: A Report to the Universities* (Washington, 1948), p. 4. Also United Nations Economic Commission for Europe, *Economic Survey of Europe in 1954* (Geneva, 1955), p. 136.

regional centers of production, Weber examines locational problems for a single industry, followed by an analysis of interindustry relationships.

Under the assumption of uniform density of the relevant variables throughout an area, there will be a tendency toward the concentration of an individual industry if cost economies can be attained by merging several intersecting or contiguous market areas into one. Such an outcome requires that the reduction in production cost should outweigh the additional cost of transporting the product to greater distances. Reductions of production cost are said to follow from the predominance of agglomerative over deglomerative factors. An agglomerative factor is defined as "an 'advantage' or a cheapening of production or marketing which results from the fact that production is carried on to some considerable extent at one place, while a deglomerative factor is a cheapening of production which results from the decentralization of production."[11] Agglomerative factors include economies of scale attainable in a large plant (firm) and advantages resulting from close association of several plants, such as development of technical equipment (specialized machines, repair facilities), development of labor organization (skilled labor force), marketing factors, and savings in general overhead cost (gas, water, transportation). Deglomerative factors are said to originate in the rise of land rent which is caused by the increased demand for land at the place of agglomeration.[12]

At the second stage of the argument, Weber removes the assumption of independence between the locational pattern of individual industries and considers the impact of the interaction of industries on location. Industrial interrelationships result in the concentration of various processes, connected through the use of materials, labor, economic overhead, auxiliary activities, etc. The agglomerative factors operating in individual industries and the interrelationships of industrial processes, then, both contribute to the concentration of manufacturing activity at a few locations.[13]

Some of the ideas contained in Weber's theory of location have been further developed by August Lösch, P. Sargant Florence, and E. M. Hoover.[14] On the basis of their contributions, natural resources, transportation possibilities, and external economies can be singled out

11 Weber, *op. cit.*, p. 126.
12 *Ibid.*, pp. 127–34.
13 *Ibid.*, chap. vi.
14 Cf. references in n. 4 and 5.

as the main determinants of the development of a region. Among these factors, external economies and transportation costs will be examined in the following.

External economies were discussed in Chapter 7 without consideration given to locational factors. At this point, we shall distinguish between mobile and immobile external economies.[15] The external economies belonging to the former group are not bound to a certain location, whereas immobile external economies are localized. Florence gives the well-sounding name of "economies of juxtaposition" to immobile economies and explains that "juxtaposition allows lower transportation costs and easier communication: (*a*) from the suppliers to the demanders of materials or products, and (*b*) between one specialized process in production and another; and (*c*) allows specialized auxiliary services on the spot to be fully used."[16] These advantages of juxtaposition or, to use the Weberian terminology, economies of agglomeration comprise the availability of economic overhead facilities (transportation, gas, electricity, water supply, waste disposal, etc.), the availability of a skilled labor force, the ease of exchange of technical information, and the existence of linked processes (vertical and horizontal specialization, auxiliary services, etc.).

The economies of agglomeration provide significant advantages for the further growth of an industrially developed region. Other things being equal, new firms will tend to be located in those regions where external economies can be appropriated. These economies contributed, for example, to the previously mentioned development of the Birmingham metal trade and of textiles in Lancashire, as well as to the concentration of the French silk industry in Lyons, cutlery in Thiers and Nogent, etc. The absence of external economies is a substantial obstacle in the way of economic development in underdeveloped regions. Although Rosenstein-Rodan's estimate, according to which 70–80 per cent of the capital needs of underdeveloped areas should go into social and economic overhead,[17] appears to be exaggerated, overhead capital and interindustry relationships certainly play an important part in regional development.

The diseconomies of agglomeration should also be mentioned at

15 This distinction was first advanced by E. A. G. Robinson in *The Structure of Competitive Industry* (London, 1931), p. 142 (p. 124 in the American edition, published by the University of Chicago Press, 1958).

16 *Investment, Location, and Size of Plant,* p. 52.

17 "Les besoins des capitaux des pays sous-développés," *Economie Appliquée,* January–June, 1954, p. 82.

this point. Diseconomies arise as the further influx of capital leads to the congestion of urban areas, overcrowding of transportation facilities, increased cost of social utilities, and rising factor prices. Such diseconomies have especial importance in a metropolitan area and lead to a divergence between social and private productivity. Entrepreneurs base their investment and production decisions on private profitability and take into account the agglomeration economies appropriated by the firm, whereas the external economies and diseconomies created through the activity of the enterprise are not subject to cost calculations. At a later stage of agglomeration, diseconomies may outweigh the economies originating in the firm's activity. In this case, private profitability overstates social profitability, and corrective action becomes necessary. Such a situation has arisen, for example, in some areas in Britain, where a licensing system on new investments has been applied to remedy the situation.[18]

Agglomeration economies are also affected by improvements in transportation and communication. Developments in the field of transportation have a twofold effect on agglomeration. Arguing along Weberian lines, one would say that lower transportation costs enlarge the market area and contribute to agglomeration. On the other hand, an improvement in transportation (and communication) facilities reduces the economies of juxtaposition, since the advantages of specialization will not require proximity. For example, factories manufacturing parts and accessories need not be located near the user plant. Considering the importance of this last-mentioned factor, one is inclined to agree with E. A. G. Robinson, who maintains that the proportion of mobile to immobile external economies is steadily increasing and that, consequently, the advantages of industry concentration show a declining trend.[19] The decentralization of the French automobile industry can serve as an example. The continuation of this trend may result in a reduction of regional imbalances.

In connection with the economies of agglomeration, François Perroux's discussion of the poles of development deserves consideration. As we noted in a previous chapter, a key industry (*industrie motrice*) and industries linked to it form a pole of development. The

18 Cf. M. Fogarty, "The Location of Industry," in *The British Economy, 1945–1950* (London: Oxford University Press, 1952), pp. 269 ff. Similar corrective measures are being used in Paris, although with less consistency. See Romus, *op. cit.*, p. 221.

19 *The Structure of Competitive Industry* (Chicago: University of Chicago Press, 1958), p. 124. For a different opinion, see Florence, *The Logic of British and American Industry*, pp. 85, 89.

growth of the poles is determined by the growth of the key industries, and, in turn, the poles have a profound effect on the economic structure and the development of a region. Perroux writes: "A market area grows and develops by reason of the action of the poles and not exclusively nor principally through the reduction of real costs in small units of equal size and through the increased number of such units. A market area is a complex of *poles* situated in *their* environment."[20]

Perroux's conception is broader than the concept of agglomeration economies as commonly understood. While most writers have stressed price-cost relationships, Perroux notes the importance of induced technological change in the process of regional development and also includes noneconomic factors among the variables considered. Emphasis is laid on the psychological and sociological effects of the poles of development, for example. Perroux believes that the growth of a region may be greatly influenced by the creation of a "growth mentality" attributed to the emergence of a key industry.

One of the frequently used examples of the poles of development is the role of the iron and steel industry in the Ruhr. Another is the regional development centered around the newly discovered gas at Lacq (France). Besides the construction of factories for the utilization of gas and the pipeline for its transportation, this discovery has contributed to the establishment of a sulfate factory, petrochemical works, and thermal installations. The concept of the poles of development has also been utilized in the discussion of industrialization of certain regions in Brazil.[21]

In the American literature, the concept of the "industrial complex" is comparable to Perroux's poles of development. An industrial complex is defined "as one or more activities occurring at a given location and belonging to a group of activities which are subject to important production, marketing, or other interrelations."[22] A concrete evaluation of industrial complexes is given for the case of the Puerto Rican refinery-petrochemical-synthetic-fiber industries.[23] The study examines various possible alternatives from the point of view of

[20] *La coexistence pacifique*, Vol. II: *Pôles de développement ou Nations?* p. 346. See also "Note sur la notion de 'pôle de croissance,' " pp. 307–20.

[21] Cf. M. Penouil, *Note sur quelques aspects de la politique d'aménagement du territoires* (Paris, 1958), p. 29, and J. R. Boudeville, "Contribution à l'étude des pôles de croissance brésiliens: une industrie motrice—la sidérurgie du Minas Gerais," *Cahiers de l'Institut de Science Economique Appliquée*, Série L, No. 6, June, 1957.

[22] W. Isard and E. W. Schooler, "Industrial Complex Analysis, Agglomeration Economies, and Regional Development," *Journal of Regional Science*, Spring, 1959, p. 21.

[23] Cf. n. 3 above.

their locational advantages and disadvantages. Aiming at numerical estimates, the authors pay little attention to nonquantifiable elements and to the impact of the establishment of such an industrial complex on the growth of the region as a whole. In this sense, their work is confined within narrower limits than Perroux's hitherto largely unfilled framework.

Patterns of Regional Development

The *Economic Survey of Europe since the War* reads: "No single country would be regarded as having a well-integrated economy as long as glaring disparities persisted between the levels of development and standards of living in different areas within it."[24] This statement indicates the double problem that many less developed regions face: lower incomes and rates of productivity growth inadequate to lessen regional disparities. Lower incomes, *per se,* would not give cause for concern if a higher rate of growth acted in the direction of reducing regional disparities. Similarly, lower than average rates of growth would not be regarded as undesirable if the region had higher than average per capita income.

With regard to interregional differences in income levels, two main determining factors should be distinguished: (*a*) low productivity per head in all industries of the region and (*b*) a high percentage of low-productivity industries in the region. The importance of the first factor is stressed by Viner, in whose opinion "the real problem . . . is not agriculture as such, or the absence of manufactures as such, but poverty and backwardness, or poor agriculture and poor manufacturing."[25] The second factor has received emphasis in the discussion of regional disparities in the United States, where it has been shown that about 80 per cent of the variation in per capita incomes can be explained by differences in occupational distribution.[26] "Problem" regions can be characterized, in general, by the operation of both factors. On the one hand, lower productivity in given industries is generally prevalent in such regions; on the other, industries with a lower growth

24 (Geneva: United Nations Economic Commission for Europe, 1953), p. 218.

25 Jacob Viner, *International Trade and Economic Development* (Oxford: Clarendon Press, 1953), p. 52.

26 F. A. Hanna, "Analysis of Interstate Income Differentials: Theory and Practice," in *Regional Income,* Studies in Income and Wealth, No. 21 (Princeton: Princeton University Press, 1957), pp. 113–61. Also H. S. Perloff, "Interrelations of State Income and Industrial Structure," *Review of Economics and Statistics,* May, 1957, pp. 162–71.

potential and stagnant or cyclically unstable industries can usually be found in lagging regions.[27]

In line with our previous reasoning, disparities in income levels could not persist if low-income regions exhibited higher than average rates of productivity growth. Some light can be thrown on this possibility if we examine patterns of regional development in different countries. Regional disparities in the United States will be of interest in this connection. In the period 1880–1950, time series on regional per capita incomes—with the exception of the period 1920–30—show a steady decline in income disparities in this country (see Table 4).

TABLE 4

DIVERGENCES IN PER CAPITA INCOME LEVELS OF NINE REGIONS
IN THE UNITED STATES, 1880–1950*

	Arithmetic Mean Deviation of Regional per Capita Incomes from National Level (*Per Cent*)
1880...	45.6
1900...	36.6
1920...	25.7
1930...	31.1
1940...	25.0
1950...	16.9

*SOURCE: R. A. Easterlin, "Long Term Regional Income Changes: Some Suggested Factors," Regional Science Association, *Papers and Proceedings*, Vol. IV (1958), p. 315.

This decline of interregional income differentials in the United States can be attributed to migration, to shifts in the composition of output, to shifts of location affecting some industries (textiles, cigarettes), and lately to increased government spending in the South. At the same time, locational shifts in iron and steel manufacturing and the decline in the relative importance of food and clothing consumption adversely affected the poor areas. Hoover expresses the opinion that recent trends indicate a continuing process of equalization in the degree of industrialization, as well as in the interregional distribution of industry and population.[28] It should be noted, however, that, because of the "relapse" during the 1920's, interregional discrepancies

[27] On Europe, cf. *Economic Survey of Europe in 1954*, p. 139. For a detailed classification of problem regions, see E. M. Hoover and J. L. Fisher, "Research in Regional Economic Growth," *Problems in the Study of Economic Growth* (New York: National Bureau of Economic Research, 1949), pp. 189–93.

[28] Hoover, *op. cit.*, pp. 161–65; also Regional Science Association, *Papers and Proceedings*, Vol. IV (1958), pp. 316–24.

in income levels were about the same in 1940 as in 1920, and the convergence of per capita incomes after 1940 can be attributed in large measure to government spending. These results imply that agglomeration economies often counteract the workings of the competitive mechanism. Although labor migration has been a powerful equilibrating force in the United States, technological and pecuniary external economies appear to have hindered the equalization of income levels through capital movements. Resource depletion and discovery and shifts in consumption patterns can also be mentioned as forces that may counteract the equilibrating tendencies. The latter factors have contributed to the relative decline of formerly thriving regions, such as parts of New England, the Great Lakes Cutover Region, and the Southern Appalachian Coal Plateaus in the United States.[29]

Agglomeration economies weighed more heavily in regional development in Italy, where it has been observed that capital movements from the backward South to the more developed North were a dominant feature of Italy's economic history. This movement of funds was intimately related to the absolute decline in Southern Italian manufacturing during the decades following the unification of the country and to the movement of financial and monetary centers to the North.[30] Besides the absolute decline in manufacturing, the relative position of the South with regard to average per capita national income has also deteriorated, and the absolute increase in income levels over the last hundred years has been small.[31]

In 1950 the Cassa per il Mezzogiorno was set up, and subsequently, in 1954, the so-called Vanoni Plan was announced to foster the economic development of Southern Italy. In the following years, efforts have been made to lessen Southern Italy's disadvantage with respect to social and economic overhead capital, but the measures instituted have been rather limited. As a result, although per capita

[29] See S. E. Harris, "New England's Decline in the American Economy," *Harvard Business Review*, Spring, 1947, pp. 348–71, and Hoover, *op. cit.*, pp. 200–204.

[30] Cf., e.g., Alessandro Molinari, "Southern Italy," *Banca Nazionale del Lavoro, Quarterly Review*, January, 1949, pp. 25–47.

[31] Available data show that in 1951 per capita income in the South was 47.7 per cent of that of the North, while housing standard was 65 per cent, per capita meat consumption 44 per cent, and milk consumption 22 per cent. See Giuseppe di Nardi, "The Policy of Regional Development. A Case Study: Southern Italy," *ibid.*, September, 1960, p. 239; and UN Economic Commission for Europe, *Economic Survey of Europe in 1953* (Geneva, 1954), p. 132.

income levels have increased faster than before, regional disparities of growth rates have not been reduced, so that absolute discrepancies between income levels increased further.[32]

In regard to the European economy, the United Nations Economic Commission for Europe has undertaken a comparative study of interregional disparities in income levels in various countries. The results indicate that regional differences in per capita incomes are much larger in the less developed countries of Europe, such as Spain, Portugal, Greece, and also Italy, than in the highly industrialized economies (United Kingdom, Germany). In addition, there is some evidence that disparities have been growing in the former group of countries in recent years, whereas some degree of equalization has been observed in more advanced economies.[33]

Regional problems have received attention in recent years also in Latin America. Among others, the northeast area and the San Francisco Valley in Brazil and the state of Caldas and the Cacan Valley in Colombia are regarded as backward regions. Development plans have been formulated to assist these areas; yet, in the absence of coordination in development planning, these efforts have had only limited success.[34]

The evidence presented gives support to the view that interregional disparities in income levels have a tendency to decrease in advanced economies, but they often show signs of deepening in countries on a lower level of economic development. These differences in trends can be attributed to various causes. One could argue that in less developed countries the limited amount of new investment goes primarily to regions where the availability of related industries and social and economic overhead capital offer higher returns and that the spreading of advances made in more developed regions is hindered by the lack of an adequate interregional transportation and communication system, as well as by sociological and psychological rigidities. On the other hand, in advanced economies, a highly developed price system permits the exploitation of wage differences, transportation and

---

[32] See Pasquale Saraceno, "The Vanoni Plan Re-examined," *Banca Nazionale del Lavoro, Quarterly Review*, December, 1957, p. 379, and di Nardi, *op. cit.*, p. 239.

[33] *Economic Survey of Europe in 1954*, pp. 138–42. France does not fit the pattern. Here relatively high average incomes are associated with large interregional disparities.

[34] S. H. Robock, "Regional Aspects of Economic Development," *Regional Science Association, Papers and Proceedings*, Vol. II (1956), pp. 51–63.

communication facilities are improved, the proportion of mobile external economies increases, and a more equitable allocation of overhead capital is likely to be achieved.[35] It should also be noted that, at least in Europe, conscious regional policy is considerably stronger in advanced industrial than in underdeveloped countries. This, in turn, can be attributed to the fact that developed economies possess larger funds that can be used for such purposes.[36]

Economic Integration and Regional Policy

In recent years there has been considerable discussion on the probable effects of integration on regional trends. The relationship between agglomeration economies and regional development in an integrated area was first examined by Herbert Giersch and Maurice Byé. Giersch maintained that, by reason of agglomeration economies, the abolition of restrictions on trade and factor movements would strengthen the attractiveness of highly industrialized centers for both labor and capital; Byé also argued that, as a result of economic integration, some regions (or countries) might gain, while others would lose.[37] Similar views found expression in the publications of the UN Economic Commission for Europe. Using the Italian unification as an example, the Commission argued that "in the absence of positive intervention . . . disparities in income levels, once established, have a vicious tendency to become more pronounced."[38] With regard to European integration plans—the ECE concluded—"this is tantamount to saying that the gap between levels of development in the high-income and the low-income areas of Europe would continue to widen,

---

[35] Similar reasoning was used by Gunnar Myrdal, who maintained that at a higher stage of development the positive "spread-effects" emanating from a developed region become more pronounced and outweigh the negative "backwash-effects." The spread-effects include increased demand for the backward regions' products, transmission of technological information, etc., while the backwash-effects comprise capital movements from underdeveloped to more advanced regions and changes in the locational pattern favoring the developed areas. See *Economic Theory and Under-Developed Regions* (London: Duckworth, 1957), chap. 3.

[36] One should not expect a uniform pattern of regional development in every country, however. The interregional transmission of growth in any particular case is intimately related to the extent of the demand for the products of underdeveloped areas and is also conditioned by the political and social environment. The latter factors are given emphasis in A. O. Hirschman, *The Strategy of Economic Development* (New Haven, Yale University Press, 1958), chap. 10.

[37] Giersch, *op. cit.*, p. 91; Byé, "Customs Unions and National Interests," *International Economic Papers*, No. 3, pp. 225–26. Also "Localisation de l'investissement et communauté économique européenne," *Revue Economique*, March, 1958, pp. 188–212.

[38] *Economic Survey of Europe since the War*, p. 218.

which could hardly be regarded as an achievement in economic integration."[39]

Recently, regional problems in an integrated area have received emphasis in François Perroux's writings. Perroux asserts that integration and the development of backward regions are incompatible and maintains that a policy aimed at integration favors the regions possessing poles of development at the expense of the presently underdeveloped regions. With regard to the European Common Market, Perroux expresses the view that "the policy of the so-called integration does not assert itself to the benefit of an abstract Europe, but very concretely, to the benefit of the Ruhr and of those industries which are most directly animated by it."[40] In Perroux's opinion, integration would intensify agglomerative tendencies in a European Common Market, benefiting Germany and the Benelux countries, whereas the West and South of France and most of Italy would be the losers.[41]

The arguments displayed by Perroux and others pointing to polarization in an integrated economic area cannot be dismissed lightly. Nevertheless, agglomerative tendencies acting in the direction of higher regional disparities and, in the Common Market, the economic attraction emanating from the Ruhr might have been somewhat overrated. Two considerations seem to be neglected by those who lay great emphasis on the intensification of regional imbalances in an integrated area: first, the impact of the abolition of trade and other barriers on frontier regions; second, the possibility of beneficial effects of increased interregional intercourse for poor regions.

With regard to the first, Giersch noted that regions near to national borders that had hitherto suffered as a result of barriers to commodity and factor movements would develop after the abolition of the frontiers.[42] Economic integration, then, would reconstitute the

[39] *Ibid.*, p. 220. See also *Economic Survey of Europe in 1953*, p. 137.

[40] *La coexistence pacifique*, Vol. II: *Pôles de développement ou Nations?* p. 261. See also *L'Europe sans rivages*, p. 274.

[41] "Les formes de la concurrence dans le marché commun," *Revue d'Economie Politique*, January–February, 1958, p. 359. Also "Les pôles de développement et l'économie internationale," *Les Affaires Etrangères* (1959), pp. 287–305. For a similar opinion, cf. André Thiéry, "Modificaciones que se producirían en la localización geográfica actual de la actividad económica europea como consecuencia de una eventual integración de las economías nacionales en una perfecta unidad," in *Estudios sobre la unidad económica de Europa*, Vol. VI: *La localización de las actividades económicas en Europa después de la integración unitaria* (Madrid, 1957), pp. 808–11. The opposite conclusion is reached in Jean Chardonnet, "Unificación económica europea y modificaciones en la localización geográfica actual de la actividad económica," *ibid.*, pp. 757–59.

[42] *Op. cit.*, p. 91.

natural regions cut across by national frontiers, and this change would contribute to the growth of these regions. This consideration is of especial importance in Europe, where the more prosperous regions of each country tend to be located near the European economic center— the Ruhr—and the poor regions of countries close to this center are separated by national frontiers from the rich regions of countries more distant from the Ruhr.[43] Thus the less developed former frontier regions will gain after unification, although the regions situated at the periphery of the area are likely to lose.

Aside from the case of the former frontier regions, the "spread-effects" emanating from highly developed regions would also benefit the backward areas in the framework of a European union. We have pointed out above that historical evidence appears to support the proposition that the spread-effects tend to become more powerful at a higher stage of development. These may take the form of increased demand for the underdeveloped regions' products, rising proportion of mobile external economies, transmission of technological knowledge, and relocation of plants in response to wage differences.

The described factors can be relied upon to counteract the polarization tendencies in a union of developed economies and are likely to lead to a reduction of regional disparities, *on the average*. Nevertheless, this does not mean that the relative position of *some* low-income regions may not deteriorate. In the European Common Market, for example, such consequences might follow in the absence of regional development policies in Southern Italy and in some parts of Southern France. Under these circumstances, the continuation and, in some instances, also the intensification of regional policies appear to be necessary in the countries participating in the Common Market. At the same time, by reason of the increased interdependence in the economic activity of these countries, individually applied measures for regional development will not achieve this purpose but may partly cancel each other. Consequently, the effective application of regional policies requires their coordination in an integrated area.[44]

In contradistinction to the case of developed economies, inter-regional differences in social and economic overhead capital are

---

43 Cf. *Economic Survey of Europe in 1954*, pp. 137–39.

44 For a similar conclusion, see *Economic Survey of Europe in 1954*, pp. 170–71; Tibor Scitovsky, *Economic Theory and Western European Integration* (Stanford: Stanford University Press, 1958), p. 134; and Romus, *op. cit.*, pp. 334–37.

greater and, in general, agglomeration economies are likely to be more important in the underdeveloped countries of Latin America. Hence the often voiced claim that, in Latin America, the freeing of tariff barriers will aggravate interregional inequalities and may also impede the development of backward regions, can have some validity.[45] Policies for regional development, then, will have especial importance in this area.

The Objectives and Tools of Regional Development Policies in an Integrated Area

Growth of per capita incomes, full employment, and stability are the most frequently mentioned goals of regional development policy. In determining these policy objectives, the region is often regarded as an independent entity, without consideration given to the economic interdependence of regions. Such a conception frequently leads to demands for equal income levels in every region and for regional self-sufficiency. Actually, regional issues cannot be considered separately from problems of a national economy or, in the case of economic integration, of an integrated area.

The main goal of economic integration has been said to be an increase in welfare. This objective can also be applied to regional development planning, by evaluating alternative policies on the basis of their contribution to higher welfare for the economy or for the integrated area as a whole. The reader will recall that we have defined welfare as consisting of a real income and an equity component. Consequently, not only the increase in national income per head but also interregional disparities are to be taken into account in judging the effects of different policies. As in the case of countries with differing income levels, it can be argued that the marginal utility of income is likely to be higher in poor than in rich regions. This would imply that an income transfer from developed to underdeveloped regions may be considered beneficial even if gains in the latter regions do not exceed losses in the former.

Given the objective of an increase in welfare, we can comment on the usability of the various tools of regional policy for achieving

[45] *Progress Report on Inter-Latin American Trade and the Regional Market*, covering the period June, 1957, to April, 1958 (UN Economic Commission for Latin America, 1958), p. 27; and S. S. Dell, *Problemas de un mercado común en América Latina* (Mexico, D.F.: Centro de Estudios Monetarios Latínoamericanos, 1959), p. 56.

this goal. Two main forms of policy measures will be distinguished here: encouragement of labor migration and government assistance to the relocation of industries.

In Chapter 4 we criticized the view that labor imbalances in an integrated area can be cured by development programs without reliance on migration. At the other extreme, some argue that, instead of employing "artificial" measures to boost the development of laggard regions, interregional labor migration should be relied upon to even out regional income differentials. In line with this reasoning, Otto Eckstein maintains that we would overestimate the benefits of investment projects in laggard regions if the wiping-out of local unemployment was included in the projected gain and that selection of projects on this basis would actually lead to a slowing-down of economic growth, since labor would not become available where needed.[46] Such reasoning is deficient in two respects, however: it does not take into consideration the resistance to migration that is due to psychological and sociological factors and disregards the possibility that, under certain circumstances, a decline in population may depress living standards in the region of emigration.

Various factors can contribute to the latter result. External economies are "lost" if existing educational and transportation facilities and various kinds of social utilities cease to be fully used as population declines. The maintenance of these facilities would then inflict an additional burden on the remaining population on a per capita basis. Some of these installations might even be shut down, in which case less would be provided for those left behind. The burden carried by the working force would increase further as a result of changes in the age composition of the population. In addition, the quality of the labor force would deteriorate if primarily skilled workers migrated. Finally, the region of emigration would suffer an injury because human investment in the form of raising and educating children would be lost through emigration.[47]

The decline of population may also trigger off a cumulative deterioration of living standards. Depopulation is bound to bring about a drop in investment activity—or even negative net investment—and thus the possibilities for productive employment will be further re-

[46] *Water-Resource Development* (Cambridge, Mass.: Harvard University Press, 1958), p. 33.

[47] The experience of Ireland can be used to illustrate these points. Cf. Joseph Johnston, *The Sickness of the Irish Economy* (Dublin, 1957), pp. 18 ff.

duced; and, at the same time, the increased burden of the upkeep of social, educational, and other facilities results in higher taxes, if transfers from other regions are not forthcoming. Higher taxes and the uncertainty accompanying depopulation could produce a capital flight, contributing to the creation of "an atmosphere which paralyzes technical and economic progress."[48]

On the other hand, the adverse effects of these factors will be counteracted if emigrants' remittances or transfers from developed regions ease the burden of the reduced population in the backward region or if mostly the unemployed migrate and with their entire families. Under such circumstances the fiscal burden of the region is reduced by the amount of unemployment compensation and relief payments the emigrants had previously received, and thus the decrease in its surplus population can have a beneficial effect on the regional economy. Finally, the arguments for migration are strengthened in the case where the natural increase of population provides the emigrants.

These considerations suggest that—although an important part of regional policy—the encouragement of interregional migration, by itself, often does not provide a satisfactory solution for curing regional imbalances. Reliance should therefore be based on encouraging the movement of industries. In general, if a region is not at a great natural disadvantage (such as mining regions after the depletion of deposits), laggard regions can be developed by various forms of transfers (provision of social and economic overhead capital, subsidies, etc.) and also through loan guarantees or the dissemination of information on investment possibilities.

In order to determine the impact of transfers on economic welfare, these should be evaluated in their effects on future income growth in the transferor and the transferee regions as well. This criterion, however, does not provide us with a precise method for measuring and comparing costs and future benefits of alternative regional policies. Perhaps this is the reason why, in evaluating regional projects, the opportunity cost of an investment, consisting of the returns to factors in alternative uses, is often left out of account. This omission

---

[48] *Economic Survey of Europe in 1954*, p. 145. It has been noted that in a number of European countries, such as the United Kingdom, Germany, and Sweden, differences in local taxation have had perverse effects on the location of industry either because a chronically low level of income necessitated higher tax rates to meet local expenses and this made the place unattractive as a location for new industries or because depression in one major industrial branch led to higher taxation to meet increased expenditure for unemployment relief (*ibid.*, p. 152). See also Myrdal, *op. cit.*, pp. 23–24.

is conspicuous in the literature dealing with regional problems in an integrated area. The usual argument refers—in some form or other—to the agglomeration economies of developed regions that impede the industrialization of backward territories. The conclusion is then reached that the "hidden subsidization of the highly industrialized regions involved in the present distribution of social capital" should be remedied by open subsidies.[49] Such a view fails to consider that the alleged "hidden subsidization" of developed regions does not usually involve an interregional income transfer, whereas the "open subsidy" amounts to a transfer. New enterprises in a developed region, for example, will appropriate external economies that would have remained unused otherwise. On the other hand, the creation of overhead capital or the subsidization of industries in a backward region has an opportunity cost in the form of alternatives forgone. The use of economic calculus in such cases is one of the yet-to-be-solved problems of economics.[50]

The disregard for the alternative cost of regional development programs is also manifest in the literature on regional multipliers, where existing input-output relations are projected, disregarding capacity limitations and factor scarcities.[51] The calculation of the multiplier by inverting an input-output matrix is of greater usefulness if unemployed resources are available in the backward region. But also in this case bottlenecks can restrict regional expansion, or, alternatively, increased import leakages can reduce the value of the regional multiplier.

In setting forth the objectives of regional policy in an integrated area, the need for remedying imbalances in the industrial structure of regions is often argued.[52] The correction of imbalances in a region's industrial structure should not lead, however, to the fetishization of the idea of "balanced" development. Excessive preoccupation with balanced development would jeopardize the gains from specialization

---

[49] *Economic Survey of Europe in 1954*, p. 166.

[50] For an attempt to evaluate regional projects quantitatively, see F. V. Krutilla and O. Eckstein, *Multiple Purpose River Development* (Baltimore: Johns Hopkins University Press, 1958).

[51] Cf., e.g., F. T. Moore, "Regional Economic Reaction Paths," *American Economic Review, Papers and Proceedings*, May, 1955, pp. 133–48, and W. Z. Hirsch, "Inter-Industry Relations in a Metropolitan Area," *Review of Economics and Statistics*, November, 1959, pp. 363–69.

[52] For such a proposal, see Pierre Uri, "Harmonisation des politiques et fonctionnement du marché," *Revue Economique*, March, 1953, pp. 169–87.

that are based on the diversification of economic activity between regions. Regional policy-makers have long been haunted by the memory of the depression in the 1930's, when regions specializing in industries that were most affected by the depression suffered particularly. It is the author's conviction that the damage of possible recessions to certain regions can be remedied at less cost to the society by antirecession policies and transfer payments rather than by forgoing the benefits of specialization.[53] Nevertheless, there is need for balanced development in the sense that none of the factors affecting the growth of a region should be permitted to act as a bottleneck in the way of economic development; furthermore, efforts should be made to exploit all the hidden resources of a region.[54]

Among the various forms of transfers for the purpose of developing laggard regions, the provision of overhead capital and the subsidization of industries are of main importance. The former comprises the supply of public utilities, transportation facilities, and social and educational services; the latter may take the form of favorable treatment in transportation and in placing government orders, provision of capital, low rentals of industrial buildings owned by the government, tax reduction, and outright subsidies. In most European countries both groups of measures have been employed to some extent, although France and Italy are lagging in the application of the latter group of measures.[55] In general, one may say that although in some situations the employment of the one or the other may be sufficient, the coordinated application of both would lead to better results. In the case of Southern Italy, for example, it is noted that the provision of overhead capital, by itself, is not sufficient for economic development and should be supplemented by other measures.[56] One is inclined to agree with the view that, "far from being alternatives, the two broad types of intervention—the provision of basic investments and the implementation of industries—are complementary. . . ."[57]

The above-mentioned forms of transfers are more effective in their effects on the development of backward regions if accompanied

[53] This does not mean that the establishment of manufacturing industries in regions narrowly specialized on a few agricultural products may not be desirable for economic growth.

[54] For example, the establishment of a textile factory would give employment to women in a region where existing industries employ mostly male workers.

[55] Romus, *op. cit.*, passim.

[56] Saraceno, *op. cit.*, pp. 375–86, and di Nardi, *op. cit.*, pp. 215–66.

[57] *Economic Survey of Europe in 1954*, p. 165.

by information and publicity measures, state guarantees of private loans, and the creation of financial institutions to channel savings into productive investment outlets. Furthermore, as we argued above, for the full effectiveness of these measures, their coordination is necessary in an integrated area. The outlines of a coordinated regional policy can be found, for example, in the treaty establishing the European Common Market, but the actual implementation of these provisions remains to be seen.

HARMONIZATION OF

SOCIAL POLICIES

La politique économique a besoin d'une justification sociale, tout comme la politique sociale doit tenir compte des limitations économiques.

—*Le travail dans le monde* (Geneva, 1953), p. 44

Wage Differentials within a Union

The bogey of wage equalization for avoiding distortions in competitive cost relationships raised its head again in the discussion on economic integration.[1] It has been asserted, for example, that the French manufacturing industry would be at a disadvantage in the European Common Market, by reason of its allegedly higher wage level. Also in Latin America, some contend that low-wage countries would have a competitive advantage in a free trade area.

Several generations of economists have taught that, under conditions of balanced trade, wage differentials will indicate differences in the marginal productivity of labor,[2] and they have conclusively shown that, for the purposes of evaluating competitiveness, not wages but unit costs, comprising labor, capital, and other cost elements, are relevant. For the economy as a whole, differences in unit costs are reflected in the exchange rate, while interindustry disparities appear as the immediate causes for international trade. Thus wage differences, per se, do not present any "advantages" or "disadvantages" in international trade.

In a customs union, where restrictions on factor movements are maintained, free trade is likely to reduce differences in wage levels

[1] In the literature on social problems of an economic union, the expressions "harmonization" and "equalization" are often used interchangeably. In the present study the concept "harmonization" will be employed to denote a policy aimed at the reduction of differences in wages, social policies, etc.

[2] Note that social benefits are not considered until the next section.

but will fail to equalize wages between countries.[3] Freeing of factor movements would further reduce wage disparities, although psychological and sociological obstacles to migration and incomplete information on job possibilities would continue to account for wage inequalities, as demonstrated by North-South disparities in the United States. Nevertheless, in view of our argument, inequalities in wage levels will not falsify competitive-cost conditions and there is no need for equalizing wages. On the other hand, a policy aimed at forcible equalization in an integrated area is bound to have harmful effects, since it would lead to balance-of-payments difficulties and unemployment in the absence of factor mobility, and it would give rise to undesirable capital movements if factors were free to move.

Similar arguments can be used to deal with the assertion that, in the absence of a harmonization of wage policies, no individual country would be able to improve the living standards of its workers. A rise in wages is not constrained by the absence of concerted action but rather by the extent of the growth of productivity, and wage increases will not show uniformity so long as differential rates of productivity growth persist. At the same time, prices being determined on the common market, differential movements of wages unaccompanied by changes in productivity are scarcely possible. The bargaining power of the labor unions is restricted thereby, since the unilateral granting of higher wage demands would squeeze the profit margins of the entrepreneurs and result ultimately in reduced sales and unemployment. The disciplinary action of the market would, then, contribute to the avoidance of cost inflation. On the other hand, the often proposed industry-wide collective bargaining for the economic union as a whole[4] would create an unstable bilateral monopoly situation and would be conducive to cost inflation. Disagreements between the bargaining partners or the threat of cost inflation, in turn, might evoke government intervention in wage settlements, leading to wage and price fixing which, short of comprehensive planning, would sacrifice the allocative function of the price system.

It has also been argued that differences in the length of the working week would put the country with a shorter statutory working period at a disadvantage, as and when business conditions necessitated

3 The reader will recall here the discussion presented in Chap. 4.
4 Cf., e.g., the views expressed by Professor Byé in his note appended to the *Ohlin Report* [International Labour Office, *Social Aspects of European Economic Co-operation* (Geneva, 1956)], p. 137.

overtime work. In André Philip's opinion, these "artificial elements" can be eliminated only if hours of work and overtime rates are standardized.[5] At the insistence of French negotiators, such a provision has been added to the Treaty establishing the European Economic Community, where the French statutory workweek and overtime payments were adopted as a yardstick.[6]

An excellent criticism of the alleged need for the harmonization of working hours and overtime rates has been given in the *Ohlin Report*. Noting that international differences in working hours and overtime payments can be deemed to reflect the community's preferences in regard to income and leisure, the Report points out that wage rates, hours of work, and overtime rates act as three interdependent variables in determining the wage pattern. It follows that harmonization with respect to one particular element, such as working hours or overtime payments, is likely to distort, rather than correct, competitive cost relationships.[7]

The example of the European Common Market can be cited to confirm this conclusion. Among the participating countries, a 40-hour workweek is in force in France and 45–48 hours in other economies. But the length of the actual workweek in France has been—with little variation—above 45 hours since 1951.[8] In effect, the overtime premium has come to be regarded as a part of normal wages, an element in the wage pattern, by employers and workers alike. Consequently, in the absence of changes in hourly wage rates, the introduction of overtime premiums for work performed after 40 hours in the other countries of the Common Market will disturb the existing competitive-cost pattern and will need to be corrected through future changes in wage rates.

Another argument calls for the equal treatment of male and female workers throughout an integrated area. If, for example, in one country equal wages are paid to men and women, cost relationships are alleged to be distorted in the absence of such rules in other participating economies, since the former country will be at a disadvantage in industries employing female labor in higher than average

[5] "Social Aspects of European Economic Co-operation," *International Labour Review*, September, 1957, p. 251.

[6] *Protocol relating to certain provisions of concern to France*, II, p. 1.

[7] Pp. 70–71. For a similar argument, cf. Alfred Frisch, "Frankreich's soziale Belastung im Spiegel der europäischen Zusammenarbeit," *Wirtschaftsdienst*, June, 1955, p. 342.

[8] *International Labour Review*, Statistical Supplement, June, 1960, p. 152.

proportion and at an advantage in industries using mostly male workers.[9] Again, at the persistent demand of the French, the principle of equal remuneration for equal work as between men and women has been accepted for the European Common Market.[10]

From the economic point of view, the equalization of wage rates paid to men and women can be desirable only if the "natural price" of male and female labor is equal and if institutional obstacles have obstructed the equalization process on the market. The natural wage of men and women, however, is mostly unequal, since the supply and demand conditions of male and female labor differ and there is only a partial overlapping between their markets. On the one hand, the earnings of women usually constitute a supplement to the family's earnings; on the other, the demand for labor in any region depends on the industrial structure of the region and is often stronger for male than for female work. Consequently, the ratio between wages paid to men and to women in comparable jobs may differ from country to country and from region to region. In some countries, such as the Benelux states, a smaller percentage of women seek employment; in others (e.g., Germany), a higher fraction. At the same time, demand for female labor is greater if light industries predominate and almost nonexistent in mining regions.[11]

The equalization of the *ratio* of female to male wages in the framework of an economic union would create unemployment in regions where the natural price of female labor was lower than the average and would bring about a scarcity of female labor in the opposite case. On the other hand, the *absolute* equalization of wages paid to men and women might give rise to unemployment of female workers in all countries affected. Although we can accept the proposition that such an equalization will remedy distortions due to different statutory arrangements between member countries, these considerations imply a less efficient solution after equalization, since the economic gain due to the disappearance of intercountry differences may well be outweighed by the loss resulting from the raising of female wages above their natural level. In effect, such a provision could not

---

9 Cf., e.g., Philip, *op. cit.*, p. 251.

10 *Treaty establishing the European Economic Community*, Article 119.

11 This discussion draws on Jan Tinbergen's, "Les distorsions et leur corrections," *Revue d'Economie Politique*, January–February, 1958, pp. 260–61. See also *Ohlin Report*, p. 64.

only lead to unemployment of presently occupied women but could also obstruct the way toward the future utilization of a latent female labor force in heavy industrial regions through the establishment of factories employing mostly female workers.

Although economic considerations would militate against equal pay to men and women, these can be overridden by social arguments. It is often suggested that equal remuneration is a corollary of the proclaimed equality of the sexes, and in this regard France occupies a more advanced position than other countries. However, even if social arguments of this kind were accepted for the European Common Market, this does not mean that they should be applied in integration projects of less developed economies, such as a Latin-American union. In the latter case, there is little likelihood that social considerations of the equality of sexes would be given such a great weight as to overbalance the harmful economic consequences.

It can now be concluded that there does not appear to be an economic basis for harmonization, and the forcible equalization of wages, working hours, overtime rates, or female and male wages will distort competitive cost relationships rather than remedy allegedly existing distortions. On the other hand, it could be argued that if artificially low wages were paid in certain industries of some countries, such a policy would result in inefficiencies and would need correction in an integrated area. With regard to the European Common Market, André Philip contends that existing interindustry wage differentials have been underestimated and that, "by placing certain industries in an artificially favourable or unfavourable situation, such differences can lead to an ill-conceived policy regarding location of industry."[12]

It is suggested here that interindustry wage differences in the countries participating in the Common Market (see Table 5) find their origin in conditions of demand for and supply of labor in different industries, which conditions, in turn, are dependent primarily on productivity, the degree of development of an industry, the level of demand for the industry's products, and interindustry labor mobility. In the absence of governmental wage control, the above causes will account for disparities in interindustry wage patterns; hence, there appears to be no need for reducing these differences in the European Common Market or in any other integration project embracing de-

12 *Op. cit.*, p. 250.

TABLE 5

INDICES OF AVERAGE HOURLY EARNINGS IN SELECTED INDUSTRIES
OF COMMON MARKET COUNTRIES, 1955*

(Cotton Textile Industry = 100)

	Cotton Textiles	Leather Footwear	Radio-electronics	Machine Tools	Ship-building	Steel	Coal Mining
Belgium....	100	96	134	138	153	173	157
France....	100	101	137	148	128	133	151
Germany..	100	100	116	125	131	175	160
Italy......	100	91	130	132	139	175	125

*SOURCE: Absolute figures are given in International Labour Office, *Labour Costs in European Industry* (Geneva, 1959), p. 56, and are based on a large sample of establishments in these industries. No data are available for Luxemburg and the Netherlands.

veloped industrial economies.[13] On the other hand, in a union of underdeveloped countries, the harmonization of minimum-wage laws may become necessary.[14]

So far, we have considered intercountry differences in wages only. In the following we shall discuss problems related to intercountry differences in social benefits (bonuses, payments for time not worked, social security benefits, family allowances, pensions, unemployment compensation, etc.) that may be financed by enterprises or from general taxes.

Social Benefits Financed by Enterprises

Some authors consider social charges borne by entrepreneurs separately from wages and argue that differences in social charges constitute an artificial cost advantage for countries where these payments amount to a relatively smaller percentage of the wage. The conclusion is then reached that the harmonization of social benefits financed by entrepreneurs is necessary in order to avoid distortions of competitive cost relationships in an integrated area.[15] This allegation will be examined below under varying assumptions.

[13] Note also that differences in average wages are more pronounced among these countries than are disparities in interindustry wage patterns (cf. the data of Table 6, p. 218).

[14] See pp. 228–29 below.

[15] Cf., e.g., Henry Laufenburger, "Quelques aspects financiers de la Fédération Européenne," *Revue de Science et de Législation Financières*, January–March, 1953, p. 83; W. G. Hoffman, "Wirtschaft- und sozialpolitische Probleme einer europäischen Integration," *Schweizerische Zeitschrift für Volkswirtschaft und Statistik*, March, 1954, pp. 41–54. A long-run rather than immediate harmonization is envisaged in *L'intégration européenne et la sécurite sociale* (Brussels: Ligue Européenne de Coopération Economique, 1957), p. 9.

Before embarking upon the examination of the problem of social charges, it should be noted that the advocates of harmonization pay little attention to nonstatutory social security schemes. Some of these schemes are provided for in collective contracts, others are voluntarily furnished by the entrepreneur. Both comprise pension plans and short-term benefit schemes (sickness, maternity, and temporary disability) as well. Available information suggests that nonstatutory contributions are relatively high if statutory rates are low, and vice-versa. In Sweden, for example, where obligatory social security contributions amount to 2.2 per cent of wages, nonstatutory contributions are 53 per cent of statutory contributions, whereas the corresponding percentages for Germany are 11.7 and 6 per cent.[16] Since the economic effects of statutory and nonstatutory social charges are, by and large, identical, there appears to be no reason for treating them separately. In comparing social charges, we should then take into account nonobligatory contributions, too, and the corresponding benefits have to be added to the earnings of the worker.

In the previous discussion we have already noted that not wages but rather unit costs should be estimated in evaluating competitiveness. Labor costs per hour comprise wages and social charges, whereas hourly labor costs divided by average labor productivity will give labor costs per unit of output. Thus, for the entrepreneur, wages and social charges are but two elements of labor costs and should not be considered separately. This would suggest that, similarly to our conclusions with regard to wages, the harmonization of social charges is not desirable either. As the authors of the *Ohlin Report* expressed, "so long as we confine our attention to international differences in the general level of costs per unit of labour time, we do not consider it necessary or practicable that special measures to 'harmonise' social policies or social conditions should precede or accompany measures to promote greater freedom of international trade."[17]

The thesis expounded in the *Ohlin Report* appears to be based on the presumption that social security payments borne by the entrepreneur are ultimately shifted to wage earners. Wages in countries

---

[16] "Cost of Non-Statutory Social Security Schemes," *International Labour Review*, October, 1958, pp. 388–403 and *Ohlin Report*, p. 33. The data do not include days off with pay. Nonstatutory social security schemes are also of importance in some Latin-American countries. Cf. "Gradual Extension of Social Insurance Schemes in Latin American Countries," *International Labour Review*, September, 1958, p. 275.

[17] *Ohlin Report*, p. 40.

where social charges had risen—it is argued—increased less than they would have increased otherwise, since producers would have been able to pay higher wages in the absence of a payroll tax.[18] Actually, there is some negative correlation between wages and social charges in the countries of the Common Market, and intercountry disparities become less pronounced if wages plus social charges, rather than only wages, are compared (Table 6). The correlation becomes stronger,

TABLE 6

AVERAGE HOURLY EARNINGS AND SOCIAL CHARGES IN THE
MANUFACTURING INDUSTRIES OF COMMON MARKET COUNTRIES*

	Average Hourly Earnings, in Swiss Francs	Obligatory Social Charges and Cost of Days Off with Pay as Percentage of Wage	Wages plus Social Charges, in Swiss Francs
Belgium............	1.91	29.4	2.47
Germany...........	1.74	21.5	2.11
France.............	1.56	37.0	2.13
Netherlands........	1.38	26.2	1.74
Italy..............	1.22	67.7	2.05

*SOURCE: *Ohlin Report*, p. 33. Wage data refer to 1954, obligatory social charges to 1956, cost of days off with pay to 1952–53. The French figures have been corrected for the devaluation of the French franc in 1957, since the new rate was deemed to correspond better to an equilibrium rate. With the exception of days off with pay, nonobligatory social charges were not included, by reason of the paucity of information.

and differences in earnings are further reduced by including social charges, if data on the member countries of the European Free Trade Association are also added.[19] Yet the negative correlation between wages and social charges only suggests the shifting of the cost of social charges to the wage earners but cannot provide any proof. To establish this proposition, we have to inquire into its validity under varying assumptions with regard to price and wage flexibility and the impact of social benefits on the supply of labor. First, we shall consider the case of social charges borne uniformly by all industries under the assumption of factor immobility.

Under perfect price and wage flexibility, any increase in social charges would be shifted to the wage earners *if* they regarded the

[18] *Ibid.*, pp. 67–68. For a similar conclusion, see "Taxes on Wages or Employment and Family Allowances in European Countries," *Economic Bulletin for Europe*, August, 1952, p. 46, and V. R. Lorwin, *The French Labor Movement* (Cambridge, Mass.: Harvard University Press, 1954), p. 227.

[19] *Ohlin Report*, p. 33. This result does not apply, however, to underdeveloped European countries such as Spain or Greece, since in these countries low social charges accompany low wages.

corresponding social benefits as part of their earnings. Disregarding possible differences in social charges and benefits within a given period that are due to lags, both the demand for and the supply of labor will shift proportionately as social charges increase; thus the reduction in wages will equal the amount of increased social charges, with employment being constant. Under these assumptions, there is no need for the harmonization of social charges, but no harm is done if these are equalized, since, by assumption, there would be a corresponding change in wages.

Retaining the assumption of perfect price and wage flexibility, our results need qualification if only part of the social benefits affect the supply of labor. Available information on American collective contract negotiations suggests that, for example, pension benefits or days off with pay are actually considered as part of the earnings. This cannot be said about family allowances, since the latter are in no relationship with the amount of work performed. Family allowances loom large in French and Italian social security schemes (16.75 and 31.4 per cent of the wage) and have considerably less importance in Belgium (7.5 per cent), in Holland (5.5 per cent) and in Germany (1.0 per cent).[20] The employers' contribution to family benefits has little effect on the supply of labor, and consequently only part of this cost is shifted to the worker, and another part is borne by the entrepreneur and/or the consumer.[21] The entire cost of family allowances would be shifted to the wage earner, however, if the supply of labor were completely inelastic to wage changes. Given that the supply of labor is likely to have some elasticity, some degree of harmonization appears to be necessary on this score. Nevertheless, in determining the desirable degree of harmonization in any particular case, we also have to take into account that family allowance regulations express the community's preferences in regard to family size and population growth, and the harmonization of these schemes may run counter to social *Anschauung;* while France wants to have large families, Holland may wish to reduce the birth rate.

Next, we remove the premise of perfect price and wage flexibility

[20] *Ohlin Report*, p. 149. The figures refer to employer contributions to family-allowance schemes as of January 1, 1956. With regard to Germany, cf. *Übersicht über die soziale Sicherung in der Bundesrepublik Deutschland* (Bonn: Bundesminister für Arbeit und Sozialordnung, 1958), p. 76.

[21] The reader will note that different conclusions follow if the labor supply curve is backward-bending in the relevant range. This possibility will not be considered in the following.

and introduce the assumption that prices and wages show downward rigidity. In this case, an increase in social charges in an individual country does not entail a reduction of wages but will rather give occasion to an increase in prices and a contraction of profits. As a result of price rises, real wages will be reduced, or, alternatively, entrepreneurs will be unwilling to raise wages parallel to future increases of productivity for the sake of recuperating lost profits. Consequently, after the corresponding price rises and/or increases in labor productivity have taken place, a new equilibrium will be reached where most of the cost of social programs originally paid for by the entrepreneur is likely to have been shifted to the wage earners.

It should be emphasized that the new situation is not an exact replica of the old equilibrium, since the differential rates of price rises and productivity growth, the market power of producers and unions, and the losses suffered by fixed-income receivers together determine changes in relative prices and wages. Nevertheless, in an independent national economy, the initial increase in social charges can be deemed as having been determined by the preferences of the community; hence the final outcome can also be regarded as corresponding to the community's wishes. Thus, although under the assumption of downward rigidity of prices and wages social charges might not have been wholly shifted to wage earners, it cannot be claimed that the imposition of social charges distorted cost relationships in the new equilibrium.

On the other hand, arguing from the same presuppositions, objections can be raised against forcible harmonization in an integrated area. If we accept the premise that social charges imposed in the past have been absorbed in the cost structure of individual countries, the immediate effect of an equalization of social charges would be to disturb existing cost relationships and to put at a disadvantage the exports of those member countries in which the largest increase in social charges had taken place. It appears likely that the ensuing deterioration of the balance of payments in these countries could not be remedied without a probably painful deflationary process or a realignment of the exchange rates. It can be added that a harmonization of social charges would also run counter to the preferences of the various communities as expressed by the existing situation. If prevailing opinion in Belgium opposes the expansion of social security schemes, whereas in Italy these are regarded as desirable, harmonization will be uncalled for. An equalization at the average level would be resented by both the Belgians and the Italians; the adoption of Italian standards by other countries would be even less likely to be accepted in Belgium or Germany. Finally, we should also note that past increases in social charges and benefits often did not require any adjustment in wages, since—especially in the case of nonstatutory schemes—wage increases warranted by a rise in productivity might have taken the form of higher social benefits. Forcible harmonization, on the other hand, would not be accompanied by productivity changes.

TABLE 7

SOCIAL CHARGES IN SELECTED INDUSTRIES OF COMMON
MARKET COUNTRIES, 1955*

INDUSTRY	SOCIAL CHARGES AS PERCENTAGE OF LABOR COSTS IN		
	France	Germany	Italy
Cotton textiles............	31.1	24.6	43.7
Leather footwear.........	27.2	23.6	42.8
Radio electronics........	32.1	30.0	43.9
Machine tool.............	31.9	28.3	41.7
Shipbuilding.............	33.9	26.4	44.5
Coal mining.............	41.4	35.5	49.8

*SOURCE: *Labour Costs in European Industry*, pp. 28–41. Figures are based on a large sample of establishments in these industries.

We have discussed, so far, problems relating to social charges that affect all industries uniformly in each country. Similar conclusions hold for the case when unequal social charges are borne by different industries. It can easily be seen that, as long as social benefits financed by the contributions of entrepreneurs are shifted to the wage earners, no distinction is necessary between measures of general and special incidence. Within a single country, higher social charges in any one industry would not levy a special burden on this industry but would rather cause the composition of labor costs to differ. The same reasoning applies to intercountry differences in the social charges of various industries. For example, in Common Market countries for which information is available, substantial differences exist in regard to the interindustry pattern of social charges (see Table 7); yet the maintenance of these differences will not distort cost relationships to any significant degree, provided that the cost of special measures is ultimately borne by the workers of the industry in question. Thus, under the above assumptions, harmonization of special measures would also disturb existing cost relationships rather than remedy allegedly existing distortions.[22]

So far we have not considered the possibility of factor movements in the discussion of social charges and benefits. It is alleged by some authors that, as soon as we allow for factor mobility, the need for harmonization of social charges will also arise.[23] To evaluate this proposition, we shall first assume perfect mobility of capital and introduce the assumption of labor mobility at a later point.

Maurice Byé recommends the harmonization of social charges "if capital is mobile as between one country and another, and if general or limited measures impose on a country's industries, or on only some of them, a very different level of charges from that borne by all industries, or the competing industries in another country."[24] Harmonization is desirable under such conditions, according to Byé, since the country with higher social charges would tend to lose capital to the country with lower charges, and similar results would follow in the case of interindustry discrepancies.[25] Such a proposition is untenable, however. Capital movements respond to differences in labor costs per unit of output rather than to differences in social charges. If, in an industry, higher wages *plus* social charges are not compensated for by higher labor productivity, capital will move—and rightly so. Assuming that social measures introduced in the past have already been absorbed in the cost structure, differences in the level of social charges per se would have no effect on interindustry or intercountry capital movements. On the other hand, because of inflexibilities in the price and wage structure, perverse capital movements would be initiated if social charges were harmonized. Since prices in any one country could change but little in the face of competition on the markets of an economic union, increased social charges would cut into profits, thereby giving occasion to an undesirable movement of capital. It

<hr/>

[22] The reader is reminded here that these conclusions need qualification in case some of the social benefits do not affect the supply of labor. Safety equipment in coal mining is an example. These benefits cannot be shifted to the wage earner; hence some measure of harmonization appears necessary. Finally, if higher social charges on a particular industry in a member country have not yet been corrected by differential movements of wages (e.g., because of the heavy burden of these charges), one should argue for their removal instead of forcing other countries to adopt similar measures.

[23] See Note by Byé to *Ohlin Report*, pp. 119–39, and, by the same author, "Freer Trade and Social Welfare. Comments on Mr. Heilperin's Article," *International Labour Review*, January, 1958, pp. 38–47.

[24] Note to the *Ohlin Report*, p. 129.

[25] "Freer Trade and Social Welfare. Comments on Mr. Heilperin's Article," p. 44.

can be concluded, then, that if allowance is made for capital mobility, the arguments against the harmonization of social charges are strengthened rather than weakened.

Introducing the assumption of labor mobility, we inquire into the effects of differences in social charges and benefits on migration. If all social charges paid by the entrepreneur affect the labor supply in the same way as wages do, neither intercountry nor interindustry differences in social regulations can be held responsible for migration, but labor movements will follow disparities in wages *plus* social benefits. The need for harmonization, then, does not arise,[26] and, given downward wage rigidity, harmonization would actually bring about perverse labor movements.

These findings need qualification if only a part of social benefits affect the labor supply. We have argued above that family allowances belong to this category.[27] If there are considerable discrepancies in family-benefit schemes—as there actually are among the Common Market countries—undesirable labor movements may ensue: workers with large families will have incentive to move to countries that have a more generous family-allowance system (in the Common Market, France and Italy) and single workers will migrate to the other countries of the union (in this case, Germany, Belgium and the Netherlands). In addition, workers may migrate when the size of their family changes. Thus, although the scope of migration is likely to be limited in present-day integration projects,[28] the significant differences existing with respect to family-benefit schemes in, e.g., the Common Market warrant a reduction of disparities in this field. Yet, as we noted above, the harmonization of family- benefit systems will be restricted by reason of differences in social attitudes toward this question from country to country. In addition, the harmonization of family allowances, by itself, will create further distortions, which will necessitate compensating changes in some other items.

[26] For a different opinion, see Byé, *ibid.*, p. 44. Note also that high social charges would not lead to the outward movement of *both* labor and capital, as Byé contends. If higher social charges are imposed at any given moment of time in a country, capital will be exported and labor will migrate into the country, rather than moving out. Capital and labor will move together only if and when increased social charges depressed the rate of growth of national income.

[27] This is less true for pension plans and unemployment contributions. Although the workers do not receive these immediately or may never receive them, one can argue that the workers take them into account in evaluating their earnings. (A different view appears to be held in *Labour Costs in European Industry*, p. 3).

[28] Cf. pp. 90–92 above.

After having discussed various possible cases under differing assumptions in respect to commodity and factor movements, the conclusion can now be reached that, excepting the special cases mentioned above, the harmonization of entrepreneur-financed social programs is not necessary for the proper functioning of a union, and measures of harmonization, if undertaken, are likely to cause distortions in the pattern of production and trade and will give rise to undesirable factor movements, no matter whether the social charges are of general or special incidence.

Social Benefits Financed from General Taxes

We have examined the alleged need for the harmonization of social charges financed by entrepreneurs and concluded that such a harmonization was neither necessary nor desirable. In the present section some problems connected with the incidence of social benefits financed from general taxes are discussed. First, factor immobility will be assumed; later the mobility of capital and labor will be introduced. In both cases, distinction is made between measures of general and special incidence.

State-financed social benefits of general incidence affect the distribution of income in any one country. If we assume that the introduction of social programs necessitates raising direct or indirect taxes, this will be equivalent to a redistribution of income in favor of the workers. Under *ceteris paribus* assumptions, the integration of national economies with greatly differing degrees of tax-financed social benefits may then lead to inefficiencies in production and trade, by favoring labor-intensive industries in countries with high social benefits.[29] In addition, the high level of taxation to finance social benefits is likely to discourage savings and investment. In such a case the incidence of these taxes will be ultimately borne by the wage earners, since a retardation of the growth rate may result in "overcompensation"—in the sense that the increase in real wages will fall behind wage increases in other countries.

These considerations indicate the need for some degree of harmonization of state-financed social benefits in the case of large intra-

---

[29] The reason being that tax-financed social benefits can be regarded as a subsidy to labor costs. The argument does not hold, however, if the labor supply is perfectly inelastic or if workers do not regard social benefits as part of their earnings.

TABLE 8

FINANCING OF SOCIAL SECURITY IN THE COMMON MARKET COUNTRIES, 1954*

	CONTRIBUTIONS (IN PER CENT) FROM				CONTRIBUTIONS OF STATE AND OTHER PUBLIC AUTHORITIES AS PERCENTAGE OF NATIONAL INCOME
	Insured Persons	Employers	State and Other Public Authorities	Other	
Belgium.........	18.7	43.4	32.3	5.6	4.4
France..........	16.1	62.9	19.2	1.8	3.5
Germany........	21.8	39.5	32.7	6.0	7.0
Italy............	5.8	66.9	23.7	3.6	3.8
Luxemburg......	15.7	45.2	19.4	19.7	3.0
Netherlands......	17.4	49.1	27.2	6.3	4.2

*SOURCE: International Labour Office, *The Cost of Social Security, 1949–1954* (Geneva, 1958), pp. 161–78.

union differences in these schemes.[30] Such differences are of some importance in the European Common Market, for example (see Table 8). The discrepancies are even larger between the countries participating in the Free Trade Association of the "Outer Seven." While in Portugal only 17.6 per cent of social security receipts are financed by state and other public authorities and these receipts amount to 1.3 per cent of national income, the corresponding percentages are 59.6 and 6.7 for the United Kingdom and 79.7 and 9.3 for Sweden.[31] In the Latin American Free Trade Association, state participation in social security schemes is reported to be nonexistent in Argentina, relatively small in Peru, and significant in Brazil.[32]

We should also note that the economic arguments for harmonization can come into conflict with noneconomic considerations, such as the need for compliance with preferences of the community. The extension of social security schemes undertaken in Brazil may be considered excessive in Argentina. Or, similarly, in countries such as Sweden, where the state-financed part of social security is predominant, the public would be reluctant to accept a move toward equalization over a free-trade area. The need for harmonization becomes more pronounced, however, if special measures are applied to individual industries in various countries. The financing of social programs bene-

[30] This conclusion does not follow, however, if the redistributive effect of general social security measures is exactly counterbalanced by other measures affecting income distribution.

[31] *The Cost of Social Security, 1949–1954*, pp. 161–78.

[32] *Ibid.*, pp. 178–89.

fiting certain industries from general taxes (e.g., various forms of state assistance to miners) is equivalent to a subsidy, the distorting effect of which on resource allocation is only too well known. Thus it would be necessary to remove intra-union inequalities as regards tax-financed special measures in order to ensure the proper functioning of a union.

Introducing capital mobility into the picture, the arguments for the harmonization of tax-financed social measures are greatly strengthened. Under *ceteris paribus* assumptions, if countries on a similar level of economic development, but with differing state-financed social security schemes, participate in a common market, capital will tend to move from the country with the more inclusive social security system to countries where income-redistributional measures are applied to a lesser degree. On the other hand, if labor is also mobile, a movement in the opposite direction will take place. Similar consequences ensue if special measures are applied.

It can be concluded that, under the assumption of factor mobility, the harmonization of state-financed social security schemes appears necessary also in integration projects where, in the absence of factor mobility, noneconomic arguments against harmonization are given prominence. Nevertheless, the degree of harmonization is likely to remain limited also in this case, primarily because of the significant role played by national preferences in the determination of social policies. In addition, an equalization of tax-financed social charges in a union comprising advanced and underdeveloped economies would be detrimental to the interests of the latter, inasmuch as it would impede the flow of capital from developed to backward economies.[33]

Social Policy Problems in a Union

We have discussed, so far, various social problems related to the establishment of a union. Here we turn our attention to questions of social policy after the union has been established. In this connection, reference will be made to problems of social policy for the union as a whole and to problems connected with the coordination of the member countries' social policies.

It has already been noted that the harmonization of increases in real wages is unnecessary in a union, as long as wage increases follow

[33] On this point, see Bertil Ohlin, "Problèmes d'harmonisation et de coordination des politiques économiques et sociales," *Revue d'Economie Politique*, January–February, 1958, p. 288.

the rise in productivity. This rule applies not only to raising wages but also to improvements in social benefits financed by the enterprises, since the rise of real wages can take either form. Thus, in general, an increase in any element of the labor cost, if matched by a rise in productivity, will not create distortions either within the union or for the union as a whole.

Different considerations are relevant in regard to social benefits financed from general taxes. These measures have a bearing on income redistribution and should be discussed as such. Income redistribution may proceed by raising tax rates to provide more extensive social security coverage or by making the tax structure more progressive for the sake of reducing the tax burden of the lower-income classes. In the first case, a transfer takes place from high-income receivers to the lower-income groups; in the second, the burden of taxation is redistributed at the expense of those with higher incomes. Both forms of income redistribution have, by and large, identical effects.

Divergent measures of income redistribution undertaken by the members can influence production and trade patterns and differential rates of growth. As noted in connection with the disparities in state-financed social security schemes, any act of income redistribution would favor the labor-intensive industries of those countries where such measures have been applied, if the supply of labor showed some elasticity. Furthermore, in line with our previous reasoning, the redistribution of income is likely to have an adverse effect on savings and investment in the countries affected and to reduce the growth rate in these economies. The latter consideration applies especially to underdeveloped countries, where the detrimental effects of income redistribution are more pronounced, and may jeopardize much of future growth and the potential improvement of living standards.

Further effects of the application of disparate redistributional measures are observed in regard to factor movements. Under *ceteris paribus* assumptions, any action undertaken in order to reduce income inequalities in one of the participating countries would augment the exportation of capital to other member countries and reduce capital imports. Capital movements are likely to reinforce the adverse impact of these measures on savings and will contribute to a slowing-down of the process of growth. A lower growth rate would imply a restriction of the future improvement of living standards, and, ultimately, the initial measure of income redistribution could well harm, rather than benefit, the low-income classes. Finally, if labor is free to migrate, perverse labor movements may also result from an act of income redistribution. Initially, workers would migrate to areas where social benefits were higher, but a movement in the opposite direction would take place as and when the adverse effects of income redistribution on living standards were felt.

These arguments show the adverse effects of disparate measures of income redistribution undertaken within the union.[34] If the same measures are applied in unison, different consequences will follow. Some economists argue that an increase in the share of lower-income groups in the national income will ensure effective demand and accelerate growth.[35] The latter proposition appears to be based on false reasoning by equating the Keynesian stability problem with that of growth. Under certain conditions an increase in the workers' share may contribute to stability, but at the same time it is likely to reduce the rate of saving and thereby potential growth. On the other hand, the example of postwar Germany indicates that workers will ultimately benefit from a tax reform which is conducive to saving and investment.

At this point, we should also consider the impact of minimum-wage laws on the functioning of a union. This question has especial importance in Latin America, where wages often do not rise above the subsistence level. It is sometimes argued that the setting of minimum wages would contribute to economic development, since higher incomes would ensure demand for consumer goods.[36] This argument appears to be erroneous, however; *ceteris paribus,* an increase in the share of consumption will be accompanied by a reduction in the rate of investment, which is likely to endanger, rather than facilitate, economic development. The determination of minimum wages taking into account "the financial capacities of the employers" as proposed in Uruguay, Guatemala, and Colombia[37] is not advisable either, since it would introduce arbitrariness in wage fixing and would contribute to the malallocation of resources. In addition, minimum-wage legislation—if effective—may result in unemployment and the underutiliza-

---

[34] For a more detailed discussion of the effects of disparate tax measures on capital movements, see pp. 249–51 below.

[35] Cf., e.g., Hoffman, *op. cit.,* pp. 49–50.

[36] International Labour Office, *Minimum Wages in Latin America* (Geneva, 1954), p. 3.

[37] *Ibid.,* p. 18.

tion of existing resources by raising wages above the marginal productivity of labor at the full-employment level.

These considerations suggest that economic arguments are not sufficient to establish the need for the setting of minimum wages by state action in underdeveloped countries. Economic arguments, however, will often be overridden by social considerations. In the face of imperfect labor markets, minimum-wage legislation is considered desirable from the humanitarian point of view. Nevertheless, one should be aware of the possible economic costs of such a measure.

The economic effects of widely differing regulations on minimum wages in an integrated area are comparable to those due to disparate measures of income distribution. Countries with more advanced minimum-wage legislation may lose capital to other participating economies, and their labor-intensive industries will also suffer. In the Latin American Free Trade Association, for example, Mexico and Uruguay have a more comprehensive system of minimum-wage legislation than Argentina and Paraguay and have also succeeded in its more extensive application.[38] Under these conditions, a harmonization of minimum-wage regulations appears to be necessary to ensure the proper functioning of a free-trade area in Latin America.

Finally, we should note that some degree of coordination appears to be desirable in other fields of social policy, too. To begin with, the international discussion of social problems may be helpful for future social progress, and the experience of individual countries may stimulate action in various social fields in the other participating countries as well. The need for concerted action is of particular significance with regard to the introduction of special measures. State assistance provided to miners, for example, appears as a subsidy to the mining industry; thus its application in only one country may disturb the competitive-cost pattern. On the other hand, the country in question may successfully press for the employment of such a measure in the mining industries of the other participating countries. In addition, coordination is considered desirable in respect to the assistance given to unemployed workers in industries adversely affected by the establishment of the union, as well as in connection with the measures designed to facilitate labor migration. With regard to the latter, besides ensuring equal treatment to all workers irrespective of the country

[38] *Ibid.*, pp. 9 ff.

of origin, agreement should be reached on the migrating worker's rights to old-age pension, unemployment compensation, etc., in the country of immigration. Last but not least, coordination of social policies can be helpful in improving working conditions and ensuring the workers' social rights, especially in a union of underdeveloped countries.[39]

39 For a useful discussion of these problem, cf. Albert Delpérée, *Politique sociale et intégration économique* (Paris: Librairie Générale de Droit et de Jurisprudence, 1956), *passim.*

Chapter

11

FISCAL PROBLEMS
IN A UNION

L'armonizzazione tributaria . . . non è una finalità del mercato comune, ma è un mezzo da attuare solo nel caso in cui le divergenze della fiscalità sia di natura o dimensioni tali da determinare delle distorzioni econo- miche, che non possono venir evitate con altri mezzi.
—Cesare Cosciani, *Problemi fiscali del Mercato Comune*, p. vi

Budgetary Problems in a Common Market

The budgetary problems of an integrated area are largely dependent on the extent to which decision making is delegated to central (federal) agencies or to a federal government. The spectrum runs from a free-trade area with relatively few centrally solved fiscal problems to complete integration, where the importance of the federal budget overshadows that of the state budget. In this chapter we shall deal mainly with the case of a common market in which barriers to commodity and factor movements have been removed but the participating states have largely retained their fiscal sovereignty. Most of our conclusions will apply, however, to a customs union or free-trade area, too.

The history of intercountry budgetary relations dates back to the payment of war reparations and indemnities and, in general, to the problems of international transfers between independent states. Such relationships were of a temporary character and involved, in most instances, two countries only. The sharing of the costs of international agencies, on the other hand, assumes permanence in intercountry budgetary relations. The first agreement of this kind was reached with respect to the Universal Postal Union in 1874, when state contributions to the expenses of this institution were based on various criteria, such as area, population, and the volume of postal traffic. This same arrangement was used by the Permanent Court of Arbitration at

The Hague and by the League of Nations. The latter subsequently adopted the principle of the ability to pay, although—in the absence of national income data—it had to rely on crude indicators, such as government revenue and population. A reinterpretation of the "capacity to pay" formula led later to the establishment of progressivity in contributions to the administrative expenses of the United Nations and to the program costs of the United Nations Relief and Rehabilitation Administration.

No explicit principle was used in the allocation of Marshall Plan funds. Formally, Marshall aid to various Western European countries was made dependent on their balance-of-payments deficit, but, in effect, the governments controlled the size of this deficit to a great extent. Rules for state contributions had no time to evolve in the European Defense Community, and—despite ambitious plans—no agreed formula was developed for the sharing of defense expenditures in the North Atlantic Treaty Organization either.[1] Finally, in the European Coal and Steel Community the cost of administration, subsidies, and indemnities is covered by a 1 per cent tax on the value of production.

The past experience of intercountry budgetary relations gives some indication of the budgetary problems that arise in an integrated area. In examining the latter, we have to consider, on the one hand, the need to carry out certain tasks in common and, on the other, the ways of financing common expenditures and the sharing of the cost of coordinated plans. The common tasks referred to here include administration on the union level, aid to underdeveloped regions, resettlement of workers, assistance to firms adversely affected by the union's establishment, execution of jointly undertaken projects, and apportionment of military expenditures.

The cost of administration will remain relatively low as long as the functions appropriated by central agencies are limited. However, at higher stages of integration, the proper functioning of the union will require establishing an "international bureaucracy" to deal with the various economic, fiscal, monetary, and social problems that arise in the framework of a union. Federal agencies will also deal with the problem of promoting labor mobility and assisting underdeveloped regions.

[1] T. C. Schelling, *International Cost-Sharing Arrangements*, Essays in International Finance, No. 24 (Princeton: International Finance Section, Princeton University, 1955).

In Chapter 9, we argued for the coordination of regional development policies. Since the national economies in an integrated area cannot be considered as separate units, subsidies given to some regions will affect resource allocation and growth also in other member countries and regions. Furthermore, it is conceivable that the cost of these subsidies would exceed the financial means of one country. Such considerations have induced, for example, the signatories of the European Common Market to establish the European Investment Bank with responsibility to contribute to the development of backward regions.

Common financing also becomes necessary in order to cope with problems of a transitional nature. The freeing of trade barriers will adversely affect some firms and their employees in various industries. Assistance to the reconversion of these enterprises and to the retraining or resettlement of workers should be regarded as a joint responsibility of the participating countries and be managed on the union level. In the European Common Market, these tasks are entrusted to the European Investment Bank and the European Social Fund.

In regard to projects that, by size or nature, cannot be entirely financed by individual member states, the exploitation of nuclear energy comes first to mind. The development of atomic installations within the six countries participating in the European Common Market will proceed in the framework of the European Atomic Energy Community. Projects not related to atomic energy, but surpassing the financial means of individual countries, can be financed by the European Investment Bank. Canalization and some other investments in transportation come under this heading. Compared with Europe, common financing of investment projects is likely to assume greater importance in Latin America, where the financial means available to individual countries are very limited.

Finally, if defense is considered a common responsibility and military expenditures amount to a significant proportion of national income, there is need for an agreement on the size of military budgets in the countries participating in a union, although such an agreement does not necessarily imply the integration of national armies. From the economic point of view, the coordination of military budgets is desirable in order to avoid disparities in the burden of defense. Otherwise, countries with proportionately larger military budgets would be obliged to levy higher taxes, and factors of production might move from these states to other participating countries. These considerations are of little relevance in a Latin-American union, since in the latter countries military expenditures amount to an insignificant part of national income.

The cost of common or coordinated programs in an integrated area may be tax- and loan-financed. According to the principles of public finance, tax financing of current expenditures and loan financing of investments appear desirable.[2] Thus administrative expenses and military expenditures should be tax-financed, whereas assistance to underdeveloped regions and the cost of jointly undertaken investment projects would be financed by loan issues. Among the expenses attributable to difficulties of transition, assistance granted to enterprises is in the nature of an investment and should therefore be loan-financed. On the other hand, contributions to the retraining and resettlement of workers are more likely to be considered as current expense.

Starting out with the assumption that the current expenditures of the union are financed from the tax receipts of the participating states, the benefit principle and the principle of "ability to pay" can be considered as possible methods for the apportionment of these expenses. It is suggested here that the latter principle should serve as a basis for determining the contributions, since no reliable formula can be devised to measure the benefits enjoyed by the individual member states. On the other hand, the ability of the different countries to share this burden can be more precisely ascertained.[3]

Most of the recent proposals on the allocation of internationally borne current expenses rely on national income as an indicator of capacity to pay.[4] The contribution schemes also often include an element of progressivity implied by the capacity-to-pay formula. Progressivity can be introduced into the financial arrangements by taking

2 Cf. R. A. Musgrave, *The Theory of Public Finance* (New York: McGraw-Hill Book Co., Inc., 1959), chap. 23.

3 A combination of the benefit and the capacity-to-pay approaches has been advocated, however, in R. N. Bhargava, "The Theory of Federal Finance," *Economic Journal*, March, 1953, pp. 84–97.

4 Cf., e.g., C. S. Shoup, "Taxation Aspects of International Economic Integration," *Aspects financiers et fiscaux de l'intégration économique internationale*, Travaux de l'Institut International de Finances Publiques (The Hague: Editions W. P. van Stockum & Fils, 1954), pp. 107–8. "Potential" rather than actual national income is advocated to serve as a basis of the contributions in Gerhard Isenberg, "Regionale Wohlstandsunterschiede, Finanzausgleich und Raumordnuung," *Finanzarchiv*, Vol. XVII, No. 1 (1956), pp. 77–78. One may wonder, however, how potential national income (*Tragfähigkeit*) can be measured.

national income *less* an exemption designed to cover subsistence needs as the basis of the contributions or by devising a scale based on per capita incomes.

The use of national income as an indicator raises the problem of measurement. The same problem is encountered in the comparison of state budgets. The comparability of national accounts and budgets would require the application of uniform methods in national accounting and a uniform classification of receipts and expenditures.[5] Existing differences in statistical methods used by countries participating in present-day integration projects reduce the reliability of these comparisons. In addition, the comparability of national accounts and budgets suffers from the inappropriateness of exchange rates. In France, for example, two devaluations have taken place within a short time interval, and international comparisons had to be modified accordingly. The inadequacy of exchange rates for gauging the value of the currencies in many Latin-American countries is only too well known. Under these conditions an apportionment of country contributions will be inaccurate if national income figures are converted at the official rate of exchange. To avoid this inaccuracy, Henry Laufenburger proposed that a "money of account" be adopted for the purpose of valuing national incomes.[6] It is questionable, however, what such a "money of account" would be worth in the face of changing price levels and composition of income. More reliable results can be reached by using identical sets of price weights for comparing the national income data of different countries.[7]

Contributions based on national income figures are calculated under the implicit assumption that the shape of income distribution is identical within every country. In other words, by considering the country as a "tax-paying" unit, we abstract from differences in the distribution of incomes within countries. Yet, if we accept the proposition that contributions should be based on the personal capacity to pay, it can be argued that a country with a greater dispersion of incomes should be required to carry a larger proportion of the burden. These considerations point in the direction of a unified tax system, under which all persons pay the same kind of taxes no matter whether

5 For a detailed examination of this problem, cf. A. Daussin, "Les aspects budgétaires de l'intégration économique internationale," *Aspects financiers et fiscaux de l'intégration économique internationale*, pp. 57–88.

6 "Finances fédérales," *Economia Internazionale*, February–March, 1953, p. 241.

7 Cf. p. 38 above.

the receipts are used for the purposes of the individual states or of central agencies.[8] This solution would encounter great difficulties, however. In all present-day integration projects, significant differences exist as to the size of the budget relative to national income and the types of taxes employed. The unification of the tax systems is hindered not only by technical difficulties, psychological and sociological considerations, and differences in the requirements of the budget but also by the fact that the modifications in taxes necessary to establish uniformity would disturb existing cost relationships and the final effects of such a change could not be reliably estimated, since the incidence of taxes can hardly be ascertained. Thus, under present-day conditions, the uniformization of tax-systems does not provide a feasible solution. Instead, the sharing of the cost of common expenditures can be based on national income figures and progressivity can be introduced by the use of one of the above-mentioned methods. For the financing of these contributions, a portion of the state tax receipts may be set aside, or customs duties and excise duties may be assigned for this purpose.[9] Alternatively, the example of the European Coal and Steel Community may be followed in levying a tax on the value of production or on sales.[10] A uniform percentage tax, however, would have to be amended to ensure progressivity, and, in addition, administrative difficulties would arise in its implementation in the service industries and in small-scale manufacturing.

The investments undertaken jointly by the participating countries can be financed from the proceeds of bonds issued by the union or by an investment bank of the union and also from the proceeds of securities issued by the member states.[11] In the absence of an integrated capital market, the contributions of the participating countries could be based on the scale used in apportioning current expenses.

[8] Such a solution was proposed for the case of a federation in J. M. Buchanan, "Federalism and Fiscal Equity," *American Economic Review*, September, 1950, pp. 583–99.

[9] On the other hand, in a union of countries whose main source of revenue is customs duties, the common customs revenue is likely to be greater than the cost of common expenditures; hence the apportionment of this revenue will become the principal budgetary problem. These considerations have relevance for the West Indies customs union, for example. See H. G. Johnson, "Symposium on the Report of the Trade and Tariffs Commission (Croft Report), Comment," *Social and Economic Studies*, March, 1960, pp. 29–36.

[10] The need to give autonomous powers of taxation to the central authorities of the union is argued in Bruno Visentini, "Sui poteri iniziali da attrubuirsi alla Federazione Europea in materia tributaria," *Economia Internazionale*, February–March, 1953, pp. 286–90.

[11] In the case of the European Investment Bank, bonds issued by the Bank and state contributions are the sources of financing.

Nevertheless, the benefit principle may play a greater role here, especially in the case of regional development plans. Finally, as soon as capital movements are freed, the issuance of bonds by the union or by one of its institutions can replace state bond issues, and the source of financing becomes irrelevant.

We have considered the problem of financing common and coordinated projects of countries participating in the union. In this connection, reference has been made to intercountry differences in the proportion of state expenditures in national income. Considerable discrepancies exist, for example, with regard to the countries of the European Common Market (cf. Table 9). On the basis of these disparities, it is often argued that the burden of taxation differs greatly between states participating in present-day integration projects. Nev-

TABLE 9

TAX BURDEN IN THE COMMON MARKET COUNTRIES, 1955*

	Tax Receipts as Percentage of Gross National Product in 1955
Belgium	17.1
Italy	19.6
France	21.9
Netherlands	22.9
Luxemburg	23.6
Germany	26.6

*SOURCE: Institut "Finanzen und Steuern," *Europäische Wirtschaftsgemeinschaft und Steuerpolitik* (Bonn 1957), p. 14.

ertheless, it would be fallacious to maintain that, for example, the financial burden of the Belgian taxpayer is necessarily lower than that of the German taxpayer. In comparing fiscal "burdens," one should consider the uses to which tax receipts are put. For instance, tax receipts spent for productive purposes, such as the subsidization of a railway network, would necessitate a correction of the figures. Allowance should also be made for differences in the financing of social security schemes, since in some countries mainly general tax receipts, in others employer and employee contributions, are used for this purpose. Disparities in the proportion of taxes in national income might also be caused by divergences in social preferences with regard to collective consumption. If, in two countries of identical national income, the citizens of one country put higher values on collective goods, little can be said about differences in the burden of taxation.

Leaving aside the problem of tax burdens, more fruitful results are reached if we compare the taxes that are employed in different countries (see Table 10 for data on the Common Market countries). Intercountry differences in tax systems will affect cost relationships, factor movements, and growth within an integrated area. In the re-

TABLE 10

Percentage Composition of Tax Receipts in the Common Market Countries, 1955*

	Income and Property Taxes	Turnover Taxes	Consumption Taxes
Belgium	50.7	26.5	22.8
France	38.4	41.5	20.1
Germany	52.4	26.9	20.7
Italy	32.3	21.1	46.6
Luxemburg	66.4	15.4	18.2
Netherlands	60.0	20.1	19.9

*Source: *Europäische Wirtschaftsgemeinschaft und Steuerpolitik*, p. 16.

maining part of this chapter we shall discuss the economic effects of intra-union disparities in regard to direct and indirect taxes, while the consideration of the countercyclical effects of the budget is postponed to the next chapter.

The Harmonization of Production Taxes

Indirect taxes can take the form of production and consumption taxes. While production (turnover) taxes are usually levied on intermediate goods and on final products at every stage of manufacturing, consumption taxes (often called sales taxes) are customarily assessed on commodities sold by retail traders. Thus, in the absence of tax refunds, a production tax applies to exported products but not to imports, and consumption taxes are levied on imported goods but not on exports. Presently we shall examine problems related to intercountry differences in production taxes within a union, with distinction made between taxes of general and of special incidence (in the former case, uniform taxes are applied to every commodity; in the latter, tax rates differ as between commodities).

For the case when rates of a general production tax differ between the member countries of a union, the origin principle and the destination principle have been recommended as alternative solutions. According to the origin principle, all taxes are levied in the country of origin, whereas, if the destination principle is applied, commodities are charged—or exempted—with the amount of tax differential between the importing and the exporting country. In an excellent treatment of the problem, the *Tinbergen Report* argues that, in long-run static equilibrium, the application of either principle would lead to the same result, with only the exchange rates being different.[12] For example, assuming that the rate of exchange between country A and country B was 1:1 under a 4 per cent production tax in both countries, the same exchange rate would prevail if country A levied a tax of 4 per cent, country B a tax of 6 per cent, and corrective taxes and rebates were applied on traded commodities under the destination principle. On the other hand, the exchange rate would change to approximately 1:1.02 if the modification of tax rates were accompanied by the application of the origin principle, since the rates of exchange would adjust to the disparities in price levels.

The findings of the *Tinbergen Report* imply that intra-union differences in tax rates would be compensated for, no matter whether the origin or the destination principle was applied. The practical application of the proposed solutions is beset with difficulties, however. In evaluating the usefulness of each, our conclusions will depend on whether the value of production or value added at every stage of manufacturing is used as the tax base. In the case when the tax is calculated after the value of production, the following deficiencies associated with the employment of the origin principle can be observed:

a) A multistage production tax based on the value of production becomes a differentiated tax, even if applied at a uniform rate. If two countries levy a general turnover tax at different rates, industries whose products go through a large number of stages of transformation will be at a cost disadvantage in the country where the rate of tax is higher. Let us assume, for example, that country A levies a tax of 2 per cent, country B 5 per cent, and the amount of value added at the different stages is identical for both countries. In the example of Table 11, the price ratios for the two countries will be 106 in Industry I and 103 in Industry II, bestowing a differential advantage on Industry I in country A and Industry II in country B.

[12] *Rapport sur les problèmes posés par les taxes sur le chiffre d'affaires dans le marché commun*, Commission d'experts (Jan Tinbergen, president) de la Communauté Européenne du Charbon et de l'Acier (Luxemburg, 1953), p. 24. For an earlier formulalation, see A. Bartholoni, "Union économique et disparité des législations fiscales et sociales," *Revue d'Economie Politique*, November–December, 1951, pp. 946–56.

TABLE 11

A MULTISTAGE PRODUCTION TAX UNDER THE ORIGIN PRINCIPLE
(A Hypothetical Example)

	INDUSTRY I				INDUSTRY II			
	Country A		Country B		Country A		Country B	
Value of production at stage 1..	100		100		100		100	
Turnover tax...............	2	102	5	105	2	102	5	105
Value added at stage 2........	50		50					
Value of production at stage 2..	152		155					
Turnover tax...............	3.0	155.0	7.7	162.7				
Value added at stage 3........	45		45					
Value of production at stage 3..	200		207.7					
Turnover tax...............	6.0	206.0	10.4	218.1				

b) Competitive cost relationships are also affected by the amount of value added at various stages. In general, the greater the proportion of value added in the first stages, the larger will be the total amount of tax in the final price. Consequently, within a union, labor-intensive industries will be favored at the expense of material-intensive industries in a country with the higher rate of turnover tax.

c) Since under the origin principle the amount of production tax paid depends on the number of stages of production, vertically integrated firms will pay less taxes in the same industry and will therefore enjoy a cost advantage. This cost advantage is likely to encourage the integration of firms, which may not be considered desirable by reason of its effect on industrial concentration. In addition, the multistage production tax is also an obstacle to specialization if the latter involves an increased number of exchanges.

d) Differences in tax rates can give rise to perverse intra-union factor movements, too. Given the artificial cost advantages (disadvantages) that arise from the application of the origin principle, firms in individual industries may move, depending on which country is favored by the differences in taxes in a particular industry. Undesirable movements of loan capital might follow in a similar fashion.

e) Also, the application of the origin principle presupposes the validity of the purchasing-power parity theory. Yet, since capital movements, immigrants' remittances, tourist expenditures and other nontrade items also affect exchange rates, changes in tax rates will not lead to proportionate variations in the rate of exchange. In addition, price rises following an increase in tax rates are likely to elicit capital movements responding to differences in price levels. Further possible short-run repercussions include changes in production and consumption patterns resulting from price variations. Thus the presumed long-run readjustment of exchange rates may never take place.[13]

f) Finally, even if we disregard the qualifications mentioned under the last point, the problem remains that the application of the origin principle presupposes perfect flexibility of exchange rates. If this were not the case, a change in the tax rate would create surpluses and deficits in the balance of payments of particular countries. Nevertheless, it can be surmised that past changes in taxes have already been taken care of by movements of exchange rates; thus it would be erroneous to claim that, for example, French producers would be at a disadvantage in the Common Market because rates of production taxes are higher in France than in other participating countries.[14] On the other hand, this argument assumes importance in judging future changes in taxes *after* the union has been established.

These considerations imply that the long-run argument presented by various writers has only limited validity, and in cases when intercountry differences in the rate of turnover taxes are significant, the origin principle will create distortions in competitive cost relationships and may induce perverse factor movements. In order to avoid these distortions, some authors recommend the use of the destination principle instead.[15] If the destination principle is applied, exporters receive tax rebates for the tax "embodied" in the exported commodity, and the importing country levies the same taxes that would have been paid, had the commodity been produced in the country of destination. Alternatively, the tax assessed in the exporting country may be adjusted for intercountry differences in rates at the place of importation. Under such a system there is no need for the adjustment of exchange rates, and, theoretically, rebates and compensating taxes would remove the possibility of distortions in competitive cost relationships. This method, however, has some deficiencies of its own:

[13] See Cesare Cosciani, "Problèmes fiscaux de la communauté économique européenne," *Public Finance*, No. 3 (1958), pp. 202–5, and *Problemi fiscali del Mercato Comune* (Milan: A. Guiffrè, 1958), pp. 67–73.

[14] For a different opinion, cf. Cosciani, *Problemi fiscali del Mercato Comune*, pp. 60–62.

[15] Cf., e.g., H. K. Mangoldt-Reiboldt, *Währungpolitische Probleme der europäischen Wirtschaftsintegration* (Kiel: Kieler Vorträge, 1957), p. 42.

a) First of all, there is the difficulty of measurement. C. S. Shoup explains that "in real life, it may be extremely difficult to estimate closely how much of a general sales tax is embodied, so to speak, in any particular item of export, so complicated are the processes of manufacture and the channels of commerce. Indeed, absolute precision would require taking into account sales-tax collections going far back; exported textiles have been produced on taxed steel that was itself produced by taxed machinery, and so on."[16] The same difficulties will arise in estimating the tax to be levied in the importing country. Further complications are connected with the use of imported goods as inputs at various stages of manufacturing, since taxes levied on these products should also be taken into consideration in determining the "tax content" of the final price.

b) To avoid some of the difficulties of measurement, most European countries exempt the exported commodities of the tax levied at the last stage of production only, and the importing country, too, imposes the tax payable in the final stage. Such a method will do away with the difficulties involved in harking back in time in order to determine taxes paid on previous stages of production, but, at the same time, it gives rise to distortions by reason of its incompleteness. Since in the production of industrial commodities taxes paid at the previous stages of manufacturing are often considerably higher than taxes levied in the final stage, this simplification provides only a partial remedy in the correction of disparate tax burdens.

c) It has also been noted that the destination principle may enable individual states to practice discrimination through the application of dissimilar rules in the reimbursement of taxes to different export industries.[17] Some degree of coordination in the procedure of giving rebates and levying compensating taxes may be necessary on the union level to escape such hidden subsidies.

d) Last, but not least, the application of the destination principle requires the maintenance of the customs apparatus. In fact, the necessary administrative work will be even greater in calculating rebates and compensating taxes than in assessing tariffs. The inconvenience associated with this procedure may hinder the expansion of intra-union trade, the cost of administration will result in the loss of marginal transactions, and, finally, the maintenance of customs for-

---

16 Shoup, *op. cit.*, p. 94.
17 See G. Vedel, "Les aspects fiscaux du Marché Commun," *Bulletin for International Fiscal Documentation*, November–December, 1958, p. 1336.

malities implies that tariffs can be easily reinstated at any time. The latter possibility may have a psychological effect by casting doubts on the future availability of export markets.

In the foregoing discussion we have examined the workings of the origin and the destination principles in the case of a turnover tax levied on the value of production. Our results need modification if value added at every stage of manufacturing serves as tax base. Under the origin principle, as the value-added tax is not cumulative, it will be free from those deficiencies of the value-of-production tax that are due to verticality. On the other hand, the difficulties noted in connection with fixed exchange rates would persist, and disparate modifications of tax rates would bring about distortions in competitive cost relationships as well as perverse factor movements within an integrated area.

A value-added tax will also avoid the difficulties of measurement associated with the value-of-production tax under the destination principle. The amount of tax rebate and compensating tax can now be easily calculated from the value of production in the last stage. There are no complications in connection with imported materials and intermediate products either, since these bear the same taxes as if they were domestically produced. Nevertheless, the problem of administering rebates and compensating taxes remains, and the possible adverse effects of maintaining customs procedures will not subside.

At this point we should also consider the distortions due to differences in the tax base between countries participating in a union.[18] In case the origin principle is applied, verticality and the amount of value added at various stages of production will influence the results. *Ceteris paribus,* countries that use the value of production as the tax base will have an artificial disadvantage in the production of commodities where the number of stages is large, since cumulation increases the amount of tax contained in the final price. At the same time, producers of capital-intensive commodities will have a cost advantage, and manufacturers of labor-intensive commodities a disadvantage, in countries that apply a value-added tax, considering that a large proportion of value added in the last stage of production will increase the value-added tax to a greater extent than it raises the tax calculated on the value of production. Finally, under the destination principle, the difficulties of measurement would also be greater if both tax bases

---

[18] In the European Common Market, the tax base is value added in France and the value of production in the other participating countries.

were used in the member countries as compared with the case where
the same base was used in all countries. These arguments point to the
fact that the parallel use of the two tax bases in different countries
should not be maintained since this creates greater distortions than
the employment of either of the two tax bases in all countries.

We can conclude that a production tax assessed on value added
is superior to a tax levied on the value of production, no matter
whether the origin or the destination principle is applied. This su-
periority of the value-added tax is due to the lack of cumulation in
the tax: a value-added tax will not exhibit either the distortion in resource allocation or the difficulties of measurement that result from
cumulation. Thus it will be necessary for countries that apply a value-
of-production tax to change to a value-added tax. In the process of
transition, the authorities should endeavor to keep receipts from production taxes unchanged, in order to avoid changes in the general
price level. If the latter objective is, by and large, achieved,[19] relative
prices of commodities will change in every country, contributing to a
more efficient allocation of resources in the union through the removal of artificial cost advantages and disadvantages that originated in
differences in the tax systems.

In the author's opinion, after the transformation of the produc-
tion-tax systems into a value-added tax has taken place, the application of the origin principle offers advantages over the destination
principle, by reason of the possibility of disposing of all customs formalities in the former case. It should be emphasized that, under the
origin principle, future changes in tax rates rather than existing rates
need to be harmonized; an equalization of the rates of turnover taxes
would do more harm than good, since the ensuing changes in price
levels would disturb competitive cost relationships and create balance-
of-payments disequilibria. In addition, we should take cognizance of
the possibility that not only turnover taxes but also income taxes
enter the cost of production if the latter tax is partly shifted to the
buyer. These considerations, as well as the impact of taxation on factor movements, appear to be neglected by the advocates of the harmonization of taxes directly entering into the cost of production
only.[20]

19 Precise calculation is impossible, since this would require the estimation of taxes
embodied in every commodity.
20 Cf., e.g., J. Trempont, "Les finances publiques dans un marché commun," *Revue
de Science et de Législation Financières*, January–March, 1955, p. 115.

Having examined problems related to intra-union disparities of general taxes, we turn now to production taxes of special incidence. The latter may be positive or negative, depending on whether the tax constitutes an additional charge over and above the general production tax or an exemption from the general tax (in the latter case it can assume the form of an outright subsidy). Under the origin principle, such a tax clearly distorts competitive cost relationships, inasmuch as it confers a differential advantage or disadvantage on particular industries of a country. These disparities in taxes are not remedied by flexibility in the rates of exchange, since exchange rates reflect differences in the average level of taxes only. Similarly, a harmonization of taxes in *some* branches of production would distort the pattern of resource allocation through their differential effect.[21]

It has been said that the application of the destination principle will remedy the distortions in the allocation of resources caused by differential taxes of special incidence.[22] This, however, is only partially true. Producers enjoying lower than average tax rates will have no cost advantage within the union but will maintain this advantage over other producers of the union in trade with third countries. A better competitive position, on the other hand, will enable these producers to reap economies of scale and to devise and use more advanced technological methods. Consequently, differential tax treatment would ultimately affect the competitive position of various industries in intra-union relationships as well.

These results indicate that, while the equalization of rates of a general production tax would have detrimental rather than beneficial effects, taxes of special incidence should be equalized in order to avoid the distortion of cost relationships and to ensure the efficient allocation of resources within a union. The harmonization of these taxes appears to be desirable, no matter whether the origin principle or the destination principle is applied.

Problems of Consumption Taxes in a Union

A consumption tax involves the application of the destination principle, since it is levied at the retail-trade stage. In fact, if we abstract from trade markups, a general consumption tax is equivalent

---

[21] The classical statement of problems involved in the harmonization of taxes for the case of sectoral integration was given in the *Tinbergen Report* (p. 37).

[22] *Ibid.*, p. 33.

to a general production tax levied in the last stage of production under the destination principle. Consequently, the arguments discussed with regard to such a production tax are also applicable here.

In present-day economies, a number of commodity groups bear unequal rates of consumption taxes. These excise taxes are levied, for example, on alcoholic beverages, tobacco, sugar, gasoline, luxury goods, etc. Differing rates of excise taxes between countries participating in a union will have various undesirable consequences: efficiency in exchange will be impaired, the existing customs machinery must be maintained, and there will be a danger of tax evasion.

One of the conditions of efficiency is the equality of the marginal rates of substitution between any two commodities for every consumer. The fulfillment of this condition requires identical relative consumer prices in every country, while disparities in relative prices are equivalent to price discrimination. Efficiency considerations, however, may be overruled for various reasons. First, certain commodities are regarded as luxury goods in one country and as necessities in another. In France, for example, wine is an object of everyday consumption, whereas it is more or less a luxury in the Netherlands. Second, there may be differences in national policy. One country may endeavor to cut down on the consumption of alcoholic beverages, another may apply a similar policy with regard to tobacco. Third, since excise taxes are levied, for the most part, for revenue purposes, differences in tastes will be conducive to the maintenance of inequalities in tax rates. Differences in excise taxes may become a means of disguised protection, however. If imported goods (e.g., tropical fruits) are heavily taxed and commodities that are mostly home-produced bear only a light tax, consumption is artificially channeled to home-produced goods, and the allocation of resources will be adversely affected.

In order to avoid possible tax evasion, border formalities would have to be maintained. Yet evasion may be attempted even if the customs machinery is preserved, although the possibilities of evasion will be greatly reduced in the presence of border formalities. Tax evasion may be practiced by the consumer and by the seller as well.[23] The consumer will attempt to evade taxes by buying the commodity in question in a state with a lower tax rate and sending it home, taking it

---

[23] On the possibilities of tax evasion, see Shoup, *op. cit.*, pp. 96–98, and C. T. Stewart, "Migration Effects of Sales Tax Disparity," *Southern Economic Journal*, April, 1959, pp. 434–46.

home with him, or ordering it at a mail-order house of another state. The attractiveness of committing this type of fraud depends on distance, the unit value of the items bought, and differences in tax rates. Alternatively, the consumer may claim exemption from the excise tax in a member country, have the purchase sent to his home country, and attempt to avoid paying the tax in the latter. In this case, not differences in tax rates but the absolute rate of the excise tax in the home country motivates the consumer. Evasion can also be practiced by wholesalers or retailers in the event of resale or if exemption can be claimed from the excise tax in case of foreign sales. In the former instance, differences in tax rates, in the latter, the absolute level of the excise tax gives inducement to fraud.

Shoup discusses the American evidence with respect to excise tax evasion. His findings imply that tax evasion is not likely to be practiced on a large scale in the United States. He also notes that the enactment of so-called tax comity laws, according to which states have the privilege of engaging in tax suits in the courts of other states, will be desirable in a union in order to eliminate certain sources of tax evasion.[24]

American experience suggests the possibility of maintaining differing rates of excise taxes in a union, although this is directly relevant only if rates and differences in rates are small, which is often not the case in present-day integration projects. In this context, we should note that in the German Zollverein at first compensating taxes had been levied at the former customs frontiers, but later the deficiencies of this method induced the authorities to unify the excises.[25] In the Benelux union, the rates of excise taxes have been equalized for most commodities, but equalization has not yet been achieved for alcohol, beer, sugar, and gasoline.[26]

It can be concluded that if excises are levied at the retail level and domestic authorities are effective in enforcing the assessment of excise taxes on all domestically sold commodities, the possibilities of tax evasion will be considerably reduced. Nevertheless, this will not prevent smuggling and tax evasion by consumers. The latter will depend primarily on differences in tax rates and on the cost of trans-

---

[24] Shoup, *op. cit.*, p. 113.

[25] G. Schmölders, "Der deutsche Zollverein als historisches Vorbild einer wirtschaftlichen Integration in Europa," *Aspects financiers et fiscaux de l'intégration économique internationale*, p. 143.

[26] J. Polak, "Aspects budgétaires et fiscaux de Benelux," *ibid.*, p. 163.

porting the commodities. In the European Common Market, for example, where distances are short, tax evasion is likely to be practiced especially in the case of tobacco and liquor. The appropriate remedy would be a reduction in rate differentials aiming at the uniformization of excises at some future date. The problem is less acute in Latin America, where high transportation costs give natural protection.

The Treatment of Direct Taxes

We have pointed out in the previous chapter that social benefits financed from general taxes and a progressive income tax can be regarded as different forms of income redistribution. For the low-income classes, both high social benefits and a low tax burden under a progressive tax will have, by and large, the same significance; and the high-income classes may also be indifferent as to the form of income redistribution, although they may resent the redistribution of incomes as such.

It should be emphasized here that high direct taxes and a high degree of income redistribution are by no means identical. The proportion of direct to indirect taxes will not indicate progressivity, since not the form of taxes but their incidence is relevant. A tax system based largely on excises, for example, might be more progressive than another relying on a proportional income tax. In its final incidence, every tax encroaches upon private consumption and investment, but it is often difficult to determine who bears the burden of the tax. Furthermore, one should take into account who benefits from the tax proceeds. Some of the uses of these proceeds, such as roads, waterworks, etc., are productive investments and will contribute to an increase in national income; others (e.g., administrative and defense expenditures) benefit the whole community; finally, the provision of social benefits, unemployment compensation, or low-rent housing are redistributional measures. In general, the net effect of taxes and the uses to which tax receipts are put determines to what extent a government budget alters the distribution of income.

In the previous chapter we examined the impact of income redistribution on production and trade patterns, factor movements, and growth. In the first place, disparate redistributional measures within a union would favor the labor-intensive industries in countries that have gone further in the redistribution of income and would bestow a differential advantage upon capital-intensive industries in countries with less far-reaching redistribution, provided that factor supplies are not perfectly inelastic. Also, income redistribution may adversely influence savings and investment and can thereby depress the rate of growth. Finally, income redistributional measures can have a considerable effect on factor movements. Their impact will be felt primarily on the international flow of capital and to a lesser extent on labor migration; whereas redistributional measures are likely to induce the movement of capital to countries with lower taxes through a reduction in the net return on capital, psychological and sociological obstacles will hinder labor migration. In the following, some further observations will be offered on capital movements that find their origin in intra-union disparities of regulations on direct taxes.

With regard to the international flow of capital, distinction should be made between loan capital and equity capital. Redistributional measures will have no direct effect on international lending if the owner of the capital does not migrate. High income taxes in the home country may be evaded, however, if the lender migrates with his capital, too. Finally, other things being equal, the increased demand for investment funds in the country with a lesser degree of income redistribution is likely to attract loan capital through higher long-term interest rates.

The flow of equity capital will respond to differences in the rates of corporate taxes levied on home and on foreign income, to the treatment of retained earnings, and to provisions for accelerated depreciation and the carry-over of losses. To begin with, the movement of equity capital is restricted, and perverse capital movements are often generated by intercountry differences in regulations on taxing the domestic income of foreign corporations and the foreign income of domestic corporations. Additional difficulties arise in connection with the tax treatment accorded to the subsidiaries of foreign companies. In present-day integration projects, legislation concerning these matters shows considerable disparities, and the existence of bilateral agreements on double taxation have not helped to achieve uniformity.

Aside from the problem of taxing the foreign income of corporations, disparities in regard to tax rates on corporate profits will affect the location (and relocation) of firms in the framework of a union. Other things being equal, participating countries with higher tax rates on corporate profits will lose equity capital to member states whose tax rates are lower. The experience of the Benelux union and the United States will be instructive in this regard. It has been noted that the establishment of the customs union between the Benelux states led to the movement of capital from the Netherlands to Belgium in response to differences in tax rates.[27] In the United States, too, it is observed that states compete with each other for capital through tax reductions and exemptions. Similar consequences may follow in the absence of harmonization with respect to corporate taxes in the Common Market, where tax rates on undistributed profits range from 32 per cent (Belgium) to 50 per cent (France), while on distributed profits the limits are approximately 23 per cent (Belgium and West Germany) and 50 per cent (France).

Differences in tax rates on undistributed and distributed profits also give some indication of the tax incentive to reinvest earnings. In countries like France, Italy, and the Netherlands, where tax rates on corporate profits are identical irrespective of whether profits are reinvested or paid out in dividends, there is a powerful inducement to retain earnings, since the stockholders bear a double tax on the amount actually distributed. On the other hand, lower rates on distributed profits in Belgium and West Germany would appear to have a disincentive effect on the reinvestment of profits under *ceteris paribus* assumptions. Other things are not equal, however, and provisions for accelerated depreciation encourage new investment in Germany as compared with some other members of the Common Market. At the same time, losses cannot be carried forward in Italy, while the period of carry-over is five years in most other countries.[28]

These considerations indicate the need for harmonization of tax regulations on corporate profits in an integrated area. This conclusion is further strengthened if problems related to the importation of capital from outside the union are considered. The inflow of capital will respond to differences in yields and risk; thus disparities in tax rates, depreciation allowances, etc., can exert considerable influence on its movement. Some observers expressed the opinion that, in the European Common Market, the differential effects of the inflow of funds from third countries in response to arbitrary differences in tax laws

27 Mangoldt-Reiboldt, *op. cit.*, p. 48.
28 Information on tax rates, carry-over of losses, etc., is taken from E. B. Nortcliffe, *Common Market Fiscal Systems* (London: Sweet & Maxwell, 1960), and refers to 1959.

might overshadow the possible harmful consequences of tax differences on the intra-union flow of capital funds.[29]

Having surveyed the problems related to direct and indirect taxation, the conclusion can now be reached that differing harmonization measures should be applied to various kinds of taxes in an integrated area. It is neither necessary nor desirable to equalize the rates of a production tax of general incidence, although harmonization is necessary with regard to taxes of special incidence. Also, all countries participating in a union should use value added as the tax base for production taxes. Some reduction in differences between excise tax rates will be desirable, too. In addition, the existing discrepancies in redistributional measures will need to be reduced even in the absence of the free movement of factors, and the need for harmonization increases as the liberalization of factor movements proceeds.

The possibility of perverse movements of equity capital necessitates the reduction of disparities in tax regulations on corporate profits. Yet disparities in direct taxation cannot be fully removed without a complete overhaul of the tax systems, since an equalization of direct taxes would disturb existing cost relationships, inasmuch as budget requirements call for a reduction of rates of turnover taxes in countries with low direct taxes and vice-versa. Consequently, the measures to be applied could not be prescribed for economic integration *in general* but should be specifically designed for every integration project. This requires a coordinated effort on the part of the participating countries in removing inefficiencies of resource allocation and in avoiding undesirable factor movements through carefully planned adjustments in the tax systems and coordination of all future changes in tax rates.

[29] Cf., e.g., L. Reboud, "Influence des fiscalités sur les mouvements de capitaux dans le cadre du Marché Commun," *Revue de Science Financière*, April–June, 1960, pp. 314–40.

Chapter 12

MONETARY UNIFICATION

AND THE BALANCE

OF PAYMENTS

Le Banche centrali della Comunità Economica Europea devono applicare una *strategia* comune, ma questo non significa necessariamente una *tattica* comune.

—M. W. Holtrop in *Bancaria*, 1958/1

Regional Analysis of Monetary Problems

Balance-of-payments problems of regions have often been compared with adjustments in the balance of payments of countries under the gold standard. This comparison is at the same time illuminating and misleading. It is illuminating because it focuses attention on certain similarities in the problems faced by a regional and a national banking system in case of a gain or loss of reserves; it is misleading because it tends to neglect differences in the adjustment process under the gold standard and in interregional relations.

A region's balance of payments is largely determined by commercial and financial flows of funds and by Treasury flows. The former include payments and receipts in financing interregional trade, regional payments to and from the central bank, and interregional movements of capital funds;[1] the latter comprise the purchase and sale of government securities, taxes and government expenditures, and government assistance. If a region's balance of payments deteriorates, commercial banks within the area will lose reserves and deposits in the same amount; conversely, an improvement in the balance of trade gives rise to a favorable clearing balance for the area's banks. Under a fractional reserve system, losses or gains of reserves result in multiple changes in deposits, depending on the reserve ratios of the commercial banks. Nevertheless, a reserve loss (gain) will have

[1] For a detailed classification, cf. R. E. Emmer, "Influences on Regional Credit Expansion," Regional Science Association, *Papers and Proceedings*, Vol. III (1957), pp. 166–79. Note that branch banking is not considered at this stage of the argument.

less leverage effect on the money supply in interregional relations than under the gold standard; in the latter case an outflow (inflow) of gold will be followed by a multiple change in the reserves of the central bank, which, in turn, has a magnified impact on the reserves of commercial banks.[2]

The classical interpretation of the gold standard postulated that balance-of-payments disequilibria would be cured through changes in price levels consequent upon an inflow or outflow of gold. Keynesian and post-Keynesian writers, on the other hand, have maintained that income changes are the main equilibrating variables under the gold standard. Given the assumed international immobility of factors, not much reliance has been placed on capital and labor movements as equilibrating variables.[3] The order of importance of the equilibrating factors appears to be different in the interregional adjustment process. In this connection, distinction should be made between temporary and persistent imbalances.

In contradistinction to the assumed workings of the gold standard, movements of short-term funds will correct transitional balance-of-payments disequilibria in interregional relations. Since regional banks possess easily marketable financial claims (e.g., government securities), a multiple contraction of the money supply following adverse clearings in the banks of the deficit area can be avoided. Instead of letting a reserve loss act on the money supply, banks will replenish their reserves through sales of short-term securities. On the other hand, in the surplus regions, banks possess excess reserves and will be willing to purchase the short-term papers offered.

The interregional flow of short-term capital can be relied upon to correct temporary disequilibria. However, if the drain on the reserves of an area's banks persists, it cannot be met by the sale of short-term securities alone. In the face of unfavorable expectations, the banks of the deficit region will curtail their loans to business enterprises, or, alternatively, they may not possess marketable securities in sufficient quantities to meet a persistent drain on reserves. At the same time, banks in a surplus area will use part of their excess reserves for

[2] This conclusion follows if the participants adhere to the "rules of the game," i.e., an increase (decrease) in gold reserves is accompanied by a purchase (sale) of securities by the central bank. The influence of gold movements on the domestic credit base is then magnified in accordance with the central bank's reserve ratio. Cf. Ragnar Nurkse, *International Currency Experience* (Geneva: League of Nations, 1944), pp. 66–67.

[3] See, however, J. H. Williams, *Postwar Monetary Plans* (New York: A. A. Knopf, 1947), chap. 13.

financing business expansion, in order to re-establish the desired composition of their portfolio. Movements of short-term funds, then, will not provide a remedy in the case of continuing disequilibria, although they can possibly be effective even if fluctuations are of large amplitude.

The question arises: If short-term capital movements take care of temporary disturbances only, what are the possible remedies of long-term disequilibria? Under the gold standard, price and income effects were supposed to restore balance-of-payments equilibrium. Income effects make their appearance also in interregional relations. If the balance-of-payments deficit of a region results from a decrease in exports (or an increase in imports at the expense of the consumption of home-produced goods), the foreign-trade multiplier will come into action: a fall in income leads to reduced imports. At the same time, the concomitant rise in incomes in the surplus regions will tend to increase imports, thereby assisting the regions with an adverse balance of payments. Under customarily made assumptions, however, income changes are not sufficient to restore balance-of-payments equilibrium; and, considering the downward rigidity of prices and wages, it is not likely that price changes would perform this task either.[4] There is need, therefore, for further equilibrating variables. Government transfers are often mentioned in this connection.

Data on the flow of funds in the United States show that during the past few decades Treasury flows, by and large, matched transit clearings. It would be misleading, however, to conclude from this evidence that government transfers necessarily acted as an equilibrating factor.[5] To begin with, the previously mentioned sale and purchase of government securities designed to remedy transitional imbalances take place at the volition of the commercial banks, and the Treasury supplies only the media for the transfers. We should consider, therefore, only those Treasury flows that find their origin in actions undertaken by the federal government. These include taxes, transfer payments, and government expenditures.

Federal taxes and transfers may have an equilibrating, as well

[4] This conclusion will need modification, however, if we take into account increases in productivity (see p. 267 below).

[5] The equilibrating role of government transfers in the regional balance of payments is stressed in P. C. Hartland, "Interregional Payments Compared with International Payments," *Quarterly Journal of Economics*, August, 1949, pp. 392–407. See also Comment by Rendings Fels and Reply by P. C. Hartland, *ibid.*, August, 1950, pp. 488–90.

as a disequilibrating, effect on the regional balance of payments. Income taxes and unemployment compensation, for example, can act as built-in stabilizers. If a region's deficit originated in a fall of exports, a reduction in federal taxes and an increase in unemployment benefits will assist the region. Nevertheless, these so-called automatic stabilizers would have a disequilibrating effect if the import surplus of a region found its origin in a rise in incomes. In the latter case, higher tax payments would further contribute to the balance-of-payments deficit of a thriving region.

As an example of expenditure policy contributing to interregional balance-of-payments equilibrium, government assistance to United States agriculture in the 1930's is frequently mentioned. This policy is responsible for dissimilar developments in American and in foreign agriculture during that period. Whereas the Latin American and other agricultural countries suffered large balance-of-payments deficits and were ultimately compelled to devalue their currency, the deficits of agricultural regions in the United States were to a great extent met by Treasury transfers. During and immediately after the Second World War, government expenditure policy was of importance for balance-of-payments equilibrium also in the South. In several instances, however, government expenditures have increased, rather than reduced, imbalances in regional payments. Expenditures on military equipment in surplus regions can be mentioned as an example. In such instances, private transfers have to remedy the imbalances caused by the flow of government funds.[6]

In the case of persistent disequilibria in the regional balance of payments, long-run capital movements may provide a remedy. To begin with, under Keynesian assumptions, an income and employment equilibrium can exist in an open economy without equilibrium in the balance of payments. In other words, an import surplus can be maintained if an excess of imports over exports is matched by an excess of domestic investment over domestic savings, with corresponding differences of opposite sign elsewhere. Thus disequilibria in the re-

---

[6] We have attempted to show that the equilibrating effects of government transfers cannot be taken for granted. Some observers go even further and argue that Treasury transfers *are* disequilibrating, while commercial and financial transfers appear as the equilibrating factors in interregional balance-of-payments adjustments. See the comments of Hobart Carr in *Record of the Federal Reserve System Conference on the Interregional Flow of Funds* (Washington, 1955), cited by J. C. Ingram in his Reply to R. L. Pfister's Comment on Ingram's "State and Regional Payments Mechanisms," *Quarterly Journal of Economics,* November, 1960, pp. 651–52.

gional balance of payments can be corrected by a geographical redistribution of savings through the capital market. If the balance-of-payments deficit of a region originates from economic expansion, higher yields will be obtained in this region than elsewhere, and, in an integrated capital market, differences in yields will give inducement to capital movements.[7] The westward movement of the economic frontier in the United States provides an example of this interregional flow of capital funds. The equilibrating movement of funds may take the form of migration of equity capital, direct lending, and floating of new securities in other regions, either by private or by state action.

Long-term capital movements can play an important part in curing imbalances in the regional balance of payments; yet they are not likely to restore equilibrium in chronically depressed regions. If an enduring decline in exports reduces incomes in a region, capital imports into the region cannot be expected to remedy the situation, and capital is more likely to move out. In such a case, labor migration may act as an equilibrating factor. One should not forget, however, that the equilibration of the balance of payments of a depressed region through labor movements does not exclude the desirability of government measures for assisting regional development.

Up to this point we have not considered the possibility of branch banking on a national scale. It can be easily seen that under a branch-banking system both short-term and long-term funds possess high mobility. Nevertheless, the mobility of funds does not mean that national banks will pump funds into declining regions. In a chronically depressed region, the loss of reserves will be accompanied by a withdrawal of loans rather than a replenishment of reserves. A branch-banking system may take care of fluctuations of greater amplitude than possible in a unit-bank system but will provide no remedy for structural disequilibria.

The conclusion can now be reached that, in spite of the formal similarity between regional balance-of-payments problems and the gold standard, dissimilarities in the mechanism of adjustment should warn us not to equate the two. Whereas, under the gold standard, price and income effects were said to act as equilibrating variables,

---

[7] The balancing role of long-term capital movements is emphasized in Tibor Scitovsky, *Economic Theory and Western European Integration* (Stanford: Stanford University Press, 1958), pp. 85–91.

factor movements play a salient role in remedying disequilibria in interregional relations. In the latter case, the movements of short-term funds can be relied upon to even out short-run fluctuations, while long-term capital movements and labor movements will assume importance in the event of persistent imbalances. Another distinguishing characteristic of the interregional adjustment process is that here government transfers are also operative.

Balance of Payments in a Union

In the foregoing analysis of interregional payments, the maintenance of balance-of-payments equilibrium among the regions of a national economy was regarded as the main objective. By concentrating on interregional relationships, we neglected trade relations with the outside world. On the other hand, in an open economy it is not necessary that the balance of payments of each particular region with the other regions should be equilibrated, provided that the region's balance of payments with other regions *and* foreign countries is in equilibrium. If the latter condition is fulfilled for every region, balance-of-payments equilibrium will be attained also for the national economy as a whole. In discussing balance-of-payments problems in an economic union, we again start out with the assumption of a "closed union" (a union with an insignificant amount of foreign trade) and will later proceed to the examination of problems in an open union. Differences between a closed union and an interregional payments system are observed with regard to the currency system, rules on reserve requirements, and monetary and fiscal policy.

The existence of a common currency in a national economy means that payments can be made in other regions directly with the money used in the debtor region. However, if the member countries of a union are committed to maintain the existing exchange rates in the future and are enjoined from imposing payments restrictions in intra-union relations, the difference between payment in a common currency and in freely convertible member-country currencies becomes largely a matter of convenience. Frenchmen will pay in French francs through their banks, no matter whether payment is to be made in Brittany or in the Netherlands, although in the latter case francs will be exchanged for guilders in the course of the banking operation. The argument needs little modification if the exchange rates are allowed to fluctuate within narrow limits, since the differences between expected and actual earnings will hardly surpass fluctuations in earnings due to normally observed price changes in the market.[8]

Different is the situation with regard to the leverage effect of changes in reserves. Whereas in interregional relations the creation and destruction of demand deposits is likely to follow a uniform pattern, the leverage effect within a union may vary from country to country. To begin with, while regulations on reserve requirements are likely to be identical within a country, these can differ greatly between countries.[9] In addition, central banks may bring about larger changes in the domestic money supply than what follows in the case of interregional movements of reserves, or, alternatively, they may not let fluctuations in foreign-exchange reserves act on the supply of money.

It requires little explanation that, while the decision-making units are the individual governments in an economic union, a single decision-making authority prevails within a national economy. The practical consequences of this situation depend on the degree of co-ordination of monetary and fiscal policies in a union and will be discussed at a later point. Here it is sufficient to note that homogeneous economic policies in one country do not imply that these policies affect every region in the same way.

In the opinion of the present writer, despite these differences in interregional and intra-union relations, basically the same solution applies to equilibrating the balance of payments within the area in both cases. This can be seen if we consider the role of capital movements in the adjustment process.

The reader will recall that in interregional relations the movements of short-term securities appeared as the main equilibrating factor in the case of temporary imbalances. Within a national economy, the multiple creation and destruction of deposits can be avoided through the purchase and sale of secondary reserves. Also in a union, there will be little need for the application of restrictive measures to correct temporary disequilibria in the balance of payments if there exist marketable financial claims that can be used to avoid fluctuations in foreign-exchange reserves. These short-term funds may be held by

---

[8] The possibility of introducing flexible exchange rates will be discussed in the next section.

[9] Actually, in the United States, reserve requirements are not uniform. Nevertheless, these differ according to the classification of cities rather than on the basis of geographical location.

the central banks, by commercial banks, or by financial interme-
diaries, provided that an institutional framework is created that makes
both possible and desirable the holding of foreign short-term securities. In order to achieve this purpose, various measures need to be
applied. First, restrictions on capital movements should be removed,
and the governments ought to commit themselves to maintain existing exchange rates and to refrain from reimposing controls on capital
movements; second, eligibility requirements need to be modified to
include holding of securities issued in other member countries; and,
third, facilities need to be provided for the exchange of these securities, quality standards should be established for differing types of
securities, and legal agreements should be reached for the event of
default.[10]

The described method provides for the transformation of "national" securities into "generalized" claims and is equivalent to an
increase in intra-union liquidity in the sense that the stock of short-
term securities held by financial institutions becomes a means for
settling a balance-of-payments deficit. If foreign securities are held
mostly or exclusively by the central banks, the operation of this system resembles an exchange equalization fund—a method often recommended for curing temporary disequilibria in an economic union.
There is no reason, however, why the holding of foreign securities
should be restricted to central banks. In a developed money market,
commercial banks will also engage in such operations. The financial
centers of industrialized nations will fulfill this task even better than
regional centers. One can agree with Franz Gehrels that, given the
highly developed markets of financial centers, an inflow of funds from
Paris to Frankfurt might be easier to bring about than one from San
Francisco to Kansas City.[11]

For reasons discussed in connection with interregional monetary
problems, short-term capital movements can provide a remedy only
for temporary disequilibria. If imbalances persist, movements of long-
term funds will become necessary. As we have noted before, imports
can continue to exceed exports, provided that foreign savings flow
into the country with a trade deficit. In the event of free capital move-

[10] Cf. J. C. Ingram, "State and Regional Payments Mechanisms," *Quarterly Journal
of Economics,* November, 1959, p. 630.
[11] "Monetary Systems for the Common Market," *Journal of Finance,* May, 1959, p.
313.

ments, the flow of long-term funds will play the same role in a union as in interregional relations. Nevertheless, private capital movements will not solve the problems of depressed areas in either case. Here a coordination of regional policies can provide a remedy, as suggested in Chapter 9.

The coordination of regional policies leads us to the problem: What degree of cooperation in monetary policies is necessary for the satisfactory operation of the adjustment process? J. E. Meade, among others, believes that there is need for setting up a supra-national authority to ensure a uniform central-bank and budgetary policy if we want "to make it as easy for a Frenchman to pay a German as it is for a Welshman to pay an Englishman."[12] On the other hand, Ingram argues that the removal of restrictions on capital flows and the integration of the capital markets will be sufficient to enable capital movements to fulfill their equilibrating role.[13] In commenting on this issue, we should note that even the existence of a single policy-making authority does not always imply identical results in all regions. The example of the United States may be suggestive in this connection.

It has been too often assumed that a restrictive policy initiated by the Federal Reserve Board will affect all regions in the same way. Actually, this is not entirely true, not only in regard to margin requirements for security holdings, which exert influence chiefly on the New York district, but also with respect to other weapons of monetary policy. Open-market operations carried out in the New York money market are rather slow in reaching faraway regions, and their effect may well be neutralized by other money flows, as the experience of certain districts indicated during the period of monetary restraint in 1953. Changes in reserve requirements have also been shown to have dissimilar effects in various regions.[14] Finally, small differences in the discount rates between Federal Reserve districts, too, are frequently observed.

The experience of the United States indicates that a uniform monetary policy may have differential effects in various regions and

12 "The Balance-of-Payments Problems of a European Free Trade Area," *Economic Journal*, September, 1957, p. 631.
13 Ingram, *op. cit.*, p. 631.
14 Cf. N. N. Bowsher, J. D. Daane, and R. Einzig, "The Flows of Funds between Regions of the United States," Regional Science Association, *Papers and Proceedings* (1957), pp. 139–59.

that neither these results nor differences in the measures applied are incompatible with the operation of the monetary mechanism. Another interesting example is that, although between 1953 and 1957 the money supply increased by about 50 per cent in France and Germany and only by 3 per cent in Great Britain, the inflationary effects were stronger in the latter country than in the former two.[15] These examples suggest that, given the diversities in the financial and banking structures of countries participating in a union, one need not proceed to the application of uniform measures after the union has been established.

On the other hand, the freeing of capital movements in an integrated capital market is not sufficient to ensure proper balance-of-payments adjustments in a union. The cooperation of the central banks becomes necessary, for example, with respect to discount rates. Discount-rate policies aimed at attracting short-term funds can impede the operation of the adjustment mechanism. In addition, although incurring a balance-of-payments deficit will act as an automatic disciplinary measure in the case of inflationary developments in one of the member countries, no such immediate restraint exists if deflationary policies are followed by a participating country. The application of disparate policy measures would then lead to balance-of-payments difficulties, thereby making concerted action necessary. Nevertheless, as a minimum requirement, the observation of common rules, mutual consultation, and the cooperation of central banks can permit capital movements to fulfill their equilibrating role without creating a supra-national authority.

These remarks should not be interpreted as a denial of the usefulness of setting up a supra-national authority to deal with monetary matters. The latter, however, implies complete integration, which is a further step after an economic union has been established. Total integration has certain political preconditions, the fulfillment of which is uncertain, e.g., for the European Common Market, at least for the near future. The method of adjustment advocated here does not require political integration and is therefore likely to have great practical importance. On the other hand, if the described "economic union method" gains acceptance, it will be relatively easy to find the

---

[15] See Otmar Emminger, "Les aspects monétaires du marché commun," *Bulletin d'Information et de Documentation*, August, 1958, p. 101.

transition to a single currency system. The process of monetary unification has been described by Robert Triffin and others and will not
be taken up here.[16]

In the foregoing discussion we analyzed problems of a closed
union where trade with the outside world is unimportant and therefore equilibration of the balance of payments of any member country
with the other participating countries was considered as an objective.
A closed union is not a practical example, however. In an open union,
as distinct from a closed union, the balance of payments of each
country should be equilibrated with the member countries *and* third
countries taken together, whereby the equilibration of the balance of
payments of the union is automatically ensured. Member states can
run a permanent deficit (surplus) with each other if this is balanced by
a surplus (deficit) with nonparticipating countries.

The balancing process in an open union largely conforms to the
rules devised for a closed union with short-term and long-term capital
movements as the main equilibrating factors. The coordination of
monetary policies assumes new importance in an open union, however. Without suitable arrangements for cooperation between central
banks, a country may run a deficit with third countries and finance
this deficit with capital funds from member countries attracted by
high interest rates. Furthermore, the application of coordinated governmental measures will be necessary if, on balance, the union runs
a deficit or incurs a surplus. In the latter case, capital movements
within the union cannot bring about equilibrium. Consequently, the
setting-up of a supra-national authority may be contemplated sooner
in an open than in a closed union.[17]

One of the preconditions of the system of adjustment presented
here is the existence of a highly developed money and capital market
in the participating countries. This condition is fulfilled, for exam-

[16] Triffin distinguishes the following steps leading toward the establishment of a
single currency:

a) legalization of the use of a common unit of account in the writing of contracts;
b) adoption of new national monetary units, still independent but of equal value;
c) free intercirculation of national currencies;
d) establishment of a single authority in charge of currency issues.

See his "La monnaie et le marché commun—politiques nationales et intégration régionale," *Cahiers de l'Institut de Science Economique Appliquée*, Série R, No. 3, December, 1958, pp. 1–17. Also R. Mossé, "Système et politique monétaires de l'Europe fédérée," *Economia Internazionale*, February–March, 1953, pp. 175–88.

[17] For further arguments on the need for coordination of monetary (and fiscal)
policies, see pp. 268–70 below.

ple, in the European integration projects. Different is the situation in a union of less developed economies, e.g., in Latin America. In the latter case, private capital movements are unlikely to perform their equilibrating role. Consequently, other methods need to be devised to meet balance-of-payments problems. These methods may differ from union to union, given the actual situation in different countries. In the absence of currency convertibility, a multilateral payments union with appropriate credit margins can provide a solution, while in a union of economies with convertible currencies an agreement on mutual credits will be helpful. In either case there will be need for establishing a central agency with credit-granting powers. Another possible solution would be the introduction of a system of flexible exchange rates. Some problems related to flexible rates are analyzed below.

Fixed or Flexible Exchange Rates?

In the economic literature on balance-of-payments problems, the case for flexible exchange rates has been frequently endorsed.[18] Some authors advocate the introduction of freely fluctuating rates for economic unions, too.[19] In the present context, we are not concerned with the question whether a system of fixed or flexible exchange rates provides a satisfactory solution for present (and future) balance-of-payments problems in the world economy but will rather explore their applicability within an economic union. Thus there is no need for repeating the standard arguments about rate flexibility pro and con, and we can restrict ourselves to the discussion of those issues that are relevant to our chosen topic. We shall examine the case of a union of developed economies, and some comments will be offered subsequently with respect to a union of underdeveloped countries.

To begin with, the adoption of a system of freely fluctuating exchange rates will defeat the possible use of short-term securities to even out fluctuations in exchange reserves. Not only will financial in-

---

[18] See Milton Friedman, "The Case for Flexible Exchange Rates," *Essays in Positive Economics* (Chicago: University of Chicago Press, 1953), and J. E. Meade, "The Case for Variable Exchange Rates," *Three Banks Review*, September, 1955, pp. 3–27; Egon Sohmen, *Flexible Exchange Rates* (Chicago: University of Chicago Press, 1961).

[19] Cf., e.g., L. B. Yeager, "Exchange Rates within a Common Market," *Social Research*, Winter, 1958, pp. 415–38. Professor Meade appears to prefer complete monetary unification to flexible rates, but nevertheless he endorses the latter alternative, arguing that the former is not practicable under present-day conditions. See his "The Balance-of-Payments Problems of a European Free Trade Area," pp. 379–96.

stitutions be reluctant to hold foreign securities, but monetary authorities are not likely to permit the holding of foreign short-term papers as secondary reserves in the face of an exchange risk. Flexibility in the exchange rates also increases the risk of long-term lending, and it is questionable whether the intra-union movement of loanable funds will be intensified if repayment at fixed rates is not ensured.[20]

Another argument relates to the uncertainty issue. We noted in Chapter 8 that integration favorably affects the expectations of producers because they will not have to fear that tariffs may cut off their markets within the union. Firms, then, can rely on a wider market in introducing large-scale production methods and, more generally, in arriving at their investment decisions. On the other hand, if exchange rates are free to fluctuate, producers will be reluctant to base their investment decisions on the existence of a large market, considering that the depreciation of a member country's currency is equivalent to a reimposition of tariffs.

The proponents of freely fluctuating exchange rates often argue that traders can avoid taking exchange risks by covering their position on the forward exchange market. The reasoning just given indicates that the forward market gives no guarantee for the case when investment plans are disappointed. The risk of exchange-rate fluctuations can be covered, however, in the case of transactions in process, since the exporter can sell the future proceeds forward. Nevertheless, foreign-exchange dealings for more than three months in advance are rarely possible, and, in the case of adverse expectations, a widening gap between spot and forward rates may greatly increase the cost of covering the transaction. Finally, even in the absence of adverse expectations the fact remains that operations on the forward market are time-consuming and costly, so that transactions between, for example, Metz and Saarbrücken will be discriminated against in favor of transactions between Metz and Nice.

Some authors advocate the introduction of freely fluctuating exchange rates on the basis that these provide a substitute for flexibility in prices and wages in the case when adverse shifts occur in the demand for a country's products.[21] However, exchange depreciation is a blunt instrument compared with price and wage flexibility. Advocates of

---

[20] In the case of long-term borrowing, however, guarantees on repayment in gold or in some other constant unit would reduce the lender's risk.

[21] This view was endorsed by Yeager, *op. cit.*, pp. 420 ff.

the above view implicitly base their contention on the validity of the concept of national price levels. If we can speak about a German or a French price level, then we may take price flexibility and rate flexibility as equivalent. Yet, after trade and payments restrictions have been removed between union members, the concept of a national price level loses much of its meaning. In such a situation Lösch's description of the "price-waves" may be more appropriate: any change in the trading relationship between, e.g., Paris and Stuttgart will have a continuously decreasing impact on prices prevailing at places situated between Paris and Stuttgart.[22] Exchange depreciation will then have a differential impact on different communities and thus on individual regions and individual industries within a national economy. If, for example, the demand for French wine falls, the ensuing depreciation of the French franc will improve the competitive position of French industries other than wine production at the expense of competitors in other countries of the Common Market, while wine producers will not be fully compensated for the fall in demand. Similar consequences follow in interregional relations. We have already pointed out that disparities in the economic structure are greater between regions than between the countries of the Common Market. Consequently, if exchange-rate flexibility should provide a substitute for flexibility in prices and wages, it would seem necessary to establish variable exchange rates between regions that can be regarded as homogeneous.

Yeager has actually considered the latter possibility in arguing that the undesirable consequences of a fall in demand for automobiles could be mitigated if the exchange rate of the state of Michigan were left to fluctuate.[23] This example is misleading, however, since it disregards the fact that car production is not confined to Detroit and that Michigan produces commodities other than automobiles.[24] As Yeager also realizes, his argument—if brought to its logical conclusion—would speak for establishing a separate currency for every industry or even for every firm. The shortcomings of such a "solution" need not be elaborated. And it is also doubtful whether we can follow Yeager

[22] See August Lösch, "A New Theory of International Trade," *International Economic Papers*, No. 6 (London: Macmillan & Co., Ltd., 1956), pp. 50–65.

[23] Yeager, *op. cit.*, pp. 422 ff.

[24] Actually, in 1960 only 13 per cent of all employed persons were engaged in motor vehicle manufacturing in Michigan, although this figure should be augmented by considering the suppliers of the car manufacturers.

in concluding that, in an integrated area, the necessarily arbitrary dividing line between the application of fixed and flexible "rates" should coincide with national boundaries. In Yeager's opinion, "within each member country the national currency has proved able to serve all the essential functions of money; the national currency area has proved economically large enough."[25] But the present national currency areas are the result of a number of territorial changes during past centuries; thus it is questionable whether, for example, the Netherlands can be considered as having a currency area "economically large enough" if the proportion of foreign trade approaches half her national income, and economic arguments may speak for a separate currency area in Southern Italy rather than in Belgium.

Note also that the argument according to which rate flexibility is a substitute for price and wage flexibility in the case of adverse demand shifts is based on the implicit assumption that workers suffer from money illusion: they do not accept a cut in money wages but have no objection to a reduction in real wages. Yet if labor unions are unwilling to take a cut in money wages, they will not be inclined to accept a decrease in real wages through exchange depreciation either. If this were the case, an exchange-rate–wage–price spiral might be the outcome. On the other hand, labor unions are likely to realize that excessive wage demands lead to unemployment under fixed exchange rates, since the producer in question would outprice itself on the market if these demands were met; thus intensified competition can be expected to reduce the danger of cost inflation in an integrated area.[26]

It will now be apparent that, under full-employment conditions, flexible exchange rates are not sufficient to attain equilibrium in the balance of payments without curtailing domestic expenditure through monetary and/or fiscal policy. If the latter condition is not fulfilled, the downward movement of the exchange rate will continue. One might rightly ask the question: Why could we not apply restrictive monetary-fiscal policies without flexibility in the exchange rate? And we can follow Viner in arguing that whereas under fixed exchange rates a deficit in the balance of payments may act as a restraint to in-

---

25 *Ibid.*, p. 437.

26 It is interesting to note that the advance reduction of French tariffs in trade with the Common Market countries in March, 1961, was said to be undertaken in order to discourage inflationary wage and price increases in oligopolistic industries by opening the French market to greater competition.

flationary expansion, this restraint will cease to operate under flexible exchanges.[27]

The above arguments suggest that flexible exchange rates are neither necessary nor desirable for intra-union adjustments. It is another question whether flexible rates should be applied in the transitional period. The establishment of a union will take a number of years, and the removal of tariff barriers may result in considerable changes in the balance-of-payments position of the participating countries. It can be contended that, in the absence of flexible rates, the reallocation of resources might take place on the basis of the "wrong" exchange rates and this could be the source of persistent balance-of-payments disequilibria. The latter argument would imply the need for flexible rates to ensure appropriate adjustments in the sphere of production.[28] On the other hand, flexibility in the exchange rates would hinder capital movements and would make it difficult for the firm to prepare long-term investment plans. Consequently—apart from the possible adverse effects on investment activity—the adjustment process through the flow of capital funds will encounter obstacles. It should also be added that, since the equilibration of the balance of payments depends on relative, rather than absolute, changes in money incomes, differential movements in wages may have an equilibrating effect if the period of transition is sufficiently long to allow for substantial increases in productivity.

It is difficult to choose between the possible courses of action on the basis of a priori arguments. The author believes that, considering the advantages and disadvantages of fixed and freely fluctuating exchange rates, a compromise solution is likely to be chosen. This would be to widen the limits between which the exchange rates are presently allowed to fluctuate and to require the intervention of an exchange equalization fund to reduce the amplitude of the fluctuations. The limits could be narrowed again after the end of the transitional period.

These considerations referred to a union of advanced economies with a well-developed money market. Our objections against flexible

[27] Jacob Viner, "Some International Aspects of Economic Stabilization," in *The State of the Social Sciences*, ed. L. D. White (Chicago: University of Chicago Press, 1956), p. 296. For a different opinion, see Sohmen, *op. cit.*, p. 124.

[28] Such a position was taken, for example, by Robert Triffin in "Convertibilité monétaire et intégration economique en Europe occidentale," *Economie Appliquée*, October–December, 1956, pp. 619–58.

exchange rates concerning their adverse effect on the movement of short-term and long-term funds have little relevance for underdeveloped countries, where capital movements within the union are not likely to be of any importance. In addition, the establishment of a union between these countries will supposedly require greater changes in exchange-rate parities than in advanced economies. Consequently, a case can be made for introducing exchange-rate flexibility in unions of this sort. Such an arrangement, however, would require setting up an exchange equalization account for the union as a whole, which would have the responsibility to intervene in the market in order to avoid undesirable fluctuations in the rates.

Economic Policy for Stability and Growth

In this chapter we have so far confined our attention to balance-of-payments problems in a union. This procedure has been useful for our purposes, but it is necessary to realize that external balance is part of a broader problem—that of stability and growth. In the concluding section of this chapter we shall consider, in general terms, the policy measures necessary to serve these objectives in an integrated area.

Integration increases the interdependence of the national economies participating in a union. In a common market the elasticity of substitution between domestic goods and commodities produced in the partner countries will rise, and the import leakages associated with income changes will also be larger. In other words, small variations in domestic prices, as well as fluctuations in the national income of any one country, will have immediate repercussions in the other participating economies. The integrated capital market further contributes to this increased interdependence. A liquidity crisis, easy-money policy, or changes in corporate taxes will not fail to affect intra-union capital movements and thus economic activity.

The increased degree of interdependence between the union members will have a profound effect on the transmission of cyclical fluctuations, on the intra-union repercussions of inflationary and deflationary policies of individual countries, and on the effectiveness of policies designed to combat recession and accelerate growth. To begin with, a cyclical downturn in one member country of the union will quickly affect the partner countries. Both decreasing incomes and a fall in the price level will reduce imports in the first country, and, in the absence of corrective measures, the decline in economic activity in this country may be reinforced through feedback effects from the other members of the union. Also, the increased interdependence of the participating economies acts to reinforce the discipline of the market in the case of inflationary developments in any one country. Since prices are determined on the common market, an inflationary expansion will immediately spill over into the member countries' markets and will adversely affect the balance of payments of the inflating country. In other words, the first country will not be able to "export" the inflation but will rather have to correct its action in order to escape its undesirable consequences. This will be true even in the case of a large country, as witness the recent experience in the United States, where the price increases in certain industries have had little effect on prices in other industrialized economies, while the upward tendency in prices presents a danger for the American balance of payments.

While the discipline of the market thwarts inflationary actions undertaken by any one country, no such automatic mechanism will enforce a reversal of deflationary policy on the part of a single country. The latter will be able to improve its balance of payments at the expense of the other member countries that do not follow such a policy. Although some argue that the deflating country may have an incentive to change its policy, since an accumulation of claims on other countries will be accompanied by a reduction in domestic expenditures from a given income, it should not be forgotten that accumulating interest-bearing claims provides future returns for this country.

Greater interdependence of the union members also portends a reduced effectiveness of antirecession measures undertaken individually. By reason of the high income elasticity of imports, the cost of government spending for combatting recessions in one country will rise both in terms of government expenditure required and in terms of foreign exchange lost. Also, an easy-money policy will lead to an outward movement of capital, while a reduction in tax rates is likely to have the opposite effect. On the other hand, measures undertaken by one country to check a boom—for example, through a rise in interest rates— are bound to be thwarted both because investors can borrow in the member countries and because a capital inflow will set in.

Finally, policies designed to accelerate growth will also affect the partner countries. Policies for economic growth can take the form of provisions for accelerated depreciation, other types of tax concessions to businesses, and selective monetary measures, all designed to encourage investment activity. Most of these measures will bear influence on the economies of other member countries; on the one hand, the effectiveness of this policy will be reduced as a result of a "spill-over" in the form of increased imports; on the other, aggressive policies for growth can have an adverse effect on other economies by attracting an inflow of capital from the member countries.

These considerations indicate that, in order to avoid the undesirable repercussions of unilateral changes in interest rates or deflationary policy and to make policies aimed at stability and growth effective, concerted action is necessary on the part of the economic policy-makers in countries participating in a union. Concerted action cannot be restricted to the monetary field, partly because integration impairs the effectiveness of unilateral fiscal measures, too, and partly because the combined application of monetary and fiscal policy is likely to be more effective than the employment of only one of these policies.

Concerted action in the field of monetary and fiscal policy can mean different things. It may be taken as equivalent to cooperation or may signify the establishment of a supra-national authority whose decisions would be binding for the member countries. In the present context we shall deal with the minimum requirements the fulfillment of which is necessary for the satisfactory working of a union. The proposition is advanced here that, in the face of integrated commodity and factor markets, it is necessary to have accord on basic goals, understanding in the evaluation of current trends, agreement on the strategy applied, and reciprocal consideration given to the repercussions of any unilateral action in the field of monetary and fiscal policy on the economies of the partner countries.

In the absence of agreement on basic goals, the application of conflicting measures may thwart policy making in the member countries. These common objectives are likely to include full employment, price stability, balance-of-payments equilibrium, and growth. Most observers would agree that the overriding long-run objective is growth, although this does not mean that the coordination of policies aimed at growth necessarily has priority over that of countercyclical policies. There is less agreement on the relative importance of balance-of-payments equilibrium, full employment, and price stability as policy objectives. For example, while some commentators deprecate the importance of balance-of-payments objectives as a major goal,[29] others emphasize that increased interdependence augments the importance of balance-of-payments problems.[30] It is not our purpose here to offer suggestions on the ranking of these objections but rather to emphasize the need for accord on basic objectives.

Next, there is need for an understanding in judging a particular situation and current trends. In this connection, distinction should be made between fluctuations emanating from the world economy and disturbances within the union itself. To begin with the first, the member countries ought to appraise the world situation in unison and should be prepared to coordinate any corrective action that becomes necessary. In addition, they should watch economic changes within the union and act concurrently to avoid undesirable developments. Robert Triffin suggested that this could best be done through defining "presumptive criteria or danger signals." The criteria adopted can refer to changes in employment, prices, monetary reserves, money supply, etc., and should serve to bring into action a consultative machinery to determine the policies to be followed.[31] This proposal is certainly worthy of attention in any integrated area, but it should be noted that its perfect operation presupposes a significant improvement over presently applied forecasting techniques.

Agreement on the strategy to be followed in meeting certain situations is a further matter of interest. However, as M. W. Holtrop so aptly put it, common strategy does not mean common tactics—the uniformization of policy measures.[32] To begin with, efforts to uniformize the course of the business-cycle or growth patterns are not only futile but downright harmful. Economic changes in any country depend on its industrial structure; given the inequality of these structures, we cannot expect parallel developments. And one should not forget that disparities may be even greater within a country than between countries—as indicated by the example of some Western European econo-

[29] Cf., e.g., European Committee for Economic and Social Progress, *European Business Cycle Policy* (Frankfurt), pp. 20–22.

[30] This appears to be the position taken by the staff of the Commission of the European Economic Community.

[31] *Gold and the Dollar Crisis* (New Haven: Yale University Press, 1960), p. 139. Triffin adds that in the case of closer integration some of these criteria might be institutionalized in providing ceilings on independent national decisions.

[32] "Is a Common Central Bank Policy Necessary within a United Europe?" *De Economist*, October, 1957, pp. 41–61.

mies. Disparate changes within a union may also have some usefulness, since recession in one country (region) will tend to be compensated for if overexpansion prevails in other parts of the area, and this
will reduce the task of anticyclical policy. In addition, by reason of
differences in economic structure and institutional arrangements, different means may be appropriate in meeting identical situations, and
the same action would have different results in one country than in
another. While the economy of one member state will react to general
monetary measures, selective controls are more appropriate in another, and in a third more reliance should be based on fiscal policy.

Nevertheless, these differences in "tactics" cannot amount to a
disregard of the intra-union repercussions of any action. The application of the principle of reciprocal consideration aims at avoiding
the possible undesirable consequences due to unilateral action. Therefore, it is not sufficient to agree that a particular country should follow
an anti-inflationary policy, but a broad agreement should exist on what
general measures are to be followed. Monetary or fiscal policy can
bring the same results in the domestic economy, but repercussions in
the partner countries might differ widely. Also, if one member country engages in an expansionary fiscal policy and in a contractionary
monetary policy simultaneously, domestic employment may not be
affected, but this cannot be said about economic activity throughout
the union. This brings us back to the need for coordination, which
can rightly be regarded as a partial surrender of sovereignty. But, in
giving up the right to take certain policy measures unilaterally, a country simultaneously acquires the right to expect that other countries
will abstain from potentially damaging unilateral actions. On the
other hand, this harmony of interests is not incompatible with conflicting interests in any particular case. Therefore, there appears to be
need for instituting an intergovernmental body whose decisions do not
require unanimity yet are binding for the member states.

Although coordination of policies as proposed here amounts to
the partial abandonment of sovereignty by the member states, this is
not equivalent to the establishment of a supra-national authority,
since the states would retain their freedom of action over large areas
of economic activity. In other words, as a minimum requirement, an
intergovernmental approach appears to be sufficient to ensure the
satisfactory operation of an economic union without a unification of
the institutional structure, and this alternative has the advantage of

not requiring political unification, which—at least temporarily—may be difficult to achieve. Satisfactory operation is not equivalent to optimal operation, however. The latter will require the suppression of every conceivable form of discrimination between the economic units of the member states and necessitates adopting a supra-national approach that is associated with political unification, possibly in the form of a federation of states.

SELECTED BIBLIOGRAPHY

GENERAL WORKS ON THEORETICAL PROBLEMS OF
ECONOMIC INTEGRATION

MEADE, J. E. *Problems of Economic Union.* Chicago: The University of Chicago Press, 1953.

————. *The Theory of Customs Unions.* Amsterdam: North Holland Publishing Co., 1955.

ROBINSON, E. A. G. (ed.). *Economic Consequences of the Size of Nations.* Proceedings of a Conference held by the International Economic Association. London: Macmillan & Co., Ltd., 1960.

SANNWALD, ROLF, and STOHLER, JACQUES. *Economic Integration.* Princeton: Princeton University Press, 1959. Originally published in German under the title *Wirtschaftliche Integration.* Basel: Kyklos Verlag, 1958.

SCITOVSKY, TIBOR. *Economic Theory and Western European Integration.* Stanford: Stanford University Press, 1958.

TINBERGEN, JAN. *International Economic Integration.* Amsterdam: Elsevier, 1954.

VINER, JACOB. *The Customs Union Issue.* New York: Carnegie Endowment for International Peace, 1950.

PUBLICATIONS ON ECONOMIC INTEGRATION
IN EUROPE

ALLAIS, MAURICE. *L'Europe unie—route de la prospérité.* Paris: Calmann-Lévy, 1960.

BENOIT, EMILE. *Europe at Sixes and Sevens.* New York: Columbia University Press, 1961.

CAMPS, MIRIAM. *The European Common Market and American Policy.* Princeton: International Finance Section, Princeton University, 1956.

————. *The First Year of the European Economic Community.* Princeton: International Finance Section, Princeton University, 1958.

D'ALAURO, O. *Il mercato comune europeo: ed altri saggi di politica economica.* Genoa: Lib. Bozzi, 1959.

DENIAU, J. F. *Le marché commun.* Paris: Presses Universitaires de France, 1958.

FRANK, ISAIAH. *The European Common Market: An Analysis of Commercial Policy.* New York: Frederick A. Praeger, 1961.

274

SELECTED BIBLIOGRAPHY · 275

HAINES, C. G. (ed.). *Economic Integration.* Baltimore: Johns Hopkins Press, 1957.

HURTIG, S. *The European Common Market.* New York: Columbia University Press, 1958.

MAURY, RENÉ. *L'intégration européenne.* Paris: Sirey, 1958.

PERROUX, FRANÇOIS. *L'Europe sans rivages.* Paris: Presses Universitaires de France, 1954.

PHILIP, ANDRÉ. *L'Europe unie et sa place dans l'économie internationale.* Paris: Presses Universitaires de France, 1953.

DE SAINTE LORETTE, LUCIEN. *L'intégration économique de l'Europe.* Paris: Presses Universitaires de France, 1953.

SAMPEDRO, J. L.; CHARDONNET, J.; and THIÉRY, A. *La localización de las actividades económicas en Europa después de la integración unitaria.* In the series: Estudios sobre la Unidad Económica de Europa, Madrid, 1957.

STRAUSS, E. *Common Sense about the Common Market.* New York: Rinehart & Co., Inc., 1958.

TREMPONT, JACQUES. *L'unification de l'Europe.* Amiens: Editions scientifiques et littéraires, 1955.

PUBLICATIONS ON ECONOMIC INTEGRATION
IN LATIN AMERICA

DELL, S. S. *Problemas de un mercado común en América Latina.* México, D.F.: Centro de Estudios Monetarios Latinoamericanos, 1959.

FERRERO, R. A. *El mercado común latinoamericano.* Cámara de Comercio de Lima, Peru, 1959.

MIKESELL, R. F. *Liberalization of Inter-Latin American Trade.* Washington, D.C.: Pan American Union, 1957.

UNITED NATIONS DEPARTMENT OF ECONOMIC AND SOCIAL AFFAIRS. *The Latin American Common Market* (Prepared by the Secretariat of the Economic Commission for Latin America). 1959.

URQUIDI, V. L. *Trayectoria del Mercado Común Latinoamericano.* México, D.F.: Centro de Estudios Monetarios Latinoamericanos, 1960.

CHAPTER I

ALBRECHT, KARL. *Probleme und Methoden der wirtschaftlichen Integration.* Kiel: Kieler Vorträge, 1951.

ALLAIS, MAURICE. "Fondements théoriques, perspectives et conditions d'un marché commun effective," *Revue d'Economie Politique,* Vol. LXVIII, No. 1 (January-February, 1958), pp. 56–99.

BALASSA, BELA. "Towards a Theory of Economic Integration," *Kyklos,* Vol. XIV, No. 1 (1961), pp. 1–14.

BOMBACH, GOTTFRIED. "Economic Growth and Stability in a United Europe," *Sciences Humaines et Intégration Européenne,* pp. 236–90. Leiden: A. W. Sythoff, 1960.

GIERSCH, HERBERT. "Libéralisme, dirigisme et intégration économique de l'Europe," in *Demain l'Europe sans frontières?,* pp. 69–90. Paris: Plon, 1958.

GUITTON, HENRI. "L'Europe et la théorie économique," *Revue d'Economie Politique,* Vol. LXVIII, No. 1 (January-February, 1958), pp. 324–39.

HABERLER, GOTTFRIED. "Die wirtschaftliche Integration Europas," in *Wirtschaftsfragen der freien Welt* (Erhard Festschrift), pp. 521–30. Frankfurt: Knapp, 1957.

HARTOG, F. "European Economic Integration: A Realistic Conception," *Weltwirtschaftliches Archiv,* Vol. LXXI, No. 2 (1953), pp. 165–79.

MYRDAL, GUNNAR. *An International Economy,* chaps. ii–iv. New York: Harper & Bros., 1956.

RÖPKE, WILHELM. "Integration und Desintegration der internationalen Wirtschaft," *Wirtschaftsfragen der freien Welt,* pp. 493–501.

SANNWALD, R., and STOHLER, J. *Economic Integration,* chap. iii.

SCHNEIDER, ERICH. "Lineamenti di una teoria economica del mercato comune," *Rivista Internazionale di Scienze Economiche e Commerciali,* Vol. IV, No. 2 (February, 1957), pp. 107–18.

TINBERGEN, JAN. "On the Theory of Economic Integration," *Selected Papers,* pp. 138–51. Amsterdam: North Holland Publishing Co., 1959.

WEILLER, JEAN. "Les degrés de l'intégration et les chances d'une 'zone de coopération' internationale," *Revue Economique,* Vol. IX, No. 1 (March, 1958), pp. 233–54.

———. "Les objectifs économiques d'une coopération durable," *Economie Appliquée,* Vol. VI, No. 4 (October-December, 1953), pp. 571–96.

APPENDIX

BYÉ, MAURICE. "Les problèmes posés par la Communauté européenne du charbon et de l'acier," *Revue Economique,* Vol. XI, No. 6 (November, 1960), pp. 833–65.

DIEBOLD, WILLIAM. *The Schuman Plan,* Part IV. New York: Frederick A. Praeger, 1959.

LISTER, LOUIS. *Europe's Coal and Steel Community, passim.* New York: Twentieth Century Fund, 1960.

SCITOVSKY, TIBOR. *Economic Theory and Western European Integration,* chap. iv.

STIKKER, D. U. "The Functional Approach to European Integration," *Foreign Affairs,* Vol. XXIX, No. 3 (April, 1951), pp. 436–44.

CHAPTER II

BECKERMAN, W. "Distance and the Pattern of Intra-European Trade," *Review of Economics and Statistics,* Vol. XXXVIII, No. 1 (February, 1956), pp. 31–38.

BERTRAND, RAYMOND. "Comparaison du niveau des tarifs douaniers des pays du marché commun," *Cahiers de l'Institut de Science Economique Appliquée,* Série R, No. 2 (February, 1958).

BINSWANGER, H. C. "Der Zollschutz in den Ländern der Europäischen Wirtschaftsgemeinschaft und in der Schweiz," *Aussenwirtschaft,* Vol. XIV, Nos. 1–2 (March-June, 1959), pp. 119–46. In French translation: "La protection douanière dans les pays de la Communauté Economique Européenne et en Suisse," *Cahiers de l'Institut de Science Economique Appliquée,* Série R, No. 4 (May, 1960), pp. 3–41.

BYÉ, MAURICE. "Unions douanières et données nationales," *Economie Appliquée,* Vol. III, No. 1 (January-March, 1950), pp. 121–58. The English translation, entitled "Customs Unions and National Interests," appeared in *International Economic Papers,* No. 3, pp. 208–34. London: Macmillan & Co., Ltd., 1953.

ERDMAN, PAUL, and ROGGE, PETER. *Die Europäische Wirtschaftsgemeinschaft und die Drittländer,* Part I. Basel: Kyklos Verlag, 1960.

GEHRELS, F., and JOHNSTON, B. F. "The Economic Gains of European Integration," *Journal of Political Economy,* Vol. LXIII, No. 4 (August, 1955), pp. 275–92.

GIERSCH, HERBERT. "Economic Union between Nations and the Location of Industries," *Review of Economic Studies,* Vol. XVII, No. 2 (1949-50), pp. 87–97.

———. "Einige Probleme der kleineuropäischen Zollunion," *Zeitschrift für die gesamte Staatswissenschaft,* Vol. CXIII, No. 4 (1957), pp. 602–31.

JOHNSON, H. G. "The Gains from Freer Trade with Europe: An Estimate," *Manchester School of Economic and Social Studies,* Vol. XXVI, No. 3 (September, 1958), pp. 247–55.

KREININ, M. E. "European Integration and American Trade," *American Economic Review,* Vol. XLIX, No. 4 (September, 1959), pp. 615–27.

———. "The 'Outer Seven' and European Integration," *American Economic Review,* Vol. L, No. 3 (June, 1960), pp. 370–86.

LIESNER, H. H. "The European Common Market and British Industry," *Economic Journal,* Vol. LXVIII (June, 1958), pp. 302–16.

LOVEDAY, A. "Article XXIV of the GATT Rules," *Economia Internazionale*, Vol. XI, No. 1 (February, 1958), pp. 1–16.

MAKOWER, H., and MORTON, G. "A Contribution towards a Theory of Customs Unions," *Economic Journal*, Vol. LXIII (March, 1953), pp. 33–49.

MEADE, J. E. "The Removal of Trade Barriers: The Regional versus the Universal Approach," *Economica*, New Series, Vol. XVIII (May, 1951), pp. 184–98.

————. *The Theory of Customs Unions*, chap. ii.

MIKESELL, R. F. *Liberalization of Inter-Latin American Trade*, chaps. iii–iv. Washington, D.C.: Pan American Union, 1957.

SANNWALD, R., and STOHLER, J. *Economic Integration*, chap. ii.

SCITOVSKY, TIBOR. *Economic Theory and Western European Integration*, chap. i.

TINBERGEN, JAN. "Customs Unions: Influence of their Size on their Effect," *Zeitschrift für die gesamte Staatswissenschaft*, Vol. CXIII, No. 3 (1957), pp. 404–14. Reprinted in Jan Tinbergen, *Selected Papers*, pp. 152–64. Amsterdam: North Holland Publishing Co., 1959.

————. "The Impact of the European Economic Community on Third Countries," *Sciences Humaines et Intégration Européenne*, pp. 386–98. Leiden: A. W. Sythoff, 1960.

VERDOORN, P. J. "Two Notes on Tariff Reductions," Appendix III in *Social Aspects of European Economic Co-operation*, Report by a Group of Experts (Ohlin Report), pp. 160–69. Geneva: International Labour Office, 1956.

VINER, JACOB. *The Customs Union Issue*, chap. iv.

CHAPTER III

GEHRELS, FRANZ. "Customs Unions from a Single Country Viewpoint," *Review of Economic Studies*, Vol. XXIV, No. 1 (1956–57), pp. 61–64.

JOHNSON, H. G. "Discriminatory Tariff Reduction: A Marshallian Analysis," *Indian Journal of Economics*, Vol. V, No. 1 (July, 1957), pp. 39–47.

————. "Marshallian Analysis of Discriminatory Tariff Reduction: An Extension," *Indian Journal of Economics*, Vol. VI, No. 2 (October, 1958), pp. 177–82.

————. "The European Common Market—Risk or Opportunity?," *Weltwirtschaftliches Archiv*, Vol. LXXIX, No. 2 (1957), pp. 267–78.

LIPSEY, R. G. "Mr. Gehrels on Customs Unions," *Review of Economic Studies*, Vol. XXIV, No. 3 (1956–57), pp. 211–14.

————. "The Theory of Customs Unions: Trade Diversion and Welfare," *Economica*, New Series, Vol. XXIV (February, 1957), pp. 40–46.

————. "The Theory of Customs Unions: A General Survey," *Economic Journal,* Vol. LXX (September, 1960), pp. 496–513.

MEADE, J. E. *The Theory of Customs Unions,* chap. iii-v.

MEYER, F. V. "Complementarity and the Lowering of Tariffs," *American Economic Review,* Vol. XLVI, No. 3 (June, 1956), pp. 323–35.

APPENDIX

BACHMANN, HANS. "Die Verhinderung von Handelsumlenkungen in einer Freihandelszone," *Aussenwirtschaft,* Vol. XIII, Nos. 1–2 (March–June, 1958), pp. 1–23.

CAMPS, MIRIAM. *The European Free Trade Association. A Preliminary Appraisal.* London: Political and Economic Planning, 1959.

HESBERG, WALTER. *Die Freihandelszone als Mittel der Integrationspolitik.* Frankfurt: Knapp, 1960.

LANGUETIN, PIERRE. "L'association européenne de libre–échange," *Revue Economique et Sociale,* January, 1960, pp. 5–20.

Negotiations for a European Free Trade Area, Documents Relating to the Negotiations from July, 1956 to December, 1958. Presented to Parliament by the Paymaster General by Command of Her Majesty, London, 1959.

ORGANISATION FOR EUROPEAN ECONOMIC CO-OPERATION. *Report on the Possibility of Creating a Free Trade Area in Europe.* Prepared for the Council of the OEEC by a special working party, Paris, 1957.

OUIN, MARC. *The OEEC and the Common Market.* Paris: Organisation for European Economic Co-operation, 1958.

ROUQUET DA GARRIGUE, V. "Le plan Carli et le problème des détournements de trafic dans une zone de libre-échange," *Revue de Science Financière,* Vol. LII, No. 2 (April–June, 1960), pp. 244–66.

CHAPTER IV

BALASSA, BELA. "The Factor-Price Equalization Controversy," *Weltwirtschaftliches Archiv,* Vol. LXXXVII, No. 1 (1961).

BYÉ, M., and MAGAUD, C. "Effet d'une intégration européenne sur l'immigration de la main-d'oeuvre en France," *Demain l'Europe sans frontières?,* pp. 115–27. Paris: Plon, 1958.

CAVES, R. E. *Trade and Economic Structure,* chaps. iii, v. Cambridge, Mass.: Harvard University Press, 1960.

DELPÉRÉE, ALBERT. "La mobilité du travail en Europe Fédérée," *Economia Internazionale,* Vol. VI, Nos. 1–2 (February–May, 1953), pp. 293–306.

EDDING, FRIEDRICH. "Intra-European Migration and the Prospects of Integration," *Economics of International Migration.* Brinley Thomas (ed.), pp. 238–48. London: Macmillan & Co., Ltd., 1958.

EUROPEAN COAL AND STEEL COMMUNITY. *Obstacles à la mobilité des travailleurs et problèmes sociaux de réadaptation.* Luxemburg: Etudes et Documents, 1956.

FERRARI, ALBERTO. "Il movimento dei capitali nel quadro della Comunità economica europea," *Rivista di Politica Economica,* Vol. XLIX, No. 7 (July, 1959), pp. 1160–84.

FFORDE, J. S. *An International Trade in Managerial Skills, passim.* Oxford: Basil Blackwell, 1957.

DE FONZO, FRANCESCO. "Il diritto di stabilimento nella Comunità economica europea," *Rivista di Politica Economica,* Vol. XLIX, No. 10 (October, 1959), pp. 1574–88.

GOTTLIEB, MANUEL. "Optimum Population, Foreign Trade, and World Economy," *Population Studies,* Vol. III, No. 2 (September, 1949), pp. 151–69.

HOLZER, MAX. "Die Freizügigkeit der Unternehmungen und der Arbeit," *Aussenwirtschaft,* Vol. XIV, No. 3 (September, 1959), pp. 250–65.

KÜNG, EMIL. "Freizügigkeit im internationalen Kapitalverkehr?," *Aussenwirtschaft,* Vol. XIII, No. 4 (December, 1958), pp. 331–46.

LARCIER, R. L. "Le placement mobilier dans le marché commun," *La Revue de la Banque,* No. 1 (1959), pp. 62–72; No. 2 (1959), pp. 125–41.

MEADE, J. E. *Trade and Welfare. The Theory of International Economic Policy,* Vol. II, Part III. London: Oxford University Press, 1955.

———. *Problems of Economic Union,* chap. iii.

MEINHOLD, HELMUT. "Internationale Arbeiterwanderung," *Finanzarchiv,* Vol. XVII, No. 3 (1957), pp. 384–97.

MOLINARI, ALESSANDRO. "Manpower and the Common Market," *Banca Nazionale del Lavoro Quarterly Review,* No. 47 (December, 1958), pp. 484–510.

MUNDELL, R. A. "International Trade and Factor Mobility," *American Economic Review,* Vol. XLVII, No. 3 (June, 1957), pp. 321–35.

"Obstacles to Labour Mobility and Social Problems of Resettlement: A Survey by the European Coal and Steel Community," *International Labour Review,* Vol. LXXVI, No. 1 (July, 1957), pp. 72–83.

ORGANISATION FOR EUROPEAN ECONOMIC CO-OPERATION. *Intra-European Investments.* Paris, 1951.

CHAPTER V

ALLAIS, MAURICE. *L'Europe unie—route de la prospérité,* chap. ii. Paris: Calmann-Lévy, 1960.

CLARK, COLIN. *The Conditions of Economic Progress,* chap. vi. London: Macmillan & Co., Ltd., 1957.

———. "International Comparisons of Productivity Trends," *Journal of Business,* Vol. XXXI, No. 4 (October, 1958), pp. 267–79.

DUQUESNE DE LA VINELLE, L. "Study of the Efficiency of a Small Nation—Belgium," *Economic Consequences of the Size of Nations,* pp. 78–92.

FABRICANT, S. "Study of the Size and Efficiency of the American Economy," *Economic Consequences of the Size of Nations,* pp. 35–53.

FRANKEL, MARVIN. *British and American Manufacturing Productivity,* chaps. ii–iii, vi–vii. Urbana: University of Illinois Bulletin, Bureau of Economic and Business Research, 1957.

KUZNETS, S. "Economic Growth of Small Nations," *Economic Consequences of the Size of Nations,* pp. 14–32.

MACDOUGALL, G. D. A. "Does Productivity Rise Faster in the United States?," *Review of Economics and Statistics,* Vol. XXXVIII, No. 2 (May, 1956), pp. 155–76.

MADDISON, A. "Industrial Productivity Growth in Europe and the United States," *Economica,* New Series, Vol. XXI (November, 1954), pp. 308–19.

MARSAN, V. A. "The Experience of Italy," *Economic Consequences of the Size of Nations,* pp. 151–67.

PAIGE, D., and BOMBACH, G. *A Comparison of National Output and Productivity of the United Kingdom and the United States,* chap. v. Paris: Organisation for European Economic Co-operation, 1959.

RAPPARD, W. E. "Le secret de la prospérité américaine," *Revue d'Economie Politique,* Vol. LXIV, No. 3 (May-June, 1954), pp. 389–432.

ROSTAS, L. *Comparative Productivity Levels in British and American Industry,* chap. v. Cambridge: At the University Press, 1948.

ROTHBARTH, E. "Causes of the Superior Efficiency of U.S.A. Industry as Compared with British Industry," *Economic Journal,* Vol. LVI (September, 1946), pp. 383–90.

UNITED NATIONS DEPARTMENT OF ECONOMIC AND SOCIAL AFFAIRS. *The Latin American Common Market,* Part B.

VERDOORN, P. J. "Fattori che regolano lo sviluppo della produttività del lavoro," *L'Industria,* 1949 (1), pp. 45–53.

———. "On an Empirical Law Governing the Productivity of Labor," *Econometrica,* Vol. XIX, No. 2 (April, 1951), pp. 209–10.

YOUNG, ALLYN. "Increasing Returns and Economic Progress," *Economic Journal,* Vol. XXXVIII (December, 1928), pp. 527–42.

YOUNG, J. H. "Comparative Economic Development: Canada and the United States," *American Economic Review, Papers and Proceedings,* Vol. XLV, No. 2 (May, 1955), pp. 80–93.

CHAPTER VI

BAIN, J. S. *Barriers to New Competition,* chap. iii. Cambridge, Mass.: Harvard University Press, 1958.

BLAIR, J. M. "Technology and Size," *American Economic Review, Papers and Proceedings,* Vol. XXXVIII, No. 2 (May, 1948), pp. 121–52.

———. "The Relation between Size and Efficiency of Business," *Review of Economics and Statistics,* Vol. XXIV, No. 3 (August, 1942), pp. 125–35.

BORCH, KARL. "Productivity and Size of the Firm," *Productivity Measurement Review,* No. 12 (February, 1958), pp. 47–51.

THE ECONOMIST INTELLIGENCE UNIT. *Britain and Europe,* Part II. London, 1957.

FRANKEL, MARVIN. *British and American Manufacturing Productivity,* chap. v.

JEWKES, J. "Are the Economies of Scale Unlimited?," *Economic Consequences of the Size of Nations,* pp. 95–116.

JOHNSTON, J. "Labour Productivity and the Size of Establishment," *Bulletin of Oxford University and Institute of Statistics,* Vol. XVI, Nos. 11 and 12 (November–December, 1954), pp. 339–61.

LEIBENSTEIN, HARVEY. "The Proportionality Controversy and the Theory of Production," *Quarterly Journal of Economics,* Vol. LXIX, No. 4 (November, 1955), pp. 619–25.

MANDY, P. L., and DE GHELLINCK, G. "La structure de la dimension des entreprises dans les pays du marché commun," *Revue Economique,* Vol. XI, No. 3 (May, 1960), pp. 395–413.

NATIONAL BUREAU OF ECONOMIC RESEARCH. "Cost and the Size of Plants and Firms," *Cost Behavior and Price Policy,* pp. 219–63. New York, 1943.

ROBINSON, E. A. G. *The Structure of Competitive Industry,* chap. ii. Chicago: University of Chicago Press, 1958.

SCHUMPETER, J. A. *Business Cycles,* Vol. I, chap. iii. New York: McGraw-Hill Book Co., Inc., 1939.

SMITH, C. A. "Survey of the Empirical Evidence on Economies of Scale," *Business Concentration and Price Policy,* pp. 213–30. Princeton: Princeton University Press, 1955.

UNITED NATIONS DEPARTMENT OF ECONOMIC AFFAIRS. *A Study of the Iron and Steel Industry in Latin America,* Vol. I, Part II, chap. ii. New York, 1954.

WHITIN, T. M., and PESTON, M. H. "Random Variations, Risks and Returns to Scale," *Quarterly Journal of Economics,* Vol. LXVIII, No. 3 (November, 1954), pp. 603–12.

CHAPTER VII

CHENERY, H. B. "The Interdependence of Investment Decisions," *The Allocation of Economic Resources,* Essays in Honor of B. F. Haley, pp. 82–120. Stanford: Stanford University Press, 1959.

FLEMING, MARCUS. "External Economies and the Doctrine of Balanced Growth," *Economic Journal,* Vol. LXV (June, 1955), pp. 241–56.

GILBOY, E. W. "Demand as a Factor in the Industrial Revolution," in *Facts and Factors in Economic History,* pp. 620–39. Cambridge, Mass.: Harvard University Press, 1932.

HIRSCHMAN, A. O. *The Strategy of Economic Development,* chaps. iv–vii. New Haven: Yale University Press, 1958.

HOUSSIAUX, JACQUES. "Quasi-intégration, croissance des firmes et structures industrielles," *Revue Economique,* Vol. VIII, No. 3 (May, 1957), pp. 385–411.

NELSON, R. R. "The Simple Economics of Basic Scientific Research," *Journal of Political Economy,* Vol. LXVII, No. 3 (June, 1959), pp. 297–306.

OHLIN, GORAN. "Balanced Economic Growth in History," *American Economic Review, Papers and Proceedings,* Vol. XLIX, No. 2 (May, 1959), pp. 338–58.

ROSENSTEIN-RODAN, PAUL. "Problems of Industrialization of Eastern and South-Eastern Europe," *Economic Journal,* Vol. LIII, Nos. 210–211 (June–September, 1943), pp. 202–11.

SCITOVSKY, TIBOR. "Growth—Balanced or Unbalanced?," *The Allocation of Economic Resources,* pp. 207–17.

———. "Two Concepts of External Economies," *Journal of Political Economy,* Vol. LXII, No. 2 (April, 1954), pp. 143–51.

STIGLER, G. J. "The Division of Labor Is Limited by the Extent of the Market," *Journal of Political Economy,* Vol. LIX, No. 3 (June, 1951), pp. 185–93.

STRASSMANN, W. P. "Interrelated Industries and the Rate of Technological Change," *Review of Economic Studies,* Vol. XXVI, No. 1 (October, 1959), pp. 16–22.

STREETEN, PAUL. "Unbalanced Growth," *Oxford Economic Papers,* New Series, Vol. XI, No. 2 (June, 1959), pp. 167–90.

WICKHAM, S. "Observations sur l'intégration et diversification des entreprises," *Revue Economique,* Vol. IV, No. 4 (July, 1953), pp. 485–502.

CHAPTER VIII

BYÉ, MAURICE. "Localisation de l'investissement et Communauté économique européene," *Revue Economique,* Vol. IX, No. 2 (March, 1958), pp. 188–212.

DIEBOLD, WILLIAM. *The Schuman Plan,* chap. xiv.

DIXON, R. C. "European Policies on Restrictive Business Practices," *American Economic Review, Papers and Proceedings,* Vol. XLVIII, No. 2 (May, 1958), pp. 442–51.

EDWARDS, C. D. "Size of Markets, Scale of Firms, and the Character of Competition," *Economic Consequences of the Size of Nations,* pp. 117–32.

ERDMAN, PAUL, and ROGGE, PETER. *Die europäische Wirtschaftsgemeinschaft und die Drittländer,* chap. v. Basel: Kyklos Verlag, 1960.

FAIST, THEODOR. "Die Wettbewerbsbestimmungen für Unternehmen in der europäischen Wirtschaftsgemeinschaft und in einer europäischen Freihandelszone," *Aussenwirtschaft,* Vol. XIV, No. 4 (December, 1959), pp. 297–311.

FRUMENTO, A. "Le regole di concorrenza fra imprese industriali nella Communità Economica Europea," *Rivista Internazionale di Scienze Economiche e Commerciali,* Vol. V, No. 1 (January, 1958), pp. 1–56.

GATT. *The Possible Impact of the European Economic Community, in Particular the Common Market, upon World Trade,* Trade Intelligence Paper No. 6. Geneva, 1957.

HOFFMANN, WALTHER. "Marché commun et concurrence," *Convertibilité, multilateralism et politiques de stabilisation, Cahiers de l'Institut de Science Economique Appliquée,* Série P, No. 3 (October, 1959), pp. 113–56.

HOUSSIAUX, JACQUES. *Concurrence et Marché Commun.* Paris: Editions M-Th. Genin, 1960.

KREININ, M. E. "On the 'Trade-Diversion' Effect of Trade Preference Areas," *Journal of Political Economy,* Vol. LXVII, No. 4 (August, 1959), pp. 398–401.

LISTER, LOUIS. *Europe's Coal and Steel Community,* chaps. v–viii.

MARCHAL, ANDRÉ. *Les ententes et les concentrations dans le marché commun.* Bruxelles: Services d'Information des Communautés Européennes, 1959.

PERROUX, FRANÇOIS. "Les formes de la concurrence dans le marché commun," *Revue d'Economie Politique,* Vol. LXVIII, No. 1 (January–February, 1958), pp. 340–78.

PHILLIPS, ALMARIN. "Concentration, Scale, and Technological Change in Selected Manufacturing Industries, 1899–1939," *Journal of Industrial Economics,* Vol. IV, No. 3 (June, 1956, pp. 179–93.

RÖPKE, WILHELM. "Europäische Investitionsplanung. Das Beispiel der Montanunion," *Ordo*, Jahrbuch für die Ordnung von Wirtschaft und Gesellschaft, Vol. VII (1955), pp. 71–102.

SCITOVSKY, TIBOR. *Economic Theory and Western European Integration*, chap. iii.

————. "International Trade and Economic Integration as a Means of Overcoming the Disadvantages of a Small Nation," *Economic Consequences of the Size of Nations*, pp. 282–90.

TUCHTFELD, E. "Intégration économique et progrès technique," *Demain l'Europe sans frontières*, pp. 91–113. Paris: Plon, 1958.

TRIFFIN, ROBERT. "The Size of the Nation and Its Vulnerability to Economic Nationalism," *Economic Consequences of the Size of Nations*, pp. 247–64.

VILLARD, H. H. "Competition, Oligopoly, and Research," *Journal of Political Economy*, Vol. LXVI, No. 6 (December, 1958), pp. 483–97; Comment by Jacob Schmookler and Reply by H. H. Villard, *ibid.*, Vol. LXVII, No. 6 (December, 1959), p. 628–35.

CHAPTER IX

BOUDEVILLE, J. R. "L'espace opérationnel macroéconomique—La région plan," *Cahiers de l'Institut de Science Economique Appliquée*, Série L, No. 6 (January, 1960).

CAPET, MARCEL. "Recherche de l'incidence de la Communauté Economique Européenne sur une région," *Cahiers de l'Institut de Science Economique Appliquée*, Série R, No. 4 (May, 1960), pp. 81–122.

CHARDONNET, JEAN. "Unificación económica europea y modificaciones en la localización geográfica actual de la actividad económica," *La localización de las actividades económicas en Europa después de la integración unitaria*, pp. 717–84. In the series: Estudios sobre la Unidad Económica de Europa, VI, Madrid, 1957.

DELL, S. "Economic Integration and the American Example," *Economic Journal*, Vol. LXIX (March, 1959), pp. 39–54.

EASTERLIN, R. A. "Long Term Regional Income Changes: Some Suggested Factors," Regional Science Association, *Papers and Proceedings*, Vol. IV (1958), pp. 313–25.

FLORENCE, P. SARGANT. *Investment, Location and Size of Plant*, chap. iv. Cambridge: At the University Press, 1950.

GIERSCH, HERBERT. "Economic Union between Nations and the Location of Industries," *Review of Economic Studies*, Vol. XVII, No. 2 (1949–50), pp. 87–97.

HOOVER, E. M. *The Location of Economic Activity*, chaps. v, vii, viii. New York: McGraw-Hill Book Co., Inc., 1948.

ISARD, WALTER. *Location and Space Economy, passim.* New York: M.I.T.–John Wiley & Sons, 1956.

————, and SCHOOLER, E. W. "Industrial Complex Analysis, Agglomeration Economies, and Regional Development," *Journal of Regional Science,* Vol. I, No. 2 (Spring, 1959), pp. 19–34.

LAJUGIE, JOSEPH. "Les conditions d'une politique de développement régional pour les pays du marché commun," *Revue d'Économie Politique,* Vol. LXIX, No. 3 (May–June, 1959), pp. 263–334.

MYRDAL, GUNNAR. *Economic Theory and Under-Developed Regions,* chap. iii. London: Duckworth, 1957.

DI NARDI, GIUSEPPE. "The Policy of Regional Development. A Case Study: Southern Italy," *Banca Nazionale del Lavoro Quarterly Review,* No. 54 (September, 1960), pp. 215–46.

PERROUX, FRANÇOIS. "Note sur la notion de 'pôle de croissance,'" *Economie Appliquée,* Vol. VIII, Nos. 1–2 (January–June, 1955), pp. 307–20.

ROMUS, PAUL. *Expansion économique régionale et Communauté Européenne.* Leiden: A. W. Sythoff, 1958.

THIÉRY, ANDRÉ. "Modificaciones que se producirian en la localización geográfica actual de la actividad económica europea como consecuencia de una eventual integración de las economías nacionales en una perfecta unidad," Estudios sobre la Unidad Económica de Europa, VI, pp. 789–814.

U. N. ECONOMIC COMMISSION FOR EUROPE. *Economic Survey of Europe in 1954,* chap. vi. Geneva, 1955.

WEBER, ALFRED. *Theory of Location of Industries,* chaps. iii–iv, vi. Chicago: University of Chicago Press, 1929.

CHAPTER X

BYÉ, MAURICE. "Freer Trade and Social Welfare: Comments on Mr. Heilperin's Article," *International Labour Review,* Vol. LXXVII, No. 1 (January, 1958), pp. 38–47.

DELPÉRÉE, ALBERT. *Politique sociale et intégration economique.* Paris: Librairie Générale de Droit et de Jurisprudence, 1956.

————. "Les distorsions économiques d'origine sociale et l'intégration économique," *Revue Belge de Sécurité Sociale,* January, 1958, pp. 3–20.

FRISCH, ALFRED. "Frankreichs soziale Belastung im Spiegel der europäischen Zusammenarbeit," *Wirtschaftsdienst,* Vol. XXXV, No. 6 (June, 1955), pp. 339–45.

HALD, M. W. "Social Charges in the EEC Countries: Some Economic Aspects," *Economia Internazionale,* Vol. XII, No. 4 (November, 1959), pp. 677–96.

HAMPEL, GUSTAV. *Die Bedeutung der Sozialpolitik für die Europäische Integration.* Kiel: Kieler Studien, 1955.

HEILPERIN, M. A. "Freer Trade and Social Welfare: Some Marginal Comments on the 'Ohlin Report,'" *International Labour Review,* Vol. LXXV, No. 3 (March, 1957), pp. 173–92.

HERCZEG, K. L. "Prix et salaires sur le marché européen: les disparités actuelles empêchent-elles une intégration?," *Cahiers de l'Institut de Science Economique Appliquée,* Série R, No. 4 (May, 1960), pp. 67–80.

HOFFMANN, W. G. "Wirtschafts– und sozialpolitische Probleme einer europäischen Integration," *Schweizerische Zeitschrift für Volkswirtschaft und Statistik,* Vol. XC, No. 1 (March, 1954), pp. 41–54.

INTERNATIONAL LABOUR OFFICE. *Social Aspects of European Co-operation,* Report by a Group of Experts (Ohlin Report). Geneva, 1956.

OHLIN, BERTIL. "Problèmes d'harmonisation et de coordination des politiques économiques et sociales," *Revue d'Economie Politique,* Vol. LXVIII, No. 1 (January–February, 1958), pp. 264–90.

PHILIP, ANDRÉ. "Social Aspects of European Economic Co-operation," *International Labour Review,* Vol. LXXVI, No. 3 (September, 1957), pp. 244–56.

TESSIER, JACQUES. "Les problèmes sociaux," *Revue d'Economie Politique,* Vol. LXVIII, No. 1 (January–February, 1958), pp. 230–56.

TINBERGEN, JAN. "Les distorsions et leur corrections," *Revue d'Economie Politique,* Vol. LXVIII, No. 1 (January–February, 1958), pp. 256–63.

CHAPTER XI

BHARGAVA, R. N. "The Theory of Federal Finance," *Economic Journal,* Vol. LXIII (March, 1953), pp. 84–97.

BILLE, STEN F. W. *La souveraineté fiscale des états et l'intégration économique internationale.* Amsterdam: Bureau International de Documentation Fiscale, 1958.

BUCHANAN, J. M. "Federalism and Fiscal Equity," *American Economic Review,* Vol. XL, No. 4 (September, 1950), pp. 583–99.

COSCIANI, CESARE. *Problemi fiscali del Mercato Comune.* Milano: A. Giuffrè, 1958.

———. "Problèmes fiscaux de la communauté économique européenne, *Public Finance,* Vol. XIII, No. 3 (1958), pp. 197–214.

DAUSSIN, A. "Les aspects budgétaires de l'intégration économique internationale," *Aspects financiers et fiscaux de l'intégration économique internationale,* Travaux de l'Institut International de Finances Publiques, pp. 57–88. The Hague: W. P. Van Stockum & Fils, 1954.

DESMYTTÈRE, J. "Le marché commun et la diversité des régimes fiscaux," *Cahiers de l'Institut de Science Economique Appliquée,* Série R, No. 3 (December, 1958), pp. 19–32.

INSTITUT "FINANZEN UND STEUERN." *Europäische Wirtschaftsgemeinschaft und Steuerpolitik.* Bonn, 1957.

LAUFENBURGER, HENRY. "Finances fédérales," *Economia Internazionale,* Vol. VI, Nos. 1–2 (February–March, 1953), pp. 238–51.

NEUMARK, FRITZ. "Die budgetären und steuerlichen Aspekte einer wirtschaftlichen Integration," *Aspects financiers et fiscaux de l'intégration économique internationale,* pp. 21–53.

EUROPEAN COAL AND STEEL COMMUNITY. *Rapport sur les problèmes posés par les taxes sur le chiffre d'affaires dans le marché commun,* Commission d'experts (Jan Tinbergen, president). Luxemburg, 1953.

REBOUD, L. "Influence des fiscalités sur les mouvements de capitaux dans le cadre du Marché Commun," *Revue de Science Financière,* Vol. LII, No. 2 (April–June, 1960), pp. 314–40.

SCHELLING, T. C. *International Cost-Sharing Arrangements,* Essays in International Finance No. 24. Princeton: International Finance Section, Princeton University, 1955.

SHOUP, C. S. "Taxation Aspects of International Economic Integration," *Aspects financiers et fiscaux de l'intégration économique internationale,* pp. 89–118.

STEFANI, GIORGIO. "Per una teoria tributaria dell'integrazione economica internazionale," *Rivista di Politica Economica,* Vol. L, No. 1 (January, 1960), pp. 33–84.

TREMPONT, J. "Les finances publiques dans un marché commun," *Revue de Science et de Législation Financières,* Vol. XLVII, No. 1 (January–March, 1955), pp. 107–24.

VEDEL, G. "Les aspects fiscaux du Marché Commun," *Bulletin for International Fiscal Documentation,* Vol. XII, No. 6 (November–December, 1958), pp. 321–39.

WILLGERODT, H. "Umsatzsteuern und Handelsoptimum im Gemeinsamen Markt," *Ordo,* Vol. X (1958), pp. 63–114.

CHAPTER XII

AUST, EBERHARD. *Währungsordnung und Zahlungsbilanz im gemeinsamen Markt Europas.* Frankfurt: Knapp, 1959.

EMMINGER, OTMAR. "Les aspects monétaires du marché commun," *Bulletin d'Information et de Documentation,* August, 1958, pp. 93–103.

COTTA, ALAIN. "Les taux de change flexibles dans le cadre du marché commun," *Revue d'Economie Politique,* Vol. LXVIII, No. 3 (March–June, 1958), pp. 549–89.

EUROPEAN COMMITTEE FOR ECONOMIC AND SOCIAL PROGRESS. *European Business Cycle Policy.* Frankfurt [1958].

GEHRELS, FRANZ. "Monetary Systems for the Common Market," *Journal of Finance,* Vol. XIV, No. 2 (May, 1959), pp. 312–21.

HARTLAND, P. C. "Interregional Payments Compared with International Payments," *Quarterly Journal of Economics,* Vol. LXIII, No. 3 (August, 1949), pp. 392–407; Comment by Rendings Fels and Reply by P. C. Hartland, *ibid.,* Vol. LXIV, No. 3 (August, 1950), pp. 488–90.

HOLTROP, M. W. "Is a Common Central Bank Policy Necessary within an Integrated Europe?," *De Economist,* Vol. CV, No. 10 (October, 1957), pp. 41–61.

HARROD, ROY. "Die Koordination der Währungs– und Konjunkturpolitik in einer europäischen Gemeinschaft," *Aussenwirtschaft,* Vol. XIII, Nos. 1–2 (March–June, 1958), pp. 73–83.

———, *et al.* "Möglichkeiten europäischer Zusammenarbeit in einer weltwirtschaftlichen Rezession," *Aussenwirtschaft,* Vol. XIV, Nos. 1–2 (March–June, 1959), pp. 47–59.

INGRAM, J. C. "State and Regional Payments Mechanisms," *Quarterly Journal of Economics,* Vol. LXXIII, No. 4 (November, 1959), pp. 619–32; Comment by R. L. Pfister and Reply by J. C. Ingram, *ibid.,* Vol. LXXIV, No. 4 (November, 1960), pp. 641–52.

KÜNG, EMIL. "Der Ausgleich der Zahlungsbilanz als Voraussetzung der wirtschaftlichen Integration," *Aussenwirtschaft,* Vol. XIV, Nos. 1–2 (March–June, 1959), pp. 61–67.

VON MANGOLDT-REIBOLDT, HANS KARL. *Währungspolitische Probleme der europäischen Integration.* Kiel: Kieler Vorträge, 1957.

MEADE, J. E. "The Balance-of-Payments Problems of a European Free-Trade Area," *Economic Journal,* Vol. LXVII (September, 1957), pp. 379–96.

MOSSÉ, R. "Système et politique monetaires de l'Europe fédérée, *Economia Internazionale,* Vol. VI, Nos. 1–2 (February–March, 1953), pp. 175–88.

SCITOVSKY, TIBOR. *Economic Theory and Western European Integration,* chap. ii.

TRIFFIN, ROBERT. "Intégration économique européenne et politique monétaire," *Revue d'Economie Politique,* Vol. LXX, No. 6 (November–December, 1960), pp. 58–81.

———. *Gold and the Dollar Crisis,* Part II, chap. vi. New Haven: Yale University Press, 1960.

YEAGER, L. B. "Exchange Rates within a Common Market," *Social Research,* Vol. XXV, No. 4 (Winter, 1958), pp. 415–38, and Note by M. E. Kreinin, *ibid.,* Vol. XXVI, No. 1 (Spring, 1960), pp. 105–11.

Indexes

AUTHOR INDEX

A

Abramovitz, M., 101, 102
Adelman, M. A., 169
D'Alauro, O., 274
Albrecht, K., 275
Allais, M., 8, 109n, 165, 274, 275, 280
Aust, E., 288
Austruy, J., 171n

B

Bachmann, H., 71n, 279
Baer, W., 153n, 155n
Bain, J. S., 129, 130n, 132n, 134n, 135n,
    138–39, 142, 158n, 282
Balassa, B., 1n, 3n, 13n, 81n, 82n, 175n,
    276, 279
Bartholoni, A., 239n
Bator, F. M., 144n, 145n
Beckerman, W., 41–42, 277
De Beers, J. S., 22n
Benoit, E., 274
Berle, A. A., 169n
Bertrand, R., 45, 46, 64n, 277
Bhargava, R. N., 234n, 287
Bidwell, P. W., 66n
Bille, S. F. W., 287
Binswanger, H. C., 46, 47n, 277
Blair, J. M., 128, 136n, 142n
Bok, D. C., 92n
Bombach, G., 111n, 114, 276, 281
Borch, K., 126n, 282
Boudeville, J. R., 197n, 285
Boulding, K. E., 67n
Bourgeois-Pichat, J., 89n
Bowsher, N. N., 260n
Buchanan, J. M., 236n, 287
Buchanan, N. S., 82n
Burn, D. L., 113
Buxbaum, B., 113n
Byé, M., 9, 22, 65n, 95n, 106, 164, 171n,
    183n, 202, 212n, 222, 223n, 276, 277,
    279, 284, 286

C

Camps, M., 76, 274, 279

Capet, M., 285
Carli, G., 73
Carr, H., 255n
Carter, C. F., 160–61, 168n, 176n
Caves, R. E., 81n, 279
Centro de Estudios Monetarios Latino-
    americanos, 173n
Chardonnet, J., 203n, 275, 285
Chenery, H. B., 107n, 115, 160n, 187n, 283
Clark, C., 114n, 281
Clark, J. M., 127
Claude, H., 171n
Cohen, L., 125n
Communauté Economique Européenne,
    Commission, 168n
Corson, H., 48n
Cosciani, C., 231, 241n, 287
Cotta, A., 288
Cournot, A., 12n, 21
Courtin, R., 22n, 30n

D

Daane, J. D., 260n
Daussin, A., 235n, 287
Dean, J., 124
Dell, S. S., 106n, 109n, 161n, 205n, 275, 285
Delpérée, A., 230n, 279, 286
Deniau, J. F., 274
Desmyttère, J., 288
Diebold, W., 52n, 170n, 276, 284
Dixon, R. C., 284
Dobretsberger, J., 165n
Domar, E., 101
Dorfman, R., 13n
Douglas, P., 111n
Duncan, G. A., 35–36
Duquesne de la Vinelle, L., 116n, 133n,
    134n, 281

E

Easterlin, R. A., 199n, 285
Eckstein, O., 206, 208n
Economist Intelligence Unit, 133n, 282
Edding, F., 280
Edwards, C. D., 137n, 169n, 284
Einzig, R., 260n

293

SUBJECT INDEX

A

Administrative economies, 24, 65–67, 68, 74, 177, 242–43, 244, 246
Africa, 4, 41, 69
Agglomeration, 3, 85, 95, 192, 193–97, 200, 202–3, 205, 208
Agriculture, 15, 33–34, 103
Argentina, 4n, 44, 55, 77, 140, 155, 162, 225, 229
Asia, 4, 41
Austria, 4n, 34, 42n, 43, 53

B

Backwash effects, 202, 204
Balance of payments,
in an integrated area, 212, 220, 257–69, 270–71
of regions, 252–57, 260
and sectoral integration, 15–16
and terms of trade, 63-64, 65
Balanced growth, 6, 153–54, 208–9
Bargaining, 6, 64–65, 212
Belgium, 3n, 34, 42, 45–46, 89, 116, 125, 133, 136, 141, 161, 169, 203, 216, 219, 221, 223, 250, 266
Benelux, 3, 65
production effects, 52
size, 38
taxes, 247, 250
Brazil, 4n, 44, 55, 77, 140, 141, 155, 161, 162, 201, 225
British Commonwealth, 75–76
Budgetary problems, 231–38, 254–55

C

Canada, 112, 135, 168
Capital movements
and balance-of-payments adjustment, 253–57, 258–63, 267
economic effects of, 83–84, 92
encouragement of, 92, 95–96, 98
and fiscal policies, 86, 193–94, 226, 227, 240, 249–51, 268
and monetary policies, 93–94, 268

Capital movements—*Cont.*
in present-day integration projects, 93, 98
and social policy, 93–94, 222–23, 226, 227
and uncertainty, 93–94, 183
Cartels, 9, 163–64, 167, 170–72, 173
Central American Common Market, 4, 63
competition, 173–74
internal economies, 139–40
investment, 182, 184
labor movements, 90
propinquity, 44
size, 38
trade, 54–55
Chile, 4n, 44, 77, 153, 162
Colombia, 44, 201, 228
Commercial policies
in a customs union, 21
in a free-trade area, 77–78
Common market, 2, 15, 83 ff., 94, 103, 231
Competition
defined, 164
in an integrated area, 15, 114, 119, 131, 163–67
in present-day integration projects, 169–74
Competitiveness; *see* Complementarity
Complementarity, 53, 68
and consumption effects, 60–61
controversy on, 29–30
defined, 30–32
in present-day integration projects, 33–34
Complementarity agreements, 173
Concentration, 167–69, 170–71
Consumption effects, 11, 23, 67, 68
compared to production effects, 57–59
and complementarity, 60–62
defined, 24
and optimum conditions, 59–60
and tariffs, 61
Council of Mutual Economic Assistance, 8
Countercyclical policy, 2–3, 5–6, 14, 78–79, 238, 268–73
Customs formalities; *see* Administrative economies
Customs union, 2, 3, 14, 21 ff., 74, 80,83, 103, 179, 211, 231

D

Deflation, 180, 220, 268–69
Denmark, 4n, 43, 53, 69, 75
Destination principle, 67, 238–39, 241–45, 246
Disintegration in the European economy, 5, 8, 117–18
Dynamic effects of integration, 5, 14, 22, 39, 52, 62, 88, 104–6, 118–19, 184–85
Dynamic efficiency, 13–14, 103, 108

E

Economic development, 6, 56, 118, 141, 153–56, 173, 187–88, 195, 201, 226, 228
Economic efficiency, 11–13, 14–15, 16, 21, 22–24, 67–68, 74, 80, 87, 92, 94, 246
Economic growth, 5–6, 13, 15, 88, 101, 103, 104–7, 116, 118, 144–45, 184–87, 227–28, 249, 268, 269–71
Economic integration
  arguments for, 5–6
  concept and forms of, 1–2
  and economic policy, 191 ff.
  and efficiency, 21 ff.
  fundamental problems of, 14–15
  and growth, 101 ff.
  history of, 3–4
  objectives of, 14
  and politics, 6–7, 40, 155
  and protectionism, 30, 36
  sectoral approach to, 15–17
  views on, 7–10
  and welfare, 10–13, 67–69
Economic union, 2, 16, 104, 257, 261
Economies of scale; *see* Internal economies
Efficiency in exchange; *see* Consumption effects
Efficiency in production; *see* Production effects
Elasticity
  income, 51, 269
  of labor supply, 88, 219, 227, 249
  price, 50
  of reciprocal demand, 63
  of substitution, 50, 268
El Salvador, 4n
England; *see* United Kingdom
Entrepreneurial resources, movement of, 96–98
Equador, 44
Equity, 11–13, 14, 21, 22, 24, 29, 62, 67–68, 85–86, 87–88, 205
Escape clauses, 179

Europe, 3, 4, 5, 6, 37, 52–53, 54, 109, 117–18, 140–41, 179, 187
European Atomic Energy Community, 3, 132, 233
European Coal and Steel Community, 3
  budgetary problems, 232, 236
  competition, 170–71
  economies of scale, 132–33
  investment, 184
  labor movements, 91–92
  production effects, 52
  and sectoral integration, 17
European Common Market, 3, 4, 5, 6, 10, 17, 21, 54, 65, 77n, 82, 88, 98, 117, 125n, 182, 191, 248, 261
  budgetary problems 233
  capital movements, 93, 95
  competition, 170–72
  complementarity, 33
  consumption effects, 60
  external economies, 161
  impact on nonparticipating economies, 69, 185–87
  internal economies, 117, 125n, 131-38
  labor movements, 88–91
  propinquity, 40, 42–43
  regional problems, 202–4, 210
  size, 36, 38
  social benefits, 217–23, 225
  tariffs, 45–49
  taxes, 241–43, 250
  trade, 53
  wage differentials, 212–16
European Defense Community, 232
European Economic Community; *see* European Common Market
European free-trade area, proposed, 4, 72
  Britain's position in, 75–76, 77–78
  production effects of, 49–51
  trade deflection in 75–76
European Free Trade Association ("Outer Seven"), 3, 4
  capital movements, 93
  complementarity, 34
  consumption effects, 60
  economies of scale, 138n
  external economies, 161
  impact on nonparticipating countries, 69, 187
  policy coordination, 77–79
  size, 38
  social benefits, 218, 225
  trade, 53
  trade deflection, 72–74, 76
  transportation costs, 43
European Investment Bank, 233, 236n